Poltergeists

Poltergeists

A History of Violent Ghostly Phenomena

P.G. Maxwell-Stuart

AMBERLEY

First published 2011

Amberley Publishing
The Hill, Stroud,
Gloucestershire, GL5 4EP

www.amberleybooks.com

British Library Cataloguing in Publication Data.
A catalogue record for this book is available from the British Library.

ISBN 978 1 84868 987 9

Typesetting and Origination by Amberley Publishing
Printed in Great Britain

CONTENTS

Author's Note

Poltergeists are hard to pin down. Reports of their activities and behaviour show them to be noisy, destructive, hostile, playful, gentle, mischievous, inarticulate, scholarly, and garrulous, and these contradictory qualities are mirrored in their elusiveness. For, in spite of their name, they refuse to be confined to a single category of non-human entity, but slip between ghost, demon, spirit, and a vague 'something other', often exhibiting traits of two or more such preternatural types. In consequence they form at once both a category of their own while belonging to several others, and any attempt to define them exactly and so pin them down is destined to be a failure. Most books which deal with poltergeists are concerned, if only in part, to explain what they are, usually in accordance with the prevailing intellectual substratum of the day: ghosts and demons in the Middle Ages, bursts of some kind of physical energy in the twentieth century. I have attempted no such explanation because I have approached the subject entirely from the stance of an historian, and therefore my task has been to see reports of poltergeistery in their historical contexts and from the viewpoint of their authors' purpose and the interests of their readership. Hence I have not attempted either to explain or explain away these phenomena – I leave that to those more interested in that side of things and perhaps better qualified to make such comments – but have sought rather to present poltergeists partly on their own terms and partly on those of the people who have had to suffer and deal with them. The result, I hope, will be fresh, but in a reserved rather than a speculative fashion.

1

Ghost or Evil Spirit or Something Else?
c. 500–*c.* 1200

The dead are not always quiet. While some appear and fade in silence and others sigh or speak in the familiar tones they used in life, there are some who shriek or moan or rattle chains or behave like characters out of Grand Guignol or a Gothic novel, eager, it might seem, to make their presence known by riotous behaviour in the face of their new condition, much as the living they have left sometimes howl and shout and break glasses or bottles by the graveside or at home in an excess of mourning which seeks to calm their fear and soothe their alarm at the changes death has brought. This kind of behaviour was not uncommon, as St Augustine complained at the end of the fourth century AD in a letter to his bishop, Aurelius. 'The lewd and ignorant lower classes commonly believe that these drunken orgies and wildly expensive wakes in cemeteries are not only marks of esteem paid to martyrs, but also consolations for the dead.' 'Beastliness' he called them, too, and 'indecency'.[1] So are the loud noises, flying objects, moving furniture, and all the other disturbing phenomena associated with poltergeists to be thought of as little more than the equivalent unbridled behaviour of some of the newly dead frightened by their loss of physical existence and the unfamiliar and disconcerting unknown into which they have found themselves precipitated? At first sight, provided, of course, one accepts that the dead enter upon some form of being after their bodily dissolution, and one may also think that past records provide some evidence of it. About fifty years after St Augustine wrote his letter, for example, St Germain, Bishop of Auxerre, died and his biographer, Constance de Lyon, noted an incident involving the bishop and his entourage and the attentions of something one might be tempted to call a poltergeist.

At one time, while he was travelling during winter and had spent the whole day without food and in a state of tired vexation, they hinted that as it was getting dark he should take shelter somewhere. Some way off there was a dwelling. Half its roof and ceilings had fallen in some time ago because no one had been living there, and because of neglect wild trees had grown up over it, with the result that it would almost be better to endure the cold night air than to take shelter in that [place of] danger and dread, especially since two old men who lived nearby had told him in advance that no one would live in this particular house because of the terrifying attacks which used to disturb its peace and quiet [*infestatione terribili*]. When he learned this, the very saintly [Germain] actually sought out these gloomy ruins as though they were a place of charm and comfort, and there among a large number of [rooms] which had once served as lodgings he just about managed to find one which looked habitable. He dropped off his bags there and the very few companions [he had]. They ate a light supper. The bishop ate nothing at all and then, since the night was already far advanced and while one of the clerics undertook the duty of reading [to him], overwhelmed by exhaustion and lack of food he succumbed to a deep sleep. Suddenly a terrifying ghost appeared in front of the reader's face [*umbra adsistit*], and little by little, while he was looking at it, stood upright. At the same time, the walls were being battered with showers of rocks. At that point, the terrified reader earnestly begged the priest to protect him, [St Germain] immediately sprang to his feet, carefully inspected the dreadful phantom's appearance [*effigiem terribilis imaginis*], invoked the name of Christ, and commanded him to say who he was and what he was doing there. Immediately [the ghost] laid aside its frightening façade [*terrifica vanitate*] and spoke in a submissive tone like someone asking a favour, saying that he and his comrade had been responsible for many crimes, were lying unburied, and, because of this, were harassing people since they themselves could not be at peace. He asked [St Germain] to beg the Lord on their behalf to receive them and grant them rest.[2]

Thereupon St Germain told the ghost to take him to the spot where his bones and those of his companion lay. Going ahead with a lighted candle, the ghost then led him through the major obstacles presented by the ruined buildings and showed St Germain where to look. Next day St Germain gathered together some people from the neighbourhood and they shovelled aside the rubble which had fallen there over time, and uncovered two bodies fastened together by iron chains. These last were removed and the bodies given Christian burial, after which tranquillity was restored to the house no longer subject to terrors.

There are several aspects of this narrative which deserve comment. First, it has points in common with a ghost story from the first century AD. That was told in a letter to Licinius Sura by Pliny the Younger (*Letters* 7.27) who asks 'whether you think ghosts [*phantasmata*] exist and have a specific shape peculiar to them and some kind of supernatural power, or whether you think they are illusory things, containing no real substance, and take on a visible form or appearance out of our apprehension'. Pliny says he himself is inclined to accept their reality and relates three incidents to justify his inclination, of which the second comes, not from contemporary or personal experience, but from the previous century. The philosopher Athenodoros's curiosity was piqued by a house in Athens, said to be haunted by the ghost of an old man wearing fetters on his legs and chains on his wrists. The ghost used to make loud clanking noises with the irons and terrify anyone bold or foolish enough to stay in the house overnight. Athenodoros decided to investigate and had a bed set up for him; and, sure enough, in the dead of night he was disturbed by the ghost which behaved in its usual fashion. Athenodoros noticed it was beckoning him to follow it, so he did and suddenly, when they reached a particular spot, the ghost vanished and Athenodoros marked the place with some plants and leaves so that he could find it again. Next day he came back, and when the ground was dug, people found a skeleton wearing chains round its legs and wrists. The bones were duly collected and given a decent burial, and after that the house suffered no more haunting or disturbance.

Can we say, then, that Constance de Lyon merely copied Pliny's story, changed a few details, and attributed the incident to St Germain? Not necessarily. It is true he may well have known the anecdote in question – Pliny the Younger, along with Vergil, Cicero, Varro, Lucan and Statius, was part of the apparatus of a cultivated author of the period – and while 'influence' today is perhaps capable of suggesting something teetering on the edge of plagiarism, 'influence' in an earlier rhetorical tradition can be much more positive. For the suggestion that a passage is written 'in the manner of' simply indicates the author's awareness of a desirable prose model and his ability to imitate the style of the original. Reference to the original will thus be a signal to the reader. 'Do you remember Pliny the Younger's ghost story? Well, here's my version of something similar. Am I doing it as well as Pliny, or better?'

In fact, apart from the coincidence of chains and the discovery of bones, the two stories are not sufficiently close to warrant any suggestion of copying or imitation. Constance's vocabulary, for example, illustrates a quite different experience and reaction. In Pliny's narrative there is no poltergeist. Constance, however, emphasises poltergeist activity not only through the mention of lithobolia (stone throwing), but also in his phrase *infestatione terribili*. The verb *infesto* means 'harass by repeated attacks, molest, make a place unsafe, disturb the peace, do damage', and this fits well into the range of activity associated with poltergeists. But the poltergeist itself, (supposing there actually was one in this episode), remains off-stage, so to speak. It is the dead companion of the ghost apparent, not the ghost himself, who, we are to infer, battered the walls of the building with showers of rocks. The ghost himself merely becomes visible. He is described as an *umbra*, 'a shadow, a shaded outline, the disembodied form of someone dead, a semblance', and as an *imago*, 'a likeness, a representation, a reflection in a mirror, a mental picture, a manifestation, a visible shape or form' – both words being common nouns for 'ghost' and suggesting that while the apparition was in some way insubstantial, it was also recognisable.

Still, Constance keeps on describing the ghost as terrifying, and yet it must be said that he gives no overt indication of what makes it so. Indeed, when St Germain addresses it, the ghost lays aside the *vanitas* which causes the terror and speaks as a humble suppliant. So what is this *vanitas*? 'An unsubstantial or illusory quality, emptiness, futility, foolishness, pointless pride.' Perhaps, then, the ghost's *vanitas* detracted from his *imago*, and instead of being the obvious semblance of a departed human being, it was a dim outline, a transparent suggestion of humanity, closer to what we nowadays sometimes see in films or photographs of the 'paranormal' than the solid, comprehensible shade more common to Classical or Mediaeval experience. Certainly St Germain's first reaction upon being confronted with it is to inspect its *effigiem*, its 'outward appearance' or 'likeness', as in that of a statue or painted picture, before he decides how to react. The conclusion producing his reaction seems to have been that the apparition was an evil spirit, for he invokes the name of Christ and speaks to the ghost in the manner of an exorcist, demanding to know its name – always a prime consideration in exorcism, for knowing a demon's name gives the exorcist a useful weapon he can use against it. The way the ghost appears to the lector, too, is suggestive. We are told it 'took up a position, stood near, stopped' (*adsistit*) in front of the lector's face 'all of a sudden' (*subito*), and that little by little it was 'raised into the air, set upright' (*erigitur*), almost as though it were a puppet being pulled to a standing position from the ground.[3] This last especially implies a controlling and invisible hand as well as a form and appearance at once lifelike and unnatural. Such conclusions, then, may help to account for the use of 'terrifying' to describe the ghost and its first arrival.

Under the circumstances, it is not altogether surprising that St Germain should have wondered whether he was being confronted by an evil spirit. These were not new to him; he had dealt with them before. They had attacked him personally and on one occasion, when a man who was constantly being molested by an evil spirit stole some money which was being brought to a provincial governor, St Germain took it upon himself to ensure that the money would be returned. He sent for one of those who were accustomed to suffer this kind of harassment – we are not told why he did so – and by chance it was the thief himself who turned up. St Germain celebrated Mass, prostrated himself in prayer, and immediately the unfortunate thief was lifted into the air and hung there until finally the demon inside him confessed his crime and described where he had hidden the money.[4] It is in this context, as the fourth in a series of anecdotes intended to show St Germain's power over evil spirits and therefore his saintliness, that the story about the ghost and the poltergeist appears; so it is told, as are the others, to convey a message and underline a point. Written by a priest for a priestly audience which could then use its constituent parts as illustrations in their sermons, the *Vita Sancti Germani* is an elegant example of hagiographical literature, part history, part improving tale, with somewhat more history in it than many other specimens of the same genre. Saints work miracles and overcome evil spirits. Their *Vitae* were written to emphasise these points (among others); but because they are works of elevating propaganda, they are not necessarily fiction or improvements on real life. Real life still underpins their narratives, and it is a question of how far one goes, or is prepared to go, in accepting one incident or another as having some basis in fact or probability, which determines one's interpretation of the whole or any part of the whole.

What, then, can we usefully say about St Germain's ghost and poltergeist? There is no reason to suppose that he did not encounter a ghost, or believe that he did, when he put up one night at a house widely reputed to be haunted. Nor do we need to doubt that he may have heard a shower of falling stones there at some point. If the building was derelict, falling stones are scarcely unlikely. What we do have to ask is whether the lithobolia alone is enough to indicate poltergeist activity. The word 'poltergeist', as is well known, means simply 'noisy' or 'playful spirit', and the range of behaviours attributed to it as a result of its relatively long historical record have been summed up by Alan Gauld as follows.

The two commonest major classes [of poltergeist phenomena] are perhaps those of percussive sounds – raps, taps, thumps, thuds, crashes, bangs, and bombinations – and those of object movements – the tilting, displacement, movement, lifting and hurling of objects, generally small objects, but sometimes weighing several hundredweight. Other sorts of phenomena which have been attributed to poltergeists include communication by means of a code of raps; inundations of water, mysterious outbreaks of fire; interference with electrical equipment; the playing of musical instruments; cutting or tearing of clothes or soft furnishings; frightening or interference with animals; imitation of sounds, including the sound of the human voice; arrangement of objects into patterns; the appearance of lights, luminosities, misty figures, phantasms, etc., including the phantasms of animals; and the beating, wounding or biting of particular individuals.[5]

But although combinations of noisy and physical phenomena may suggest poltergeist activity, it is clear from his name, derived from *poltern*, 'to crash about, make a racket, bang', that only one of these will be sufficient for the purpose. So a shower of stones is indeed enough to warrant our calling the dead companion of St Germain's ghost a poltergeist even though, while we do so, we link the term to a dead person's spirit, a connection which will become less clear and perhaps less appropriate as we examine the poltergeist in later historical periods. As far as the ghost is concerned, this identification with the dead presents no problem. St Germain's first reaction was to regard it as a potential demon, and his second to accept it as a ghost. Interestingly enough, he ignores the lithobolia and asks no questions about the ghost's companion, but this may simply have been owing to Constance's decision to concentrate the narrative upon three actors – St Germain, the ghost, the lector – rather than four. When it comes to effectiveness in paranormal anecdotes, less is often more.[6] But we also need to bear in mind that noisy phenomena may be interpreted differently at different times. Showers of stones, for example, are a fairly frequent feature of certain moments during Livy's *History of Rome*, but these, as their contexts make clear, were regarded by the Romans simply as omens and not as the work of discarnate entities. Moreover, they usually appeared in company with other portents.

> In Sicily the javelins of several soldiers caught fire; in Sardinia, the staff of office held by an eques who was going round the [town] wall on his watch caught fire; fires blazed up at frequent intervals on the shores; two shields sweated blood; soldiers seemed to be struck by lightning-bolts and the sun's orb appeared to grow smaller. *At Praeneste burning stones fell from the sky*; at Arpi small round shields were seen in the sky, and the sun fought with the moon. At Capena two moons rose during the daytime; the waters of Caere flowed mixed with blood, the very spring of Hercules ran spattered with bloody stains, and at Antium, while some people were reaping, ears of corn stained with blood fell into their basket. At Falerii the sky seemed to be torn apart as though it had developed a large fissure and an enormous light shone through it.[7]

Such showers, in fact, occurred in a general, not a specific manner. They fell upon public places, such as the Aventine Hill in Rome, and were not directed at separate individuals or households in a domestic setting. Nevertheless, showers of stones coming unexpectedly out of the blue did set a precedent for those acquainted with Classical literature, and the notion of such lapidary falls' taking place to convey a message or warning would clearly have been adaptable (if necessary) to Christian contexts in which individuals for whatever reason were targeted.

Precedents, indeed, should always be borne in mind when one is dealing with any form of occult literature. An anecdote told of Caesarius, Bishop of Arles, and dated by the recording historian to 530 AD, for example, is similar to that related of St Germain.

> Helpidius, a physician and deacon, and a man very close to royal power and secular service, was not only exhausted by the attacks of devils [*diabolica infestatione*] consisting of various ambuscades [*insidiis*], but was also quite frequently assailed by a shower of rocks in his own house. He begged the holy man of God [*Caesarius*] to consider him worthy of being set free from this persecution by his prayers. [So] he who was going to be declared a saint entered Helpidius's house, sprinkled it liberally with holy water, and set it free from the dangerous periods of harassment to which it was usually being subjected. The result was that no such thing ever happened there again.[8]

The vocabulary echoes that of Constance in the devil's *infestatio* and the 'showers of rocks', but carries it a stage further with the reference to ambuscades. *Insidiae* is essentially a combination of military term ('ambush, disposition of troops in concealment so as to effect a surprise attack') and hunting ('a trap set for a wild animal, a snare'). Here, too, there is no doubt that the agents of the hostile activity are evil spirits, so the steps taken by Bishop Caesarius – once again reminiscent of those used by an exorcist – are entirely appropriate. Warfare, of course, is a most suitable and expected way to describe the relationship between the demonic world and the human. The subtext of hunting, however, is an interesting and sinister concept since it puts the demon in a position of almost ineluctable power – the hunter who is more or less certain to trap his quarry. So while the context, part historical, part hagiographical, is much the same as that of the *Vita Sancti Germani* and the authors' intentions in recording their anecdotes are the same, or at least broadly similar, the anonymous author's emphasis upon warfare underpinned by a suggestion of hunting means that his anecdote is more disturbing, in as much as a man has been attacked in his own house and feels helpless in the face of non-human aggression. Had it not been for the intervention of St Caesarius, we are led to infer, the attacks would have continued and Helpidius subjected to persecution without any end in sight.

This notion of helplessness before domestic hostility is brought out again in a story recorded by a priest, Eleusios, in his *Life* of St Theodoros of Sykeon. St Theodoros, a native of Galatia and later Bishop of Anastasiopolis in the same Byzantine province, was notable for his austerities, his exorcisms, and his miracles. Demons troubled him personally on many occasions, but he was able to overcome them with ease and to force them to leave other people alone as well. An incident recounted by Eleusios says that one day, while he was drawing near a monastery dedicated to Our Lady, he was met by the local royal governor, also called Theodoros, who took him home so that he could free the house from a major infestation of demons (*daemonum vexatione*). The problems they generated were manifold. While the governor and his family were having lunch or dinner, stones would be thrown on to the tables, thereby causing great fright; the upright threads on the women's looms would be broken; and the house itself was filled with such a large number of mice and snakes that no one dared enter it for terror. St Theodoros, however, went in, sprinkled holy water, sang psalms and prayed long and hard, and the house was liberated.[9]

In addition to the now increasingly familiar lithobolia, the presence of a future saint, and the use of prayers and holy water, there appear once again elements of persecutory belligerence with no apparent motive or cause, although if one identifies the source of the aggression as evil spirits, their evil nature is cause and motive enough. However, occasionally their stone-throwing may be seen as a deliberate act with meaning. In her history of and tribute to her father, the Byzantine Emperor Alexios I, Anna Komnena recounts an episode involving a stubborn heretic of the Bogomil sect, a monk called Basil, who was arrested for spreading his errors in Constantinople and confined to a little house not far from the Imperial palace. Orthodox Christians were of the opinion that Bogomils worshipped Satan rather than God, a notion seemingly confirmed by Basil's interrogation before a synod of the Church, so the wording of Anna's account should not be surprising. 'In spite of being threatened with being burned and other ill-treatment,' she wrote, 'he held tight to his demon and embraced his Satanaël.'[10] She then goes on to describe an incident of lithobolia.

> It was evening, and the stars above the open sky were flashing brightly, and the moon was lighting up the evening after the synod. About the middle of the night,

while the monk was entering his cell,[11] stones started to throw themselves against it, like hail. No hand was hurling them, nor was any human being stoning this devilish monk. It looked as though it was a burst of anger, Satanaël's attendant demons being furious and doing this in terror because [Basil] had let the cat out of the bag[12] in front of the Emperor, and let loose a vigorous persecution against their heresy. Someone called Paraskeuiōtēs, who had been appointed guard over that devilish old man so that he did not have the freedom to talk to anyone and share his filth [with them], swore the most shudderingly awful oaths that he had heard the rattling of the stones as they were being thrown on to the ground and roof-tiles, and that he had seen the stones [fall] in continuous dense clusters, one after another; but he had not observed anyone anywhere in the act of throwing them. This rush of stones was accompanied by a sudden earth tremor which had made the ground shake, and rattled the edges of the roof.[13] Before he suspected this was the work of demons, however, Paraskeuiōtēs was not afraid. But, as he said, when he saw that the stones were pouring down from above, so to speak like rain, and that the old arch-heretic had gone away and shut himself [in the house], he attributed the deed to demons and did not know what to make of it.[14]

Throwing stones, however, is one thing. Attempts to kill quite another, as is illustrated by Alcuin in his *Life of St Willibrord*, describing an incident from *c*.738.

The head of a household and his whole house were once subjected as follows to a dreadful attack by a demon which was playing games with them [*demonicae illusionis*]. From the terror it caused and the wicked things it did [*maleficiis*], they began to realise quite clearly that a maleficent spirit was living in the house. Quite without warning, it used to snatch and carry off food, clothing, and other household furniture [*necessaria*] and throw them on the fire. Indeed, it also picked up a small child which was sleeping between its parents [in their bed], and threw him on the fire as well; but the child's howl of pain woke up his parents who just managed to extract him from the fire [*eruerunt*]. The dreadful spirit did many other terrible things to this same family, and none of the priests was able to drive it away until St Willibrord, at the father's earnest pleading, cast holy water on them. He then told them to take every bit of furniture out of the house and sprinkled it with holy water, because he had a vision that the house was going to be burned down. Once they had done this, fire, starting in one of the bedrooms, attacked [*invasit*] the empty house and burned it down completely. But other things there which had been strengthened by being sanctified with holy water suffered none of their former attacks from that time forward.[15]

Here the level of malignant hostility has been ratcheted up considerably. Seizing various household objects which the family need – hence *necessaria* as opposed to ornaments or superfluities – and trying to destroy them is malicious, not mischievous, and the word for 'the wicked things it did', *maleficia*, has a sinister undertone because it is also a common term for acts of harmful magic. The notion of a family under attack is also emphasised by the use of *invasit* to describe the fire's action within the empty house – *invado* means 'assault, invade, seize possession of, usurp' – and this implied concept of the poltergeist as an agent of military aggression confirms what appears to be a growing trend of identifying it, not with a ghost, a spirit of the dead, but as a member of Satan's army of demons intent on making human lives a misery before finally destroying them. But it is perhaps the use of the verb *eruo* in connection with the parents' rescuing their child from the fire, which particularly draws one's attention. *Eruo* means 'dig up, remove with difficulty, uproot, unearth', and clearly suggests that while the demon-poltergeist may have 'thrown' the child on the fire, it had also thrust him deep into the burning logs or coals from which he was pulled *vix*, 'with difficulty'. The fear or terror inspired by such an experience is therefore different in degree and probably in kind from that inspired by St Germain's frustrated ghost, or even that suffered by the deacon Helpidius; and it seems that with each subsequent example of what looks like poltergeistery, we move further and further from being able to identify it as a ghost, and closer and closer to the Mediaeval certainty that this type of behaviour sprang from an evil spirit. This is, however, a point to which we shall return.

An episode of lithobolia in Mainz, followed by an outbreak of fires which destroyed the houses the poltergeist – here described as a 'demon' – had pelted with stones, took place in 853,[16] although it would be possible to read this as a series of malicious attacks against certain individuals, perpetrated by human rather than demonic agency. Nevertheless, we do not have enough information to be sure either way and so it will be best to keep an open mind in considering this and similar instances. Perhaps the ultimate identification of a poltergeist with a member of the demonic world comes in the *Annals* written by Rudolf, a priest and monk from the monastery of Fulda (died 865). In them, under the year 858, he records an episode relating to a house not far from the city of Bingen.

[There], a malignant spirit gave a clear sign of its wickedness. First, it threw stones and knocked against the house walls as though it were using a hammer, and thus proved highly disturbing to the people living there. Then it began to

17

speak clearly, and stealthily reveal to certain individuals things it had stolen, after which it started to foment quarrels among the local inhabitants. Finally, it roused everyone's feelings against one man, as though everyone else was suffering this kind of thing because of the sinful things he was doing; and in order to excite greater hatred of him, whenever this man entered any house, the malign spirit immediately burned it down. Therefore, of necessity, the man and his wife and children were forced to live out of doors in his fields because all his neighbours were afraid to receive him under their roof. But he was not allowed to remain there in safety because, once he had gathered all his crops and stacked them together, the scoundrelly spirit came along and, without warning, set the lot on fire. But so that he could placate the feelings of his neighbours who wanted to kill him, he demonstrated by [the trial] of red-hot iron that he had no part in any of the crimes which were being alleged against him.[17] So priests and deacons were sent from Mainz, with relics and crosses, to drive the malignant spirit out of that place. But while they were reciting litanies and sprinkling holy water in the house where [the spirit] was raging in a particularly ferocious manner [*saeviebat*], the ancient Enemy threw stones and drew blood from several of its inhabitants who were beginning to assemble there. It was not long, however, before the attack [*infestatione*] stopped.

But once those who had been sent for left, this same enemy uttered doleful words [*edidit lugubres sermones*] to many people who heard him [do so] and, designating a particular priest by name, claimed he had been under his cap at the very time holy water was being sprinkled in the house. To those crossing themselves out of fear [he said], 'He is my very own slave, and anyone who is surpassed by him [in wickedness] is his slave, too, because not long ago, at my suggestion, he slept with the daughter of the proctor of this town.' No human being knew about this before, except those who had carried out this crime. So it is clear that, as the true text says, 'Nothing is hidden which will not be revealed';[18] and the hostile renegade spirit [*apostata spiritus infestus*] did not stop doing these and similar wicked things in the foresaid place for three full years, until almost every single building had been set on fire and burned to the ground.[19]

Lithobolia and fire-raising now seem to be component parts of this type of experience, with actively hostile intent to ruin and then destroy; and this the Bingen demon-poltergeist, described as *nequam*, 'morally worthless, depraved', seeks to do by turning his neighbours against him, a severe kind of persecution in a society in which family and neighbourhood networks were of the utmost importance to the individual and, indeed, provided the essential context of his or her life, without which that life was robbed not only of viability but also of meaning. The poltergeist's behaviour, indeed, strikes one as being, if not out of control, at least savage in its ferocity. The verb *saeviebat*, used to characterise its actions during the attempted exorcisms, means 'behave ferociously, rage, be violent', and its noun *saevitia* refers to the action of cornered wild animals, or the fearsomeness of storms, or the intensity of suffering caused by illness and disease.

But most notable is the spirit's identification as Satan himself – 'the ancient Enemy' (*antiquus hostis*) and 'renegade spirit' (*apostata spiritus*) – and his willingness to speak. The other poltergeists have been silent, as poltergeists usually are; this one, however, Satan or not, speaks, speaks coherently, and is heard by more than one person. What he says – the revelation of what appears to have been a rape, although that has to be inferred from the expressions he uses – is clearly intended by the author to confirm his status as a demon, for demons know things which are hidden from human beings, whether past or future actions or events; but the manner of his saying it is distinctive and worth brief comment. *Edidit lugubres sermones: edo* means 'eject, emit, give birth, perform, utter, pronounce, deliver a message, disclose, declare, publish'. We have therefore the sense of someone using a voice somewhat louder than that appropriate to normal conversation, a voice raised to make a formal announcement – not exactly that of a town-crier, more that of an actor delivering a speech from centre stage. *Sermo*, however, almost contradicts this. It refers to 'anything one says, informal address, conversation, dialogue, gossip, dialect', and thus implies (but does not, of course, require) a lowered tone of voice, suitable for the exchange of pleasantries or confidences. A secret boomed out in public suggests that the speaker is in an emotional state either past caring what he or she does, or angry enough to calculate that the disclosures will do damage to the object of his or her fury; and it is clear which of these two better fits the demon-poltergeist. *Lugubres sermones* tells us how he sounded to the many who were listening: 'doleful, plaintive, gloomy, sinister'. *Lugubris* is an adjective closely connected with mourning, and mourning in the ancient world was extremely noisy, expressed by ululation, howling or drawn-out cries of grief. These were not necessarily genuine expressions of sorrow – one could hire professional mourners who would make these noises on one's behalf – but reassurances to the dead that they were missed, and thus safety measures for the living whose shrieking misery would prevent the newly dead from becoming angry at the thought the living were indifferent to his death and returning to vent that anger by doing them harm. Essentially, then, *lugubris* might suggest false grief, but false with a purpose; and if we apply this to the demon-poltergeist's delivery, we may infer that his tone was exaggeratedly sorrowful, and that the sorrow was hardly likely to be sincere.

Another spirit, who may or may not have been the Devil himself, committed sacrilegious violence against a holy man, St Godric, in an effort to stop him reciting the Divine Office. He is called 'the abominable, wicked Enemy' and *diabolus*, which is translatable as 'a devil' or 'the Devil' according to context, and Reginald, a monk of Durham, who wrote a biography of St Godric, tells us that one evening, while St Godric was praying upon his knees,

The aggressive Enemy saw this, but saw it with ill will, and, entering the church, kicked up a racket with excessive violence [*nimio furore bachatur*] against the servant of God. But [St Godric] was not in the least frightened by this and was unwilling to interrupt his appointed task because of any of the devil's deceitful tricks [*fallaciae praestigiis*]; nor did he turn his eyes to look at the demon's face [*in larvalem faciem*]. Taking offence at this, [the demon] soon resorted to other deceitful images [*figmenta*], picked up the pyx which contained the consecrated Hosts, and threw it with all its might at the man who was lying prostrate in prayer. But when he remained unmoved and was unwilling to look back, the devil boldly repeated his offence, picked up a vessel containing wine, and struck him once more. The contents spilled over him. Then [it threw] the water-cruet with its water, and after that whatever had been above the beam to which the veil of the holy cross had been attached. He collected all these things one by one and threw each of them separately.[20] But when the man of God did not rise from his prayer, [the devil] began to vent his rage by gnashing his teeth, and soon boiled over completely with greater indignation. It tore the wood to which the cross had been fixed from the wall at the far end and threw it at him, along with the rest of the [church's] furniture. But [St Godric] could not be stopped from making his devotions and, prostrate in prayer, irritated his enemy, now running riot, to an intolerable degree. The whole of that night, [the devil] laughed uproariously at him and, stirring up furies to distract him in every way possible, set in motion all the deceitful images belonging to his repertory of mocking insults. But finally, having achieved nothing and thoroughly embarrassed, it went away, leaving behind it such a great stench that the human sense of smell could scarcely have borne it. However, not a single one of all the things the Enemy had torn from their secure fastenings showed signs of any damage. Not even the figure on the cross, which was very delicate, was chipped anywhere.[21]

Once again it is worth commenting on some of the language. The intolerable din made by the devil is characterised by the verb *debachor*. This refers us back to the Maenads or Bacchantes, followers or worshippers of the Greek god Bacchus, who used to consume large quantities of wine in honour of their patron during his major festival, and roam into the countryside where they had licence to behave without restraint. Shrieking, screaming, yelling, violent behaviour of all kinds thus became associated with them and gave rise to the verb, 'behave like a Bacchant', which is used here to indicate the level of noise the devil was making. *Furor* is essentially 'extreme anger, raving madness', and *nimius* means 'excessive'; so putting the three together gives us some notion not only of how much noise, but also what kind of noise the devil was using in its effort to stop St Godric from praying. 'The demon's face', *larvalem faciem*, is an interesting phrase. *Larva* is a word for a ghost or mask or skeleton, and originally referred to the spirit of a dead human being. Now, the rest of the context suggests that St Godric was being persecuted by a demon, not by a ghost, but it is worth noting how closely (if subconsciously) the two may still have been associated in the twelfth century, as though the ancient fear that the angry dead could transmogrify into evil and dangerous entities had not altogether disappeared from popular belief.

But it is Reginald's references to *praestigia* and *figmenta* which are especially notable. A *praestigium* is a conjuring trick or illusion, and a *figmentum* a fiction, a deceit, an unreality. One of the common arguments used by demonological writers was that the Devil was a master of trickery and was able to introduce illusory images into a person's mind, so convincing that the person thought they were real. So the 'deceitful tricks' which St Godric ignored are, literally translated, 'the illusions of [i.e. caused by] deceitful behaviour', and the hurling of the pyx, wine-vessel, and water-cruet 'fictions' or 'unrealities'. What, therefore, is Reginald telling us? That there was indeed a demon who tried to interfere with St Godric's devotions, but that the damage to church appurtenances he appeared to do was not happening in reality, only in images and sounds the demon was planting in St Godric's head? It would seem so; and when we are told that none of the objects supposedly thrown with violence showed the slightest sign of damage, this suggests either that they had been restored miraculously to their former condition the moment the demon departed, or – more likely, in view of Reginald's *praestigia* and *figmenta* – that they had never really been disturbed in the first place. We have actually come across this before in Alcuin's *demonicae illusionis*, 'a demon playing games'. *Illudo* means 'make a fool of, play games with, trick', and its noun *illusio*, 'apparition, hallucination'. Alcuin's context suggests quite strongly that we are to interpret his demon's attack as a genuine, physical assault; but the possibility of demonic deception is there undoubtedly underlying the phrase and cannot be ignored.

Reginald's demon is silent. The one operating near Bingen was not, and we now find that such entities are described more frequently as speaking, although with varying degrees of coherence and intelligibility. Nevertheless, these stories should keep us on our guard in case we misunderstand what we read. A history of the bishops of Le Mans, for example, appears to tell us about one which was particularly articulate.

In the time of Bishop Hugues who was alive in 1135,[22] people heard a spirit in the house of Prévôt Nicolas, which frightened the neighbours and those who were living in the house, by making a racket and horrifying noises, as though it had thrown huge stones against the walls with a crash which shook the roofs, the walls, and the wainscots. [The spirit] would move dishes and plates from one place to another, and no one saw the hand which was causing these movements. This spirit [génie] would light a candle even though it was nowhere near the fire, [and] sometimes when food had been put on the table, [the spirit] would scatter bran or ash or soot in order to stop anyone from touching it. Amica, the Prévôt Nicolas's wife, got some thread ready to be made into cloth. The spirit twisted it and made such a mess of it that all those who saw it could not get over their astonishment at the way this had been done.

Priests were summoned and they sprinkled holy water everywhere and told everyone present to make the sign of the cross. On about the first and second night, they heard something like the voice of a young girl who, drawing sighs from the bottom of her heart, said in a mournful, broken voice that her name was 'Garnier'. She addressed the Prévôt. 'Oh dear, where have I come from? From what far away country, through how many storms, dangers, snows, cold, fire, and bad weather have I arrived at this spot? I haven't been given the power to harm anyone, but guard yourselves with the sign of the cross against a troop of evil spirits who have come here to do you injury. Have a Mass of the Holy Spirit said for me, and a Mass for the dead; and you, my dear sister-in-law, give some clothes to the poor on my behalf.'

They asked [the spirit] several questions about things past and future, and its replies were very much to the point. It even made itself clear on the subject of several people's salvation and damnation. But it was unwilling to take part in argument or discussion with the learned men who were sent to it by the Bishop of Le Mans. This last is well worth noting and makes one suspicious of this apparition.[23]

Here we are back to lithobolia and tiresome naughtiness, and the flow of the narrative makes it appear almost as though the spirit was misbehaving in order to provoke the Prévôt into sending for priests, since their exorcistical ministrations would make it manifest in some way, or at least be able to communicate. However, it is notable that Calmet's text – almost certainly a French translation or adaptation of a Latin original – uses the word *génie* at one point to designate the spirit. This will be the Latin *genius* which refers to the spirit of a particular family, the personification, so to speak, of that family's peculiar identity, associated especially with the living head of the household. This may explain why the spirit addresses the Prévôt's wife as 'sister-in-law', a claim of metaphorical rather than actual relationship. If, on the other hand, the spirit actually was Amica's dead sister-in-law, it would clearly be a ghost and thus an entity with poltergeist-like behaviour, such as we have noted before. Certainly this is how the subsequent 'conversations' understand her. Asking for Mass, especially a Requiem Mass, to be said is a common request made by Mediaeval ghosts, as is the injunction to perform an act of charity on her behalf. Ghosts, too, were questioned about the afterlife, so this much of the account is strongly suggestive of a ghost rather than a poltergeist or an evil spirit, and indeed the passage specifically seeks to reject this latter identification. Even the warning about the imminent threat from evil spirits and the coherence of its replies to questions can be paralleled by the behaviour of Mediaeval ghosts. So we are left with three further features which are worthy of some comment.

The spirit's puzzlement with regard to where it has been and the highly physical experiences it has endured on its return to earth strike a convincing note if one considers or speculates upon the changes felt by a newly dead entity. Precipitated from a material to a spiritual existence, accustomed to a physical body and then finding itself without one, used to the modus vivendi of physical living and with no experience of how to 'live' in the spirit, a ghost's natural reaction can be guessed: fear tinged by curiosity and panic. No sooner arrived, however, than required to return to the physical world in its altered state, the spirit is at a loss and either does not or cannot explain where it has been. This is persuasive as a picture of what may be thought to be a newly dead person's reaction to its double change of circumstance. It makes far less psychological sense if the spirit is a demon or a poltergeist.

However, the narrative ends with a note of scepticism, and here perhaps one needs to bear in mind that the spirit was not visibly manifest, but heard only as a voice similar to that of a young girl. Now, the practice of ventriloquism was well known to the ancient and Mediaeval worlds, and so it is possible to wonder whether someone was casting his or her voice – not necessarily in a malicious attempt to deceive, but maybe out of a sense of genuine inspiration or possession. In these latter cases, the voice would have been accepted as that of a real spirit taking and using a human body and its vocal cords as the only means it had to achieve coherent communication. But the author of the *History*, or perhaps Calmet himself, reserves judgement and is suspicious of a spirit which appears to be unable certainly unwilling – to engage in learned discourse with a number of theologians, thereby encouraging the reader to wonder whether the voice-casting (if that is what it was) was not a mischievous human experiment rather than a genuine channelling. This is a point to which we shall return in a moment. Meanwhile, we need to make another one. A first and even second reading of the anecdote may lead us to think that there is a disjunction between the poltergeist episode and the remainder, and that the author (or Calmet) is actually reporting two different incidents while making it seem, by accident or design, that the two constitute one. Thus, the poltergeist half presents us with nothing out of the way for its genre. Lithobolia, even though in this case it is described as apparent, '*as though* [the spirit] had thrown huge stones', interfering with meal times, and transporting objects are all standard features of poltergeist activity, and indeed we have met them already in other episodes from this period. But before we agree we ought to separate the poltergeist from the ghostly voice, or attribute the voice to trickery, it will be worth our while to look at two other episodes by way of comparison.

Gerald of Wales (*c.*1146–*c.*1223) wrote an account of a journey through his native country during 1188, made as part of a recruitment campaign for the Third Crusade. He completed his narrative in 1191, and has this to say of an incident in Pembrokeshire.

It has happened that unclean spirits [*spiritus immundos*] have communicated with human beings, not visibly, but in ways capable of being apprehended by the senses. First in the house of one Stephen Wiriet, then at a later date in that of William Nott, they demonstrated their presence on more than one occasion by throwing filth and other things round the place, whereby they seemed to be playing games [*illudere*] rather than doing people harm. The one in William's house used to ruin the linen and woollen clothes of its host and his guests by ripping them and making holes in them. No careful precaution was able to protect them from these discomforts, and no bar against the inside door, either. In Stephen's house there was a great marvel still, [for the spirit] was accustomed to hold conversations with the humans, and when people were abusive to it – as most of them were by way of amusing themselves – it would reproach them publicly for things they had done since they were born, which they would rather had not been heard or known about by others.

If you ask why this happened, I do not take it upon myself to ascribe a reason for it, unless this is a common portent (as it is called) of a sudden change from poverty to riches, or (more likely) riches to poverty and complete ruin, as actually happened to both these men not long afterwards. But I do think there is one thing worth noting. Neither by sprinkling holy water – no matter how far one sprinkles it nor how much one uses – nor by recourse to any of the Church's rites and ceremonies are places cleansed of this kind of apparition [*ab illusionibus huiusmodi*]. Furthermore, while the priests are entering such places with fervent prayers, under the protection of a processional cross as well as holy water, they are among the first to be insulted by having filth thrown at them immediately. From this it seems clear that sacramentals as well as rites and ceremonies protect us from harm, but not from actions which are not malicious [*innocuis*], and from injuries, but not from apparitions [*illusionibus*].[24]

Here these spirits are designated 'unclean, squalid, guilty', and although at first this may suggest they are being equated with demons, their actions seem to rule this out. Throwing 'filth' (the Latin *sordes* refers to dirt of any kind, but especially human secretions) and 'other things', and ripping up clothes is a nuisance rather than wickedness, and again the verb *illudo*, 'play games', is used to describe the kind of action being inflicted and endured. Thus, as Gerald himself says, these spirits seem to be intent on mischief rather than malice, and to that extent have something in common with fairies – at least, certain types of fairy – who, as Robert Kirk observed in his *Secret Commonwealth*, 'do not all the harm which appearingly they have power to do', and if they do turn out to have harmed human beings, 'acted not maliciously, like devils at all, but in sport, like buffoons and drolls'.[25] Their behaviour is, in fact, reminiscent of the fairy-poltergeist described in an English pamphlet of 1650, *The Strange Witch at Greenwich*, who delights in 'putting the husband's breeches upon his wife's head … throwing the boy's cap into the chimney's smoke … [and] breaking earthen pots … with other such reakes [*tricks*] and mad merry pranks'.[26] One notes, too, that while the spirit enters into conversation with human beings, it is the humans who are unpleasant and therefore the embarrassment they suffer at having their lives revealed in public is entirely their own fault. Knowledge of the details of those lives, of course, derives from the spirit's preternatural ability to know everything, past and future, which aligns it with the spirit from Le Mans which was evidently expected to know such things.

Gerald's attempt at an explanation of both incidents is pretty feeble. Presumably, since William and Stephen both suffered reversal of their fortunes and since, in the Mediaeval view of things, this will not have happened merely by chance, their discomfort at the hands of non-human entities could reasonably have been seen as a warning that their circumstances were going to change for the worse; but such an interpretation speaks of remarkable intellectual ingenuity on their part and is hardly very convincing. Gerald's more general remark, however, is interesting. Such sacramentals as holy water and the sign of the cross, he says, have their limits. They protect, but only up to a point. (Here one thinks of Sinistrari's observation that 'the kind of incubi called *folletti* in Italian, *duendes* in Spanish, and *follets* in French, do not obey exorcists, have no respect for sacred things, and display no fear when these come near them'.)[27] The context of Gerald's remarks is that of exorcism and reveals what appears to have been a common assumption that any preternatural activity was potentially demonic in origin, and therefore needed the Church's ministrations to counter it. Again, however, Gerald uses the verb *illudo* and the noun *illusiones* to describe the relationship between the spirits' actions and their human recipients. Does this throwing of filth and other objects, and the apparent converse across the threshold of different planes of being, take place in actuality in the same way as human throwing of filth and human converse happen in the physical world by and between human agents, or are they both or individually hallucinations – real to the participants, and real in their separate spheres, but unreal in relation to the physical world? These questions need further discussion, but what we can say at this point is that while both the Le Mans and the Pembroke spirits are said to be responsible for poltergeist-like behaviour and to have engaged human beings in conversation, it is clear that the Pembroke spirits are two in number and that the behaviour of one is different from that of the other. One wreaks physical havoc, the other talks to humans. Again, neither was visible, so the possibility that the voice of the second was the result of ventriloquism must be borne in mind, although such an explanation should not be taken for granted.

A second example of a talking spirit comes from a chronicle by Ralph of Coggeshall, a Cistercian monk, who continued a long-standing historical record belonging to his monastery. Coggeshall is in Essex, but the events to which he refers in this episode, dated to the decade between 1189 and 1199, took place in the neighbouring county.

> At Dagworth in Suffolk during the reign of Richard [I], an extraordinary spirit made itself felt [*fantasticus spiritus apparuit*] on many occasions over a long period of time in the house of Lord Osborne of Bradwell. She spoke to the said knight's household, imitating the sound made by a one-year-old child's voice, and kept referring to herself as 'Malkin'.[28] She used to claim her mother was staying

with her brother in a nearby house, and say that they found fault with her and told her off, which was why she was leaving them and taking it upon herself to talk to human beings. She would do and say amazing things, and things which were enough to make people laugh, and a number of times revealed the things other people had done and kept secret. At first the knight's wife and his entire household were terrified by her verbal communications [*colloquiis*], but later on, after they had become accustomed to what she said and the daft things she did [*ridiculosis actibus*], they began to talk to her with confidence and a sense of intimacy, and asked her a good many questions. She used to speak English in the Suffolk dialect, but sometimes [she would speak] Latin and discuss Scripture with the knight's chaplain – something he himself roundly swore to me was true.

She could be heard and sensed, but not seen at all except for one occasion when a little girl, who had earlier pestered and begged her to show herself in visible form, saw her in the likeness of a tiny child wearing a white dress. The [spirit] was unwilling to agree to her request at all until the girl swore, by the Lord, that she would neither touch nor take hold of her. She revealed that she had been born in Langham, and that when her mother took her with her into the open field where she and others reaped the corn, and left her by herself in one part of the field, she was snatched up and carried off by another woman and had remained with her for seven years already. She also said that after another seven years she would come back to live with human beings as she had before, and that she and others wore a hood which rendered them invisible. On many occasions she would demand that those in the house [give her] things to eat and drink. These were put on top of a particular chest and would not be found any more.[29]

Once again, let us notice the terminology used of this entity. The description *fantasticus* is potentially ambiguous. The word is a borrowing from Greek and refers to the ability to produce the appearance of something. It is derived from *phantasia*, 'a presentation, true or illusory', which is where the potential ambiguity comes in, but in fact its common meaning – 'an image, especially a psychic image' – throws a greater emphasis on the illusory component. In part of his dialogue *The Sophist*, Plato discusses the relationship between reality and appearance, and uses *phantastikos* to describe actions which are imitative of others. 'Whenever anyone uses his own body to appear to be like yours, or his voice to resemble yours closely, this [kind of] strongly imagined presentation is called mimesis' (267A). He also links it with a piece of wonder-working or a conjuring trick, *to thaumatopoiikon*, literally, 'the creation of something which makes people astonished' (268D). Here then we are back with the suggestion that the Suffolk spirit belongs to the puzzling zone between illusion and reality, however one defines 'reality' at this juncture, and that a degree of deliberate illusion-making or sleight-of-hand may be involved; and in this connection it is interesting that the spirit was extremely concerned she should not be touched. Why not? Are we to draw some kind of parallel with the ethereal hands, jangling tambourines, and luminous trumpets which manifested during some nineteenth-century spiritualist séances, quite often discovered to be fraudulent exhibitions of human dexterity rather than spirit apparition? We must not jump to conclusions, of course, but *fantasticus* does point, however uncertainly, in that general direction. Beyond saying so much, however, we cannot go.

Since we are told specifically that, with one exception, the spirit could not be seen, Ralph's *apparuit* cannot be saying she was visible, only that she was apprehensible by the senses, which is indeed one meaning of *appareo*. So what did she do to make herself apprehensible? She spoke – and it is interesting that she is said to *imitate* the voice of a one-year-old child, since 'imitation' implies an older person's conscious effort to make such sounds, and underlines the mimetic component of *fantasticus* – and indeed entered into conversation with the people in Lord Osborne's house, 'conversation' being the principal meaning of *colloquium*.[30] She also did things. This is the other method by which people apprehended her presence, but we are told only that she carried out actions, *actus*, and that they were daft *ridiculosi*, 'capable of arousing laughter, funny, comic'. Clearly they were enough to reassure her audience after its initial fear, brought on by an immaterial and extremely child-like voice which was trying to engage it in conversation. Perhaps that was their purpose, for we are not told they involved any destructive or mischievous aspect which would have destroyed the confidence and sense of intimacy [*confidenter et familiariter*] which developed between the humans and the spirit. One may also note that if the spirit could not be seen, her antics – or rather perhaps the results of her antics – could be, and the obvious implication is that she was moving objects in a way, or in a series of ways her audience found amusing. Moving objects, of course, is one of the things poltergeists do, although their actions tend more often to be mischievous or destructive; so if we were to call this Dagworth spirit a poltergeist, or even poltergeist-like, we should have to account for the absence of that malignance so commonly attributed to that type of spirit.

'Speaking Latin' indicates that the spirit was probably not the seven- or eight-year-old child the spirit claimed to be, although we are not informed how much Latin she spoke or what was its quality. The 'and' of 'sometimes [she would speak] Latin and discuss Scripture with the knight's chaplain' is ambiguous. Does it link two different and unrelated statements – (a) she spoke Latin, (b) she discussed Scripture – or does it join two parts of a single action: she spoke Latin while she was discussing Scripture, in order to discuss Scripture, with the chaplain? We cannot really tell. Speaking in the Suffolk dialect may, of course, be attributed to her being Suffolk-born, but there are one or two other details which may make us wonder whether, once again, we are dealing with some kind of fairy, for, as Robert Kirk tells us, 'their apparel and speech is like that of the people and country [*district*] under which they live'.[31] Fairies, it is well known, abducted babies and these babies sometimes came back to resume their human life after spending several years in fairy-land, during which time they might acquire unusual knowledge or powers. Christian Livingston's daughter, for example, 'was taken away with the fairy folk' and told her mother (one presumes telepathically) how to cure people's ailments, as Christian herself averred. 'All the knowledge she had was from her daughter who met with the fairies.' Parents neglecting to make the sign of the cross over their children, especially at night when they put them down to sleep, could also prove dangerous, for the omission allowed fairies to come and take the child away 'in a blast of evil wind'.[32] Leaving out food and drink which then disappeared smacks of customary care to keep the fairies benevolent, too – Sicilian fairies were particularly fond of honey-cakes – and the hood of invisibility serves to emphasise another common fairy trait, that of not being seen. Kirk, indeed, calls fairies 'a people to us invisible'.[33] The woman who abducted this child, then, may or may not have been human and a spirit – a fairy, for example, or at least some entity which, for the time being, had adopted some fairy traits.

Two possible interpretations of the Dagworth spirit thus present themselves: one produced by the use of ventriloquism to simulate an unseen being's speech, and perhaps the employment of illusionistic tricks to make objects move or appear to move; the second resting upon aspects of fairy lore. As the episode is formulated on its telling, these two possibilities appear to be almost independent of each other, the ventriloquism and poltergeistery dominating the first part of the narrative and the fairy lore the second. But quite clearly the author's suggestion is that we are dealing with one spirit, not two, and so ventriloquism and fairy lore – if either is to be entertained as a means to explain the story's phenomena – must be regarded as potential explanatory aspects of one and the same agency.

We embarked on a discussion of the Pembroke and Dagworth spirits to see if they could shed light on the spirit from Le Mans. In this last we were presented with a problem of whether to separate the narrative into two distinct parts, one involving lithobolia and other poltergeist-like activity, the other conversations with human beings, which might be attributable to the use of ventriloquism. In the Pembroke case there are undoubtedly two spirits, and the author, Gerard of Wales, raises the question, via his use of the words *illudo* and *illusiones*, of what we are to understand by 'reality' and 'illusion' or 'fantasy'. In the Dagworth case, the word *fantasticus* in a sense mirrors *illudo* and *illusiones* and suggests that we bear in mind the possibility of human intervention intended to produce or control the episode. Unlike Le Mans, however, it is fairly clear that in Dagworth only one spirit is involved and that it is responsible (barring human agency) for both the poltergeist-like actions and the spirit-conversations. What we learn from comparison of these three episodes in particular, then, is not so much the desirability of working out exactly how many spirits may have been involved, as the necessity of getting to grips with narrators whose choice of vocabulary seems to suggest the possibility of deliberate human involvement, while at the same time presenting the episodes in a way which is clearly meant to be and to be received as truthful, and it is important we try to establish how we, in turn, should be reading these narratives before we go on to study more of them.

2

Is There Anybody There?
Early Poltergeist Narratives and their Audience

The early and disparate anecdotes we have been considering may be far removed from one another in time and geography, but they do share a number of features. Most, for example, are contained either in reverential *Lives* of saintly or important figures, or in *Annals* whose principal aim was to convey to their readers a particular and favourable impression of some public institution. The mischief described, whether prankish or theatrical or murderous, is perpetrated by non-human entities, some of whom ask for assistance, some of whom seem to act for the sake of the action rather than for any ultimate purpose, and all of whom can be brought under control by prayer and the Church's sacramentals. It is taken for granted that non-human entities exist and that they are capable of operating in the realm of physical matter although some of the authors raise possible questions about the actuality of the phenomena or their non-human source. These common features are linked by the mischief or violence which characterises the non-humans' actions, and indeed it is this distinguishing mischief or violence which suggests the possibility of poltergeist rather than any other kind of spirit-source for the episodes of lithobolia, fires, moving objects, and domestic or sacrilegious damage.

Nevertheless, it is the context of these anecdotes which is particularly important in determining why the authors thought they could usefully and pertinently recount them, as well as being a notable factor in the authors' choice of narrative vocabulary. Chronologically, the stories cover a period of nearly seven centuries (*c.*500–*c.*1200), and while their comparative rarity may seem to owe something to the vagaries of survival rates among manuscript sources, these sparse examples may also suggest that perhaps the phenomena they describe were not especially common. If that is so, of course, the interest and significance of the anecdotes would be correspondingly enhanced for both authors and readers alike. Geographically they tend to come from northern and western Europe (the principal exception being that told of St Theodoros from Anatolia) and we may ask ourselves whether there is any possible reason for this, such as their accompanying or following the slow northern and western advance of Christianity among the pagan peoples of Europe, or whether it was merely chance which caused northern and western writers to note these peculiar incidents. It is certainly worthwhile examining the first point a little further, for it is notorious that the Christianisation of Europe took place piecemeal over a long period of time – Christianity was not finally and officially accepted in Lithuania, for example, until 1385 when Grand Duke Jogaila was baptised under the name of Ladislas in the cathedral in Krakow – and that the missionaries' successes varied considerably both in the extent and depth of their achievements. In the middle of the sixth century, for example, Martin of Braga wrote an epistolary sermon, *De correctione rusticorum* ('Healing Countryfolk through Chastisement') which describes what he saw as people's backsliding from the faith to which they had notionally made a solemn and life-changing commitment.

> How can any of you, after renouncing the Devil and his angels and his evil works, now return again to worship him? Because what is burning candles at stones and trees and springs and the place where three roads meet but worshipping the Devil? What is making divinations and auguries and observing the days of idols but worshipping the Devil? What is observing the days of Vulcan and the first days of each month, decorating tables and hanging up laurels, watching one's foot, pouring out fruit and wine over a log in the hearth, and putting bread in a spring, except worshipping the Devil? What is women invoking Minerva while they are weaving, keeping Fridays for weddings, and working out which day one should set out on a journey, except worshipping the Devil? What is muttering spells over herbs and invoking the names of demons in incantations, and many other things it would take me too long to say, but worshipping the Devil? Yet you do all these things after you have renounced the Devil, after you have been baptised, and in returning to the worship of demons and to their evil works you have betrayed your faith and broken the pact you made with God. You have abandoned the sign of the cross you received in baptism and pay attention to the signs of the Devil [which appear in] little birds and sneezing and much else.[1]

About two hundred years later, an appendix to the resolutions of the Council of Estienne (742/43) listed thirty practices and beliefs which may possibly have pertained to the north-eastern fringes of the Merovingian kingdoms. Therein, along with 'the sacred rites of Wotan and Thor ... amulets and [magical] knots ... incantations' and 'idols made of dough and rags', we read also of 'sacrifice which is offered to any of the saints ... [a plant] which good people call Our Lady's Bedstraw' ... and pretending that 'dead people of any kind are saints' – and odd mingling of overtly pagan practice and Christian terminology which on the one hand may, as Yitzhak Hen says of the list as a whole, be 'no more than a guide for further reference whenever some doubts as to the nature and origins of certain customs rose', but on the other illustrate the way paganism and Christianity were doing their best to settle down as bedfellows (with Christianity increasingly the more dominant of the two) during these early Mediaeval centuries, precisely the period during which our first 'poltergeist' narratives made their appearance.[2] But we find a similar situation at the end of our period, too, for in the early thirteenth century the French Dominican Etienne de Bourbon complained about people's still mixing religion, magic, and remnant paganism.

> Insulting to God are superstitions which pay divine honours to evil spirits, or to any other created being – as idolatry does, and as wretched women, sorceresses, do when they seek health by worshipping elder-trees or making offerings to them, despising churches or the relics of the saints, carrying their children thither or to ant-ills or to other things in pursuit of health. People were doing this kind of thing recently in the diocese of Leiden. I was preaching there against acts of sorcery, and hearing confessions, and many women confessed they had taken their children to Saint Guinefort. Since I believed this was a saint, I asked about him and was told, after much reluctance on their part, that he was a greyhound ... Equally insulting to God are such things as using the sacraments, or sacramentals, or sacred things, or things pertaining to the worship of God, as instruments of sorcery, as may be seen in the example of a peasant keeping the Body of Christ in his beehive.[3]

This kind of attitude towards religion, the non-material worlds, and their mutual interpenetration seems to have endured in spite of the efforts of generations of earnest, and to a greater or lesser extent effective, missionaries. Sometimes the misunderstandings which allowed theologically incorrect behaviour or belief to flourish were the result of those missionaries' well-meaning attempts to illustrate a difficult concept. When, for example, in the fifteenth and sixteenth centuries, they wanted to convey the notion of God's physical presence in the Eucharist while at the same time emphasising His majesty and ineffable glory which were not themselves physical, but could be represented in symbolic terms, they enclosed the Host in the monstrance, a golden vessel shaped and decorated as a sun with rays streaming outwards from the crystal 'window' which allowed the faithful to see the transubstantiated wafer. Since people were expected and instructed to bend the knee in worship of God thus made manifest in a type of physical form, we cannot be surprised to learn that there were those who took this symbolism seriously and actually worshipped the real sun, calling it 'Saint Orient' and offering it prayers. But we cannot lay blame for other kinds of misapprehension or dogged adherence to traditional behaviour, if blame there needs to be, entirely on the shoulders of the priesthood. People were perfectly capable of deviating from strict Christian theology by their own unaided efforts. Thus, as late as the seventeenth century, the preacher Michel Le Nobletz found that in Lower Brittany people regularly used practices which assumed a co-existence of ancient paganism and modern Christianity. Women would sweep the church and cast the dust into the air, hoping thereby to procure a favourable wind for their menfolk who were at sea; people might threaten the statues of their local saints with a whipping if the saints did not do as they prayed for, and indeed carry out that whipping if they felt disappointed or thwarted in their wishes; prayer – usually the *Pater Noster* – was offered to the new moon, and pieces of bread and butter were thrown into public fountains as a sacrifice; some people, too, emptied their house of water after a death, for fear the soul of the recently departed might drown if they did not do so, and warmed stones near the fire on the vigil of the Feast of St John the Baptist so that the ghosts of their ancestors could come and warm themselves.[4]

This last reminds us of how close and how closely connected were the material and non-material worlds. Spirit-beings of various kinds might enter and leave the human sphere almost, it seems, at will and there were examples both Scriptural and popular for humans leaving their own plane and entering some spirit Other. The prophet Elijah, for example, was taken bodily one day while he was walking with Elisha. 'And as they still went on and talked, behold, a chariot of fire and horses of fire separated the two of them. And Elijah went up by a whirlwind into heaven' (4 Kings 2.11). Enoch, too, 'was translated that he should not see death: and was not found, because God had translated him' (Hebrews 11.5). Classical literature provided the Middle Ages with another example in Ganymede, a Trojan youth borne off to Olympus to serve the divinities there with the nectar and ambrosia which kept them (and now, presumably, him) youthful and immortal; and in his Christian epic, Dante describes how he himself woke from sleep and was physically transported up to and beyond the gates of Purgatory.[5] The dead, too, were part of a single community of those who had passed away and those who were still living, for until changes in religious confession during the sixteenth century were accompanied by changes in burial practice which overtly separated the dead from the living by giving their corpses ground deliberately removed and set apart from the rest of the community, the living and the dead were neighbours, family, friends. The dead were therefore honoured, feared, cared for, and frequently consulted, and in the eyes of lay folk at least, the post-pagan Christian teaching of Purgatory often merely adapted earlier beliefs to the newer theology. Symbolic of this relationship between the worlds were cemeteries for, as Jean-Claude Schmitt has observed,

> [A cemetery was] an intermediary place, and it played a mediating role: the living had to go through it constantly, not only when they went to church or returned from church, but also when they went from one end of the village to the other or, in town, from one quarter to another. They went by it, travelled through it, and attended to leisure or mercantile activities in it, activities which apparently had little relationship to death or the dead. At least this was the opinion of theologians and preachers, whose opinion sometimes differed from that of the simple curates. In particular the Church constantly castigated dancing in churches and cemeteries as being 'pagan', 'superstitious', or 'indecent' … In the face of Church rituals, the young dancers stomping in rhythm on the ground of the dead communicated with their dead relatives and their ancestors. They danced in the cemeteries as the dead themselves were believed to dance during the night and just as the 'danse macabre' occurred in them, as was sometimes portrayed on the walls of the nearby church or in the ossuary of the cemetery. Thus the cemetery was an oneiric and fantastic place.[6]

But people lived cheek-by-jowl not only with the dead and spirits of one kind or another, all of whom might somehow traverse the gulf which should have existed (but apparently did not) between the worlds of spirit and flesh. For beneath their feet, or around them in woods and fields and caves, or above them on hill-tops and mountains, there existed liminal worlds inhabited by fairies, trolls, elves, gnomes, and the other 'descendants' of the Classical *genii loci* ('spirits of the locality'), who were equally demanding of respect and fear from humans, although Christian saints might well ride roughshod over these expectations. So, when St Collen was invited to visit the king of the fairies in his palace at the summit of Glastonbury Tor, he went, but refused the king's offer of food with the remark that he and his court were nothing more than demons; and he followed this with a douche of holy water which made king, court, and palace vanish immediately.[7] St Collen's attitude and behaviour, then, are entirely consistent with those of Bishop Caesarius, St Theodoros, St Willibrord, and the priests from Mainz and Le Mans. Non-saintly people, however, could profit from association with fairies, as Agnes Hancock claimed. Summoned to appear before the Bishop of Bath and Wells in August 1438 on a charge of practising curative magic, she explained that 'she heals children who have been touched or harmed by spirits of the air, which are generally known as "feyry"', and that 'she has communication with these unclean spirits, and seeks answers and advice from them when she wishes'.[8]

It is perhaps not surprising, then, to find that official (principally ecclesiastical) attitudes towards beings from other worlds or states of existence can be ambiguous.[9] Even if the practice of magic might clearly be wrong and therefore condemnable under most circumstances, what were churchmen to say about appearances of the dead? If ghosts came in answer to deliberate invocation by human beings, of course, that was necromancy and self-evidently sinful. But what was one to say if a ghost, especially that of a dead relative or friend, came of its own accord? Could all such apparitions be dismissed out of hand as demons? Surely not, for the temporary release of a soul from Purgatory into the material world lay in the hands of God and was thus entirely licit. What, too, of visions of the blessed? Could they all be no more than demonic illusion? Fairies, elves, and the like did not fit easily into a Christian picture of creation, either, and in consequence were not always susceptible of a clear-cut admonition. The Sicilian *donas di fuera*, for example, were fairy-like creatures with the feet of a cat or a horse, and used to visit people's houses at night to poke their noses into clothes-chests and eat some of the food if there had been a party of some kind. They could be spiteful if offended, but helpful if treated with respect, and seemed to be particularly fond of children, to whom they never did harm. Similar in many ways to fairies, they also behaved in others which resembled those of witches, so they seemed to represent a peculiar form of crossover between non-human entities and humans, a state which will have made their assimilation into official Christian cosmological thinking a somewhat difficult task. Parallel to these were the *bonae res*, 'the good things', recorded by Guillaume d'Auvergne. They too were female, came into people's houses at night, consumed the food and drink left out for them by the householders, and left behind good fortune in return. But their Latin name or title betrays uncertainty about their status. *Res* is a word with a remarkably wide range of possible meanings: 'event', 'situation', 'an actual fact', 'property or possessions', are merely a few. It takes its cue, in fact, from its context, and the fact that these females are referred to by such a term seems to indicate that the writers – for there were more than just Guillaume – did not quite know how to describe them.[10]

Churchmen's writing on these occult matters therefore sometimes reflects its writers' uncertainty; but their impulse, of course, was either to condemn belief in these beings or to designate the beings themselves as demons. 'Superstition' on the one hand and 'demon-worship' on the other thus provided churchmen with neat condemnatory categories into which, however, the teeming variety of non-human entities surrounding, entering, interfering with, or assisting humanity could not quite conveniently be thrust; and while it comes as no surprise to find that the churchmen we have seen dealing with poltergeist-like spirits treated them as though they were simply demons and could be controlled or dismissed by methods appropriate to that genus, it is also clear – as it was to many churchmen, too – that 'demons' need not be their only option by way of explaining these phenomena. For example, there was available to influence their thinking a long tradition, going back well into Classical times, of 'the angry dead', which could enable them to identify these early apparent poltergeists as particularly enraged ghosts rather than demons. Such ghosts might be angry because they realised they had lost their previous physical existence and were resentful at the loss, or they might be feeling insulted or neglected by the living. Pausanias, for example, records what is evidently a piece of local history, that while Odysseus was driven hither and thither by gales in the Mediterranean, he came at last to the city of Temesa, where one of his sailors became drunk, raped one of the local girls, and was stoned to death by the citizens. Odysseus was not in the least perturbed by the loss of his man and sailed away on the next available tide; but the ghost of the man they had stoned kept killing the Temesans, old and young, male and female alike, until he was finally defeated in hand-to-hand combat with an ex-boxer called Euthymos. Pausanias was shown a picture containing the artist's impression of the ghost: a male figure deepest black in colour with a most frightening general appearance and a wolf's skin for a garment.[11]

Now, as Tertullian later remarked of those who had died before their time or by violence, 'it seems credible that those souls in particular whom a cruel and untimely death has violently and unfairly wrenched from life should contribute to violence and injustice, as if in retaliation for their hurt'.[12] Indeed, ghosts with some grudge against the living were quite likely to use terror in order to get their real or supposed wrong righted. Lucian (admittedly a writer with satiric purpose) tells one such story whose main thrust illustrates the point, even if the details are, and are meant to be, fictitious. It involves a haunted house in Corinth.

> Terrors had long rendered the house uninhabitable. If anyone occupied it, he was immediately frightened out of his wits and fled from it, chased out by some terrifying, panic-instilling ghost. So it was by now falling in and the roof was in disrepair, and there was absolutely no one bold enough to enter it. When I heard this, I took up my books (because I have a good many Egyptian books dealing with this kind of thing) and went to the house at about bedtime. When my host found out where I was heading – straight into foreseeable trouble, as far as he was concerned – he tried to discourage me, and fell just short of physically restraining me. But I picked up my lamp and went in on my own. In the largest room I put down my light, sat on the floor, and began to read quietly. The ghost materialised and attacked. He thought he was up against some average bloke and expected me to flee in terror, like the others. He was squalid, had long hair, and was blacker than the darkness. He stood opposite me and put me to the test. He attacked me from all sides, hoping he could beat me on one of them, and transformed himself now into a dog, now into a bull, now into a lion. But I called on my most blood-curdling spell, one in the Egyptian language, drove him into a corner of the room, and by its means made him disappear. I noted the spot at which he sank down into the ground, and then rested for the remainder of the night. By morning, everyone was in despair, thinking they would find me dead, like the others. But, against all expectation, I came out of the house and went to Eubatides with the good news that he could now live in a house which had been purified and emptied of its terrors. I took him along, together with a large number of other people who wanted to come with us because of the miracle, brought them to the place where I had seen the ghost sink into the ground, and told them to get forks and spades and dig. After they had done this, some six feet down they found buried there a mouldering corpse with only its bones in place. So they took it out of the ground and gave it proper burial, and from that time onwards the house ceased to be troubled by ghosts.[13]

These Classical precedents can be paralleled in later literature, and not only from Europe, and while reverence for the dead can be seen everywhere, fear is not far away. Traditionally, it seems, the dead are emotionally unstable, powerful enough on the one hand to help the living, but equally ready, if provoked or angered, to terrorise them into a more complaisant or respectful frame of mind. In this they seem to share something of the same nature as fairies whose relations with human beings may be benign or malevolent; and if one thinks of certain Scottish witches who claimed to recognise dead people in the company of fairies; or the early fourteenth-century romance *Sir Orfeo* in which part of the population of the fairy kingdom is described as consisting of the ghosts of those who have died a violent death; or the custom of offering food and milk at ancient burial chambers to appease or please the fairies, it is clear that the experience of the mutability of mood among the powerful of the earth provided an equal expectation that the powerful of other worlds or planes of existence might be, indeed would be, similarly temperamental.[14]

Nevertheless, one has to ask whether the poltergeist falls into the same category. We know why ghosts are angry. Very often they tell us, or the reason for their actions is apprehensible enough. The ghost of Hamlet's father wanted revenge for his murder; in the case of Lucian's ghost, proper burial. But if poltergeists are particular examples of the angry dead, what are they angry about and how can one divine their message? Take, for example, another Classical story from Suetonius's *Life* of the Emperor Augustus.

> His tiny nursery – it's the size of a pantry – is still being shown [to visitors] in his grandfather's villa near Velitrae, not far from Rome, and local opinion believes he was actually born there. Religious awe prevents anyone from entering this room unless he has to and has undergone purification, because a long-standing notion has taken hold of [people] that those who go near it without due care and attention are struck by a kind of cold shivering and dread. These things have recently been confirmed, as well, because when the new owner of the villa went to bed in that room – either without thinking or because he wanted to see what would happen – after a very few night hours [had passed], he was thrown out of bed by a sudden powerful force (he didn't know what it was) and was found half-dead in front of the door along with his bedspread.[15]

Was this Augustus's ghost, angry that someone had ventured to intrude upon his sacred space in so casual and disrespectful a fashion? Suetonius does not suggest this. In fact, he contradicts it. The force which propelled the new owner out of bed and out of the room was *incerta*, 'uncertain, undetermined': neither the owner nor anyone else could explain what it was. Likewise, we should hesitate before suggesting that Suetonius doubts the veracity of the story he is re-telling. The 'long-standing notion' (*opinione veteri*) could be translated as 'old fanciful belief' were this the only use of *opinio* in the passage. But Suetonius also refers to the 'local opinion' (*opinio tenet vicinitatem*) that Augustus was born in the small room used as his nursery and, while this *might* be a mistaken belief, there is nothing either unlikely or foolish about it. What is more, that there is something untoward and sinister informing the room has recently been 'confirmed' (*confirmata*, from *confirmo*, 'establish, corroborate, settle, demonstrate the truth of'). So the greater probability is that Suetonius is simply recording, without critical or dismissive undertone, a well-known story connected with the Imperial villa still being visited by tourists. If, then, the source of that violent power is not an angry ghost, we have an unexplained energy capable of directing itself – unless we are to posit yet another unknown as its point of origin and control – against a human being and a physical object (the bedcover) in a manner which looks, from the outside at least, as though it is consciously hostile. It is also clear that it is either energy deriving from the physical plane (in which case there is no immediate puzzle about how it can operate in that plane) or it is energy coming from another – that is to say, non-material – plane, in which case the age-old question of how it can operate simultaneously in two entirely different planes raises itself once again.

Another difference between such a force and an angry ghost is that the ghost's anger can be met and dissipated, either by finishing the unfinished business which has made it angry, giving its physical remains proper burial (as was done with St Germain's angry and frightening spirit or, in the case of the child-entity from Le Mans, making further provision for the soul after death) or, in the case of the *vrykolax* – the resurrected decaying body of the dead individual bringing fear to its neighbourhood – destroying the corpse and thereby putting an end to its rampages. A poltergeist, however, or poltergeist-like entity, seems to be impervious to such solutions and therefore the likelihood of its being or emanating from an angry ghost is much diminished. So were the saints and priests right in thinking that those episodes we met earlier were caused by a demon rather than a ghost? Certainly the spirits' response to holy water and prayers in several of the instances suggests the possibility. Caesarius laid Helpidius's 'devils' in just such a fashion; St Theodoros did the same for his local governor, as did St Willibrord for a whole family, although in the case of the attacks on St Godric, it was the saint's persistence in prayer and refusal to be distracted therefrom which caused the assaults to stop. Bingen, however, provides us with two separate but related incidents. Priests were able to put a stop to a spirit's raging, but only temporarily. It soon resumed its activities and carried on, either impervious to other attempts to get it to cease, or free to continue because the exorcisms were not renewed, thereby perhaps helping to illustrate Gerald of Wales's remark that neither holy water nor exorcisms appear to have any effect on certain types of entity. So if we were to try to account for these episodes – not a particularly wise thing to do, since we lack so much vital information about them and are dependent on a single source and therefore single viewpoint – we might say that the spirits of St Germain and Le Mans look rather like ghosts, the spirit described by Ralph of Coggeshall quite like a fairy or a human abducted to fairy-land, Gerald's spirit like a poltergeist (although there must be reservations here, as in almost all these cases), and the remaining five like demons of one kind or another.

That said, however, we have to bear in mind that we are in the hands largely of ecclesiastical writers whose aim in recording these anecdotes, overtly or subliminally intentional, is to exemplify the sanctity of the subject of their *Vitae*, or to demonstrate the power of the Church over non-human entities. They may be talking to each other, or providing, via those same texts, illustrative exempla which could be used in sermons. In either case, they seem to have interpreted the phenomena they record in terms which they and their possible lay audience will have understood. Ghosts, fairies, and demons were natural parts of the cultural exchanges of the period and hence provided comprehensible and convincing explanations for what would otherwise have been uncomprehended and disturbing intrusions into everyday experience. But we also noted one other aspect of some of these narratives: the language of possible illusionism, suggesting the presence of a conscious and deliberate agency behind the sights, sound, actions, and voices. Now, here we need to be careful not to equate manipulation of people's experience through, let us say, prestidigitation, tricks of light, or ventriloquism, with knowing and intentional fraud. I have drawn attention elsewhere[16] to incidents which are capable of more than one interpretation. The Rood of Boxley Abbey, which attracted a large number of pilgrims each year because it moved its eyes and lips, was 'found' in 1538 to have been worked by strings made of hair. But the 'discovery' came in the midst of the dissolution of the English monasteries at just that moment when justification for pulling down religious houses and dispersing (or sometimes hanging) their inhabitants coincided with Henry VIII's declaration that he and not the Pope was head of the Church in England. The authorities therefore had clear motives for 'finding' and publicising their 'discovery' that the monks had been deceiving credulous laymen and women for years; and while one must acknowledge the possibility that those authorities were right and that fraud had indeed been perpetrated, we should also bear in mind that the laymen and women who formed the bulk of the pilgrim-audience were not necessarily naïve or stupid, and were well accustomed to devices which made images and statues move or appear to move. Religious pageants, for example, which everyone attended, regularly used mechanisms which allowed clouds bearing God to descend and ascend, the figure of Christ to rise from His tomb at Easter, and the Holy Spirit to come down in the shape of a dove; and from

1354 people could see an automated bronze cock belonging to the clock of Strassburg Cathedral, which crowed and moved on the hour, every hour.[17] To be sure, these devices would have been obvious to the onlookers, but so too may those used at Boxley, and if those attending religious pageants were not deceived into believing that they were witnesses to an actual descent or ascent of God or a genuine apparition of the Holy Spirit, but merely co-operated intellectually and emotionally with the mechanics of a devotional exercise expressed in theatrical mode, so too may the pilgrims to Boxley have co-operated with the intentions behind the moving eyes and lips of the Rood.[18]

[Likewise], there are holes in the west front of Wells Cathedral opening on to a singers' gallery within which allowed the voices of seven choristers to ring out across the cathedral green whence they were answered antiphonally by others. The congregation outwith the cathedral would have seen only the brightly-painted statues of angels from whose immediate proximity the singing would have seemed to emanate. What these various devices suggest is that people were well used, both in the Middle Ages and later, to devices of one sort or another calculated to present opportunities for a suspension of disbelief, in essence a suspension not dissimilar to that which a modern audience brings to a conjuror or illusionist. Is the modern illusionist trying to deceive the audience? Yes. Is the audience aware of this and do people willingly accept it as part of the performance? Yes. In what way, then, were the monks of Boxley guilty of deception?[19]

If they were exploiting stupidity, they were criminally guilty. If not, if their working of the Rood figure was known to or suspected by the audience who accepted the mechanism as a means of stimulating their imaginations to a more intense devotion, then the answer should be 'No'. Why did pilgrims go to Boxley in large numbers, year after year, unless they genuinely believed they were witnessing a miracle or wonder? Because theatre is theatre and religious theatre is religious theatre, and people's reactions to religious theatre in particular were (and are) complex, not simple, and certainly not simple-minded. If a static painting or image of Christ or the Virgin was capable of elevating the minds of spectators (accustomed, let us remember, to the expression of religious devotion through elaborate liturgy and religious teaching through the media of pictures and statues), and rousing thereby appropriate devout reaction, how much more efficaciously would a moving image work to that same end? This being the purpose, neither the monks of Boxley nor their many audiences would have had fraud in mind. Quite the opposite, in fact.[20]

When it comes to illusion therefore we must be prepared to acknowledge that people in the Middle Ages and early modern period were likely to have quite sophisticated reactions to illusion deliberately produced. They could see the strings, or know they were there, but be prepared to overlook them for the sake of co-operating in a higher purpose. In the poltergeist-like cases we have been examining, however, there is nowhere any suggestion of such illusion-making: no strings, no tricks of light, no prestidigitation. Nor is the context one of religious drama or secular entertainment. Whatever the illusion might be – if illusion was indeed involved – it was of a different kind and the thus the more noticeable and disturbing. We may also probably set aside the notion that the voices heard at Le Mans and in Pembrokeshire were produced by ventriloquism. In neither case do they seem to have issued from a visible human source, and a visible human source was requisite for at least one of the possible performances of this kind. The reason is that during these early periods ventriloquism was associated either with demonic possession or with necromantic magic or fraud. In the first, when the invading demon speaks, it is through his human instrument, even though (as one might expect) the voice is usually not that normally employed by the human, but a distorted version of it, as Samuel Willard recorded of his possessed servant, Elizabeth Knapp. 'After exercise I was called, but understood not the occasion till I came and heard the same voice, a grum, low, yet audible voice it was … I then called for a light to see whether it might not appear as a counterfeit, and observed not any of her organs to move, the voice was hollow, as if it issued out of her throat.'[21] In the case of necromantic magic or fraud, the favourite example was that of the witch of Endor's raising the ghost of Samuel for King Saul and allegedly giving him voice through her own efforts. As the Protestant propagandist Reginald Scot explained, 'this Pythonist being *ventriloqua*, that is, speaking as it were from the bottom of her belly, did cast herself into a trance, and so abused Saul, answering to Saul in Samuel's name in her counterfeit hollow voice'.[22] The fraud which Willard suspected and to which Scot alludes was not, of course, unknown and could certainly fool some people, as is shown by a case of early fifteenth-century Berne.

> There was a fraticello in the city of Berne … who got up at night in his house and, using stones and wood, pretended that some spirit was present. In this way, to the astonishment of many people there each night, he claimed – and many believed him – that either some divine revelation must be taking place, or that a ghost or evil spirit was abroad. Not infrequently he changed his voice and in wailing tones, like the ghost of a dead man who had been well known in the city,

43

he answered those who asked him questions, saying he was the ghost of a certain recently dead person, either that of someone known to him or of a stranger to whom he would give a name. He persuaded [his audience] that he would go on pilgrimage to particular saints' shrines on behalf [of those souls] ... and while he was travelling to these saints' shrines on behalf of those forementioned souls, he got quite a bit of money.[23]

Yet here again, context is important. The fraticello was pretending to be a ghost and that is how his audience understood his efforts. The 'young girl' of Le Mans certainly fits at least some of the specifications for a ghost, with her request for a requiem Mass and charitable gifts to the poor, but it was the voice's unwillingness to engage in theological discussion with learned men which aroused the writer's suspicion that all might not be as it seemed.[24] If this was a fraud, it does not appear to have been uncovered. The Pembroke spirit, however, is different, not only because its bad behaviour seemed not to be directed towards any particular end, but because when it spoke, it spoke of entirely secular subjects, answering human abusiveness in fact, with intimate details embarrassing to the abusers. Was this the knowledge of a local – a friend, a neighbour, a relative – of these individuals, or was it preternaturally derived? It is noteworthy that the audience was not overawed by or afraid of the spirit in Stephen Wiriet's house, since they were quite prepared to be rude to it. Did they know it was a game (*ludus*) and that the voice came from one of their own and not from beyond? One might be prepared to entertain this as a possibility were it not for the author's silence on the matter. Had such a solution been known or suspected or later discovered, as in Nider's case from Berne, it is reasonable to suggest that the author would have mentioned it. As things stand, the author admits he does not know the cause and tentatively links the manifestations to a complete upset in the temporal fortunes of the men who had suffered the spirit attentions. It is therefore not for us, whose knowledge of the people involved and the circumstances surrounding the episodes extends no further than what we are told in this anecdote, to pretend any clearer insight. All we can do is to note that fraudulent ventriloquism was known during this period and might well be detected, but that it is a non sequitur to infer from these points that all such spirit voices must have been fraudulent, or that, if they were produced by ventriloquism, that the intention behind the act was criminally deceptive.

But we have already noted that Alcuin, Reginald of Durham, and Gerald of Wales used words such as *illusiones* and *figmenta* in their narratives, and while their contexts do not allow us to suggest that this means some human was playing tricks on an unsuspecting (or, in the case of the writers, suspicious) audience, they do imply, and were probably meant to imply, that the spectators and auditors were indeed being deceived by demons who were either casting a glamour over their eyes and ears, or so interfering with the natural processes of sight and hearing that people genuinely thought they were seeing what was not actually there, and hearing voices which did not in fact exist. Thus, as the Dominican Heinrich Institoris explained in his *Malleus Maleficarum* (1486),

> When someone is awake, something may appear to be other than it actually is, such as seeing someone swallow a horse and its rider, or a human being transformed into an animal, or thinking that he or she *is* an animal and must go along with animals. In these cases, the exterior senses are subject to illusion and are being invaded by means of the interior senses. By the power of evil spirits, you see, illusory impressions which are capable of being apprehended by the senses, and which have been kept for a long time in the treasure-house of such impressions – that is, the memory – are drawn out to the common source of sense which deals with images. The power of evil spirits [does this], with God's occasional permission, not by means of the intellectual [capacity] in which intellectual impressions are preserved, but by means of the memory which is the keeper of impressions capable of being apprehended by the senses, and which is further back in the head. [These impressions] are so powerfully imprinted that, if someone needs to have an image of a horse or animal the evil spirit uses a vigorous effort to bring out the impression of a horse or animal from the memory, and [the person] is obliged to think that he or she is indeed seeing such an animal through the eyes of the body, an animal which does not exist outwith [his or her imagination], but gives the appearance of doing so through the vigorous effort of the evil spirit who uses these impressions as his means [of operation] … Since an evil spirit has a certain amount of power over a certain number of things (with the single exception of the soul), he can therefore make some changes in those things (when God allows him to do so), so that they appear to be other than they are; and he does this, as I have said, either by throwing the organ of sight into confusion, or by deluding it … He also works on one's power to create images, by transforming impressions capable of being apprehended by the senses, as I have just said. He also sets various humours in motion, so that things which are earthy or dry appear to be fiery or watery.[25]

Phantasmata, 'representations of realities', visual and auditory, then, can be manufactured outwith the body, or the body itself can be manipulated to produce them, the imagination – the body's treasury of images – providing demons with an ideal vehicle for creating, storing, and transmitting illusions which, to the viewer or auditor, might seem as real as anything else he or she might see or hear. For our writers, therefore, there was no question of illusion in our sense of 'unreal' image. What the people in their narratives saw and heard was real enough. The question was, did the sights and sounds exist externally and independently of the viewer and auditor, or were they generated within?

In either case, demonic activity was regarded as a likely source, and this is a natural assumption for the writers who were principally clerics and were therefore inclined to view any intrusion from another plane of being into the world of physical matter as suspicious and potentially dangerous if it could not evidently and assuredly be attributed to an angelic or divine source. The audience for their narratives may have been twofold: (i) other educated men such as themselves – their accounts were written in Latin and therefore aimed at a literate and thus limited readership; and (ii) the general public who will most likely have received these anecdotes, if they received them at all, in vernacular versions delivered during a sermon or similar mode of religious instruction. The origins of these stories, of course, lay in local gossip which was then relayed from one mouth to another until it came to the ears – or, had it been written down already, before the eyes – of the people whose individual version has become our source. What details have been left out or added, the personal religious, social, emotional circumstances enveloping the individuals to whom the events happened, and the chain or chains of the stories' transmission, are all lacking to us. The original audience, however, will have had in common points of reference which we tend to ignore or try to explain away: the possibility that demons, with God's inscrutable permission, are able to manipulate aspects of physical matter to achieve a purpose, always malevolent, of their own; the close proximity or neighbourliness which exists between the living and the dead, and which may at any moment allow the dead, again with God's permission, to return in some visible or auditory form, and appear to or communicate or react with the living; and the curious self-contained world of fairies, elves, trolls, goblins, and the rest, a world neither part of a theological construct of creation, nor a mode of existence entirely integrated into the world of physical matter. It is worth noting, therefore, that elements of all three of these referential points appear in one or other of our writers' narratives as they record their remarkable event and then seek to offer some comment, explanatory or observational, upon it. Narrators and audience lived in the same mental as well as physical universe even if personal circumstances of education if not of inclination might cause the narrator to choose to emphasise one avenue rather than another, and what they had perhaps most fundamentally in common was the firm belief that everything is connected to everything else and that therefore nothing happens without a purpose, even if that purpose cannot be detected immediately. As Rosalie and Murray Wax have expressed it:

> In describing peoples who view the world magically, Western scholars sometimes employ terms such as 'chance' or 'luck'. We think of ourselves as the believers in causal law and the primitive as dwelling in a world of happenstance. Yet the actuality is to the contrary: It is we who accept the possibility and logic of pure chance, while for the dweller in the magical world, no event is 'accidental' or 'random', but each has its chain of causation in which Power, or its lack, was the decisive agency. If a shepherd loses an animal, this is not regarded as a random event, the intersection of a roving predator and a wandering herd, but rather, there is a cause: either the lack of protective Power of the shepherd or the superior malevolent Power of an enemy.[26]

The poltergeist-like activities we have been discussing were therefore events-with-meaning, and in order to discover that meaning, it was important to uncover the agency which produced the ghost, demon, fairy, illusion, or none of these four – until some attempt at least had been made to choose between them, appropriate and effective action would not be possible; and effective action was desirable, otherwise the troublesome phenomena would continue to occur to who knew what levels of destructiveness.

3

Violence Against the Person, c.1260–c.1286

Destructiveness we have seen already in the incidents of lithobolia, fire-raising, destroying clothes, and attempted infanticide. Other attacks upon human individuals, however, could be even more frightening and take all a person's willpower and fortitude to survive. Consider, for example, an episode recorded by Guibert de Nogent (c.1055–1121/25), a Benedictine monk from the north of France. He is conspicuous among writers of the period for the quality and interest of his personal memoirs (*Monodiae*), written in c.1115, and among other recollections of his mother, he includes an incident which took place not long before he was born.

> In the dead of a dark night, as she lay awake in her bed filled with this unbearable anxiety, the Devil, whose custom it is to attack those who are weakened by grief, the Adversary himself, appeared all of a sudden and lay upon her, crushing her with his tremendous weight until she was almost dead. The pressure began to suffocate her, she was completely deprived of bodily movement, and her voice could not utter a single sound. Unable to speak but free of mind, she could only implore the help of God. And suddenly, from the head of her bed, a spirit, undoubtedly a benevolent one, began to cry out in a voice as affectionate as it was clear, 'Holy Mary, help!' The spirit spoke this way for a few seconds, and she began to comprehend what he was saying. Intensely tormented as she was, she suddenly felt that this spirit had violently hurled himself against the foe, who then rose up. The other spirit faced him, took hold of him, and threw him to the floor with a fierce noise. Their impact shook the room violently, and the servants who were usually plunged into a deep sleep were unexpectedly awakened. When divine

power had overcome the evil one, the pious spirit, who had cried out to Mary for help and had expelled the Devil, turned to the woman he had freed and said to her, 'See to it that you are a good woman!' The servant women, dumbstruck by this sudden commotion, rose from their beds to see what condition their mistress was in. They found her half dead, with her face drained of its blood and all the strength of her frail body gone. They asked her about the noise and immediately heard her tell her story; but even by their presence, their conversation, and the lighting of lamps they still had some difficulty in reviving her.[1]

There appear to be four stages in this sequence of events. First, Guibert's mother, in the late stages of pregnancy, was in a state of high tension and emotional distress, having been informed that her husband, who was absent fighting in the war between Guillaume of Normandy and King Henri I, had been taken prisoner and might well remain in confinement for the rest of his life. She felt a sharp pain and fainted and thereafter refused to eat or drink, worrying so much at the prospect of never seeing her husband again that she found difficulty in getting to sleep. It was at this point she suffered her attack of 'the Old Hag', a condition exactly described here by Guibert and sometimes alluded to as 'sleep paralysis with hypnagogic hallucinations', although one does not wish to pin modern labels on it as though such a description were the last word in accuracy.[2] It is also unhelpful to assume that her emotional state and advanced pregnancy, or her possible undernourishment or dehydration, necessarily 'produced' the symptoms of being suffocated. Something similar can be found, for example, in a case from 1983. A young man, Tom Littleton, married with children, went to bed late one night (at 1 a.m.) and had no sooner settled down than he became aware that an angry 'something' had entered the room and walked round to his side of the bed. It did not speak, but emitted two notes, one high, one low. Tom found he was entirely paralysed except for one hand which he used to wake his wife, and as soon as she was conscious and asked him what was the matter, the 'something' disappeared – or perhaps one should say, went away.[3] Interestingly enough, Tom seems to have assumed that this presence was some kind of ghost, as did his parish priest, but that may owe something to Tom's earlier experience of ghostly noises in the house, and to a lack of actual violent activity by the entity, which indeed suggests ghost rather than poltergeist as a possible source of his fright. As far as Guibert's mother is concerned, however, we should note that she was a deeply religious woman, as her son's memoirs make clear, and it makes more historical sense to listen to what she, through her son, has to say about her experience, rather than impose an 'explanation' on her and so cut out the voice which is trying to speak to us. Instead, we may care to ask questions she would have understood. Was this attack demonic, or is it possible that some other kind of spirit or entity was involved? The answer may seem obvious. The Devil, the Adversary, the Evil One, are the terms used to describe the attacking spirit, but were these the terms used by Guibert's mother, or have they been introduced into the narrative as Guibert, the monk, tells it? As it stands, it is difficult to determine.

Secondly, she heard a benevolent spirit-voice and became aware of a fight between two spirits, the one who oppressed her in the first place and the one it may be possible to characterise in contemporary terms as her guardian angel. The benevolent spirit is interesting, partly because his voice was clearly heard by Guibert's mother and its tone distinguished as affectionate, and partly because the spirit calls upon the Blessed Virgin for help before he engages the other in noisy combat. One may dismiss the notion that Guibert's mother was responsible for the cry to the Virgin and therefore actually heard her own voice, for we are told that the spirit repeated his ejaculation several times, thus allowing Guibert's mother to accustom herself to the sound, and that the voice she heard was masculine. In her understanding of the event, then, the voice was external to herself and came from an unseen source which, seemingly empowered after its prayer, wrestled its evil opponent to the ground so noisily that not only was Guibert's mother aware of what was happening, but the rest of her household was woken by the noise. The servants, then, provide witness to a part of the phenomenon, in as much as they heard a violent noise or violent noises and came to investigate. The cause of that commotion, of course, comes only from Guibert's mother, but since, from everything her son says of her, she was a deeply religious woman, it is unlikely she manufactured the incident and lied to draw sympathetic attention to herself. Thirdly, this fight, while taking place between two spirit-entities, impinged upon the world of physical matter in such a way that it created loud noises perceptible by more than one human ear: that in the initial impact of one spirit upon another, and that in the heavy contact of one spirit with the floor of the room. Fourthly, all this took place in darkness: lights did not arrive until the servant women turned up. This makes the experience auditory, not visual – not uncommon among phenomena involving ghosts and poltergeists where the source of disturbances rarely reveals itself to the sight.

Now, it seems clear that Guibert's mother's suffering the Old Hag, and her awareness of a spirit-struggle happening close to her, are not necessarily the same experience. Certainly the second reads as though it were an attempt to bring the first to an end, but while Guibert's mother was physically involved in the first, she had no part to play save that of auditor in the second. Nor is there any suggestion that her initial attacker was a poltergeist in the usual sense of the word. Her case, in fact, has parallels with that of Tom Littleton. Both experienced the Old Hag; both became aware of innate hostility emanating from what they took to be a spirit-source; both were frightened; both heard noises coming from the entity, and for both the experience happened at night and in darkness. Tom was conversant with the notion of ghosts since he had a particular interest in folklore, although how far this may have influenced or moulded his interpretation of his experience we cannot say, because he does not comment further than observing that he had never been afraid of ghosts before this episode. But does that mean he was not afraid of the *idea* of ghosts, or that he had had some kind of encounter with them, or something like them, before and had not felt fear either during or as a result of those experiences? We cannot tell from his evidence. Guibert's mother of course, would have been entirely familiar, like all her contemporaries, with the notion of spirit-visitants, and from what other things Guibert tells us about her, we know not only that she was deeply religious but also that she had a mystical strain in her which was alive, for example, to the meaning of dreams which she always interpreted in religious and sometimes predictive terms.[4] So when she underwent her Old Hag ordeal and listened to the spirit-assaults which followed, it is not surprising to find she envisaged the hostile entity as Satan, his adversary as a good spirit or angel, and heard the good spirit call on the Virgin for help.

These two spirit-attacks, then, one Mediaeval, one modern, bring us into the undefined territory between ghost and demon, an area occupied by several of the 'poltergeists' we looked at earlier and one which seems to accommodate behaviours appropriate to or expected of at least two out of those three. One very good example is that of Christina of Stommeln (1242–1312).[5] Details of her life come from her own brief dictated account, a much longer narrative written by a Dominican priest, Peter of Dacia, who knew her personally, and letters from a would-be ordinand whose account is somewhat difficult to accept in its entirety, along with other material collected in the *Acta Sanctorum*. Determined from a very early age to devote herself to Christ and somewhat extravagant in her devotions and austerities, she was thought to be possibly mad by the beguines among whom she was living, especially when they found out about her more peculiar experiences such as being convinced that the consecrated Host was a mass of maggots, or that if she swallowed the Host she might also swallow a toad. But however extravagant such thoughts may appear to be, they were not unique of their kind. Domenica dal Paradiso, for example, another highly impressionable girl, had the following experience at her first communion in 1487.

She felt that the most holy sacrament was changed in her mouth into the form of an infant which, descending into her heart, made it languish with pure delight, and then shifted its position in such a way that the head lay under her left armpit, while its feet were extended to her right side. In this way it was enthroned, as it were, upon her very heart and took possession of it. Domenica herself, meanwhile, rapt and enthralled, was sweetly crushed under the weight of this divine burden, nor could she make any movement until, with the help of her guardian angel, she was able to clasp her arm around the infant form within her, as a nurse carries a child at the breast.[6]

Still, even if we allow that Christina's negative thoughts may have been manifestations of an overworked sensibility (she was in her early twenties at the time), we are also faced with her experience of a number of poltergeist-like phenomena which cannot so readily be ascribed to a vivid imagination. The Devil used to beat her, she told her parish priest, and did it so hard that the blows could almost be heard in the local market place. 'Afterwards the demon would suddenly pull away whatever she had under her head as she lay in bed, so that her head bumped on to a box which stood below. Sometimes he got inside the pillow and there made such a disturbance that she could not sleep. Sometimes he put a stone under her head, and lifted the bedclothes off her, and if she replaced them, he again pulled them away'; and on another occasion he 'tore her feet with his fine claws, so that one day the whole parish crowded there to see the great sore places with their own eyes'. 'He gnaws at her flesh like a dog', wrote Father Maurice from the monastery at Köln, 'and bites out great pieces. He burns her clothes next to her skin while she is wearing them, and shows himself to her in horrible forms.'[7]

A little later, when Christina was twenty-six, she and a number of others were praying in church when a filthy, stinking bag flew the length of the nave and landed at their feet. Inside, and apparently unblemished by the ordure which had tainted the bag, was Christina's prayer book, stolen from her three months previously, she said, by the Devil. Nor was this the only episode involving filth. During the winter of 1268/69, as Peter of Dacia witnessed and recorded, Christina and her visitors were subjected time and time again to assaults by some hostile entity which spattered both them and the room with faecal matter. Many (but not all) of these attacks took place at night. On each occasion, however, there were witnesses and sufficient light for them to see what was happening, and when a Swedish Dominican attempted to exorcise the spirit, those present heard a violent explosive bang in the room, the candles were extinguished, and the exorcist was covered in filth. A similar drenching in faeces once took place even in the parish church, although this time Christina herself was spared the deluge. But at the beginning of Advent 1269, the entity (which Christina and others clearly identified as the Devil) turned to even greater violence. It burst down the door of her room with immense force, threw stones which hit several people present, and began to bite a number of priests – 'I saw the scar', said Christina of her parish priest. 'It was three inches long, just above the wrist' – as well as subjecting Christina herself to a barrage of stones and bones and bites. It thrust the head of a flayed cat into her mouth, ripped off parts of her clothes, and brought in a skull through which it spoke to her and the others. 'The [parish priest] told me', reported Peter of Dacia, 'that the demon sometimes placed the skull upon the ground, but sometimes lifted it up higher than the grating of the house, just as it pleased him.'[8] This violence rapidly worsened. The entity dragged Christina out of bed by her hair, wounding her sister, who tried to come to her aid, by stabbing her in the back with a sword, while all the onlookers saw, apart from the wound and the slash in her sister's dress, was Christina pinned against the canopy of the bed and the sword itself being waved about in the air by an invisible hand. When the parish priest arrived he was struck several times on the head with the blade; an attendant friar was bodily thrown out of the room; and dresses, along with household linen, which were kept not in the house itself but in a box in a church, were completely destroyed. Not long after, something ripped off Christina's shoes, along with half the skin of her feet while she knelt in prayer in the church, and cut them to pieces.

Now, if these instances constituted the whole of Christina's experiences, we should be justified in seeking to classify them as poltergeist, on the grounds that they come near to fulfilling the usual criteria for such an identification. But things are never that simple and we must add to their number various other episodes which took place alongside or in between them. When Peter of Dacia met Christina for the first time on 20 December 1267 in the house of her parish priest, she stood up to greet him and was immediately hurled backwards so forcibly that she hit her head on the wall and made the building shake.[9] There were several people present, other than the two priests, and they were also witness to Christina's being thrown into the furniture while she tried to talk to her confessor. It was on this occasion, too, that they examined her feet and discovered fresh, bleeding wounds which multiplied during the course of the afternoon. Seven people, including Peter, stayed in the house overnight, sitting in chairs to keep themselves awake so that they could observe what might happen next. Christina, too, was sitting with them and at one point gave evidence of pain near her knee. 'I have been wounded,' she said and pulled from inside her sleeve (*per manicam*) a nail covered in blood. Some time later, while the two priests were saying Mass they were interrupted by a commotion and found that Christina had produced another nail. This one was twisted and had both blood and flesh adhering to it.

Such a set of episodes is, of course, suspicious, and there can be no doubt that Christina, whose sense of personal theatre was highly developed as we can tell from her almost excessive austerities as a teenager and her extraordinary visions or pseudo-visions of the Host, may have thrown herself round the room and stabbed herself with a couple of nails she had secreted about her person. There were, indeed, witnesses and we may have expected that at least one of them would have noticed anything untoward; but we do not know whether these witnesses, or any one of them, were prepared to be hostile or sceptical (or even whether they were fully awake at the time of the nail incidents) or had stayed with Christina in the hope or expectation of seeing something unusual. Certainly Peter, who was sitting next to her when the first nail was produced, kept both nails thereafter and treated them almost as though they were holy relics. There were other episodes, too, which may draw the attention of the sceptic. In July 1268, Christina was found buried to her chin in the mud of a disused reservoir. Just before Christmas that year she complained of being burned with hot stones, and indeed one was discovered immovably lodged in her left side, although it was not hot enough to prevent others from touching it and yet sufficiently hot, along with others, to leave a good many wounds on her body. One night (she said) the Devil also thrust two sizeable willow twigs through her ankles, dragged her out of the house, and tied her to a tree, repeating the assault three days later at midday. What are we to make of these? It is always possible, of course, that she was telling lies about the stones and burned herself in private to give the impression that, however others might find them, they had in fact been hot enough to leave wounds 'so deep that you could have hidden a *prunum* [sloe] in them'.[10] She could also have taken herself to the reservoir and tied herself to the trees after mutilating her ankles.

An emotionally unstable woman eager for a certain type of attention and willing to manufacture signs of diabolic hostility towards her: it is not difficult to dismiss almost any of these particular episodes and thus taint with suspicion of fraud everything else which happened to her. But, as we have seen in the case of the Boxley Rood, an apparently simple case of deception may look somewhat different when viewed from a contemporary, rather than a modern, angle. Were the hurling backwards, the wounds on the foot, and the piercing with nails outwards demonstrations of an inward reality? In other words, if – and one should perhaps note this 'if' – Christina was inflicting these pains on herself, was she doing so with guilty intention to deceive, or was she acting out in the flesh those torments and afflictions she sincerely believed the Devil or some other hostile entity was making her suffer?

Pious enactment or intentional fraud? In view of the different psychology of our Mediaeval forebears, the former must at least be considered rather than the latter automatically assumed, for these particular events took place as part of a continuous context, a context in which, for example, during February and March 1268, Christina fell into ecstatic trances and was found to have stigmatic signs on her hands, feet, and head. These appeared with fresh vigour on Holy Saturday that year and, after lasting for about eight days, stopped bleeding, only to break out afresh each succeeding Easter until 1286 and possibly beyond. Far from displaying these stigmata or drawing attention to them, Christina sought to conceal them and was annoyed if anyone referred to them. She therefore joins company, as it were, with several other women and men – St Francis of Assisi, Blessed Angela of Foligno, St Catherine of Siena, and so on down to St Gemma Galgani in the nineteenth century and St Pio of Petrelcina in the twentieth – who have exhibited in their flesh the wounds and marks of Christ's suffering and death.[11] Now, it is well known that the mind can exercise a quite extraordinary control over the body and that hypnosis in particular can be employed to induce stigmatic phenomena in a sensitive subject. A German psychiatrist, Alfred Lechler, for example, did this with a patient of his, Elizabeth K. Elizabeth, like Christina, was in many ways emotionally disturbed to a notable extent and, again like Christina, was in her mid-twenties when she exhibited severe physical symptoms of an inner turbulence. On Good Friday 1932 she attended an illustrated lecture on the Crucifixion and this gave Dr Lechler the idea of hypnotising her with a view to reproducing Christ's stigmata in her body. By Holy Saturday his experiment had worked and Elizabeth's palms and feet showed red, swollen marks the size of a large coin with torn, weeping skin around them. On another occasion Lechler suggested she cry bloody tears, which she did; and on a third, after saying to her that a crown of thorns was being placed on her head, she winced in pain when he lightly touched her forehead. By the following morning, there were irregularly shaped puncture marks where the crown would have rested, which seeped blood within an hour.[12]

There are two points worth noting from this. First, as Ian Wilson points out, Lechler's experiments show that 'spontaneous bleedings of the type attributed to stigmatics during the last seven centuries really do happen', and secondly, that while Elizabeth K manifested her signs and symptoms under hypnosis, Christina (and her companion Mediaeval stigmatics) did not. Constant meditation by a sensitive subject upon the suffering and death of Christ may, of course, produce a condition akin to self-hypnosis, but there have been many who have meditated long upon Christ's agonies – the followers of St Ignatius Loyola, for example, encouraged to train their spiritualities by means of his highly emotive *Exercises* which lay great stress upon imagination and empathy – who have not developed stigmata at all.[13] So while there can be no doubt that Christina was – or at least had been as a teenager – emotionally unstable, and that she had a constant and intense devotion to Christ and a highly developed awareness of personifications of evil, episodes involving apparent physical attacks upon her need to be regarded with care rather than dismissed out of hand, while one bears in mind that there may be more than one explanation of extraordinary or bizarre happenings other than fraud or self-induced hysteria.

The same, for example, can be and has been said of a Romanian girl. Eleonore Zugun, who was the focus of poltergeist activity between the ages of eleven and fourteen and who, like Christina, exhibited signs and marks and bites upon her body. Eleonore was born in 1913 in Talpa, a village in northern Romania where belief in spirit worlds and the interaction between them and this one continued to be lively and active. Indeed, her grandmother was reputed to be a witch and once, when eleven-year-old Eleonore was going to visit her and found money by the roadside, which she then spent on sweets for herself, her grandmother told her that the money had been left by the Devil to tempt her and that now she would never be free of him. Was this a warning of impending demonic possession or obsession, or a piece of hostile magic (*maleficium*) equivalent to a curse? Whatever it was, the very next day poltergeist-like phenomena began to show themselves wherever Eleonore happened to be. The first was lithobolia outwith the grandmother's house; the second was movement of small objects which jumped about when Eleonore was present. Back at home, Eleonore continued to be the focus of similar activities – on one occasion, for example, a small bowl flew at a visitor and hit him on the head – and she found this so distressing that she sought refuge in a nearby monastery. Even there, however, the phenomena persisted and her family, losing what little patience it had with her, removed her thence and committed her to an asylum.

By now, of course, gossip about her had ceased to be local and it was not long before the newspapers picked up her story, as a result of which she was sent back to the monastery and placed under close observation. It was while she was there that Countess Zoe Wassilko-Senecki, a young woman with a particular interest in both occult matters and psychoanalysis, came to visit her and was so taken with what she saw, and Eleonore's personality, that the following year (1926) she brought the girl to live with her in Vienna. Here

Eleonore settled down. Her previous experiences had, not unnaturally, made her unhappy and withdrawn and, as she had had little education, she often gave the impression of being somewhat young for her actual years. Now, however, under the Countess's friendly care she became stable and her unhappiness seemed to disappear. But the poltergeistery did not, and the Countess kept a diary of its manifestations, including not only the displacement of objects but also the assaults which Eleonore was suffering upon her person: slapping, being thrown out of bed, having hair ripped out of her head, scratches and bite-marks on her face, neck, arms, and chest. These assaults did not cease when Eleonore left Vienna for a short stay in London in September 1926. There she was examined by various eminent witnesses both separately and conjointly, many of whom carefully wrote down what they had seen and heard. Thus, on Monday 4 October, Neil Gow recorded:

> 3.20. Eleonore cried out. Showed marks on back of left hand like teeth-marks which afterwards developed into deep weals. I got Eleonore to bite her right hand and noted the kind of marks caused by this bite, but could trace no similarity between this and the first alleged stigmata.
> 3.25. Eleonore gave a soft cry and pointed to her right wrist. She undid the sleeve of her blouse and rolled it up. I saw several freshly-made red marks like scratches. There were several of these, about five inches long. After a few moments they rose up into heavy white weals.
> 4.12. Eleonore was just raising a cup of tea to her lips, but suddenly gave a cry and put the cup down hastily; there was a mark on her right hand similar to those caused by a bite. Both rows of teeth were indicated.[14]

A fortnight later, Captain Seton-Kerr, a Fellow of the Royal Geographical Society, noted: 'I was present on October 5, when the so-called stigmatic markings appeared on the face, arms and forehead of Eleonore Zügun under conditions which absolutely precluded the possibility of Eleonore's producing them by scratching or other normal means'; and a report made by the National Laboratory of Psychical Research also confirmed that in its opinion, 'Eleonore was not consciously responsible for the production of the marks', and that 'under scientific test conditions, movements of small objects without physical contact undoubtedly took place'.[15] In Germany the following year, Eleonore was closely investigated by yet more doctors and psychiatrists and a documentary film of these corporeal phenomena was made in Munich, which seems to confirm the general opinion of her examiners that the phenomena were real and not produced by deception. One Munich doctor, Hans Rosenbuch, however, did not agree. He was quite sure Eleonore was a fraud and said so more than once in print, accusing both her and the Countess of manufacturing some of the scratches and marks on her person. But Alan Gauld thinks that Rosenbuch failed to prove his case. 'It is worth noting', he wrote, 'as the Countess pointed out, that Rosenbuch has nothing to say about those occasions on which phenomena took place without any suspicious manoeuvres being observed by the attentive witnesses. He simply passes them by. He was pretty clearly one of those dedicated but tiresome persons, to be found alike amongst the sceptics and the credulous, who constantly chop and distort phenomena to fit them upon some preferred Procrustean bed.'[16]

With the onset of Eleonore's menstruation in 1927, however, all her phenomena ceased and, as far as we know, never returned; 'as far as we know', because after 1930 Eleonore returned to Romania and set up as a hairdresser, after which she disappears from historical view. Eleonore thus runs counter to two theories often associated with poltergeistery: that the phenomena begin and are particularly focussed upon young girls at about the time of their menstruation and self-conscious sexuality, and that they are most remarkable in the presence of emotionally unstable and unhappy teenagers, especially girls. The parallels with Christina are interesting. Both, for example, had unhappy childhoods, but found a degree of stability later on – Eleonore while she was a teenager, Christina in her twenties – under the protection of an amiable adult willing to take them as they found them. Both attributed their sufferings to a demon. In Christina's case, she referred frequently to the Devil who was biting her and attacking her and uplifting objects, including herself, high in the air; for Eleonore, it was *dracu* – perhaps the Devil himself about whom her grandmother had warned her, or perhaps some other demon – and here it is worth recording two curious incidents noted by the Countess in her diary and later published in the short-lived *British Journal of Psychical Research*.

Once I entered my room and looked at the window. Eleonore was standing behind me. Suddenly I saw a shadow which glided down slowly in front of the window and not straight, but zigzag … Another time I was sitting with Mr Klein at the round table, while Eleonore stood with a cat in her arms at the bookstand. Mr Klein unintentionally looked at the girl, and on this occasion noticed a dark grey shadow come from behind her, pass along her right side and fall under our table upon the cushion at our feet. It was a tin box which had before stood on the washstand on the other side of the room. I had always the impression that a returning object of the kind was only again submitted to the normal laws of the physical world when it was perfectly itself again … The foregoing shadow has nothing at all to do with the appearance of the object itself. I think that the impression which this moving riddle makes is best described by the words: 'Hole in the world', which I used for it'.[17]

The second of these was clearly connected with the tin box even if, as the Countess says, it did not correspond to the shape of the box itself. The Countess herself does not connect the two incidents and does not suggest that the zigzagging shadow necessarily had anything to do with Eleonore, but connection there may have been subconsciously and connection there certainly could be in the mind of anyone disposed to remember Eleonore's *dracu* and willing to believe, with her, that the phenomena plaguing her were demon-induced or at any rate demon-inspired. Both she and Christina, of course, came from deeply religious societies and cultures in which such reference to otherworld entities in terms of Christian theology was entirely natural. This sense of community between the worlds offers perhaps the greatest difficulty for modern Western commentators on occult phenomena, but one which it is essential for them to overcome, otherwise the older mentality (not to mention the living mentality of much of the rest of the world today) will remain a puzzle and a darkness, insoluble on the one hand and impenetrable on the other. For all their chronological and cultural differences, then, Christina and Eleonore would have understood each other the moment they discussed what had happened and was happening to them because for each the Devil and the *dracu* were real, comprehensible presences and the suspected, indeed the expected source of all their tribulations.

These tribulations, too, were similar: lithobolia, personal physical assault, objects flying through the air, signs of being bitten, and other marks appearing spontaneously on the body – and in both cases, in spite of possible reservations about some of the episodes in Christina's life, the core phenomena involving both women seem to have been genuine. As Herbert Thurston points out anent Christina but with equal validity, *mutatis mutandis*, anent Eleonore, 'This was not a case in which we have merely the report of what Christina believed she had experienced when alone. The circumstances were witnessed and attested not only by the little group of her own family circle and her devoted associates, but also by the Benedictine monks of Brauweiler and by Dominicans of Cologne.'[18] So also Eleonore was witnessed and closely examined by doctors and psychiatrists who were prepared to be sceptical, as well as by friends and admirers, and even when a 'scientific' explanation for the phenomena was offered, it does not stand up to scrutiny. The Countess, who was undoubtedly a friendly admirer, nevertheless thought that the bites and other marks were somehow produced by Eleonore's unconscious mind as a form of self-punishment for powerfully developed sexual urges she fixated on her father. However, as Colin Wilson observes, 'A girl does not go on scratching and biting herself for two years because she feels guilty about her sexual desires, particularly if she finds herself transformed, like Cinderella, into the protégée of a wealthy countess.'[19] Moreover, even if one were to adhere to the notion of subconscious mind over matter, whether guilty or not, there is no accurate telling either which powers of Eleonore's subconscious mind were at work, or indeed whether the subconscious mind in question belonged to her or to someone or something else.[20] But we are here in the realms of Freudian and Jungian theorising and neither is particularly helpful in explaining Eleonore or Christina in historical terms. Rather more pertinent in Christina's case is the Church's apparent reluctance to canonise her in spite of her visions and stigmata and constant devotion to God in the midst of continual and unrelenting suffering at the hands of what she and her contemporaries called the Devil. Indeed, it may very well be precisely because of all those manifestations that the Church viewed and has continued to view her case with reservation. In sum, religion lies at the heart of the cases we have been discussing.

So, too, it can be seen as the prime factor not only in these but also in other cases separated by several centuries and a corresponding change in the prevailing outlook among educated élites. Thus, the nun Eustochium of Padua – herself the daughter of a nun and so from the start deprived of a normal family life, since she was first put into care and then obliged to live in her father's house under the resentful eye of his legitimate wife – began to exhibit from a very early age the signs of infestation by a malevolent entity referred to as 'the Devil'. After two years of alternating neglect at home and exorcism by the Church, the little girl was sent to be brought up by nuns and proved to be a devout, cheerful, and charming member of the household. For nine years she lived there more or less free from 'demonic' interference, but in 1460, when she was sixteen, the Mother Abbess died and the convent dissolved itself in the face of demands by the Bishop of Padua that it reform its hitherto lax discipline. A new abbess and new nuns then brought a very different atmosphere to the convent, and it was their more rigorous régime which encouraged Eustochium to make the first step towards taking the veil. Almost as soon as she had done this, however, her behaviour altered and she alternated between being disobedient, rude, and violent, and as devout and humble as she had been before. These changes were a prelude to what appears to have been a period of demonic possession, and as a consequence of her speeches and actions during this time she suffered imprisonment within the convent for three months as the rest of the community sought to give themselves a respite from the outrageous things she said and did during her fits. Once released from confinement, however, Eustochium was subjected to even more violent preternatural attack.

At one time he dragged her violently along the ground to the very door of the convent as if he were bent on pushing her out altogether; at other times he lifted her up high into the air and then suddenly let her drop like a stone, until it seemed a miracle that she did not break her bones. Still more frequently he scarified the skin of her neck with a network of cuts, severing the veins sometimes so that she lost quantities of blood and fainted away from sheer weakness. Constantly it happened that he tied her up with cords or bound a rough haircloth round her loins which chafed her skin intolerably. Frequently again he crushed her head or washed it with ice-cold water, covering it afterwards with damp cloths and thus producing acute neuralgia. Three or four times every day he forced her to drink great vessels of spring water, especially in the morning when she got up, his object being to injure the organs of digestion, and there were occasions when he put lime into it or varnish or some other disgusting matter; and finally on one occasion he made her eat sponge fried with stinking oil which, as the doctors judged, would alone have been sufficient to cause her death.[21]

Nor was this all. At one point, recorded her later biographer, Father Giulio Cordara, 'the evil spirit transported her on to a beam high up in the roof and there threatened to let her fall if she refused to make over her soul to him', a 'diabolic' levitation witnessed by many of her horrified sisters. This is reminiscent of Christina's being dragged out of bed and lifted up to the roof of her room while a sword, brandished by a hand unseen by the several spectators, was waved above her head. Eustochium died in 1469, her health and body fatally undermined by the attacks to which she had been subjected for the last eight years of her life.

The violent hostility directed against Eustochium may seem to resemble that of demonic obsession rather than that usually associated with a poltergeist, but it is clear, as Christina's case illustrates, that both during the period we are discussing and much later, a simple and obvious distinction between demon and poltergeist is not to be had. Compare with Christina and Eustochium, for example, the nineteenth-century cases of Marie Julie Jahenny and Dominica Clara Moes of Luxembourg. Marie Julie, like Christina, was a stigmatic and suffered assaults upon her person, and between April and September 1873 endured a particularly concentrated period of hostility which saw crucifixes and relics thrown on the floor, her clothes torn, her body scratched, and filthy rags stuffed into her mouth – all actions attributed by her and witnesses to the Devil. On the other hand, Dominica Clara, Marie's contemporary and another stigmatic, found that the entity plaguing her often acted rather more like a poltergeist than an obsessing demon. Personal items she used in her devotions would disappear and turn up again unexpectedly; large stones were thrown forcibly at her bed; crockery was broken; she was drenched in dirty water and had to sleep in a chair; her arms were covered in burns and her face with cuts; and in 1876 one of the sisters belonging to the convent of which Dominica was prioress recorded:

> One evening I heard a tremendous disturbance going on in our dormitory. I rushed up to our dear Mother who lay there ill and in bed. I had great difficulty in pushing open the door, and I found the whole room turned upside down. All the bedding of our five beds lay tumbled in confusion upon the ground. In the middle of the heap and broken to pieces was a crucifix which used to hang at our Mother's bedside, while under everything else I discovered a crown of thorns and a rosary.[22]

It seems, then, that there is, or has developed over time, a pattern of poltergeist-like behaviour which – in addition to lithobolia, transportation of objects, and other interferences with the person, such as the mutilation of clothes, all or some of which can be observed in cases where the targeted individual is not necessarily deeply religious – amounts to a sequence of violent activities directed at the body of someone for whom religion is the principal focus of her or his life and who may also be suffering emotional disturbance of a more or less serious nature. Now, this raises an obvious question. Are we to assume that the emotional disturbance provides a psychic opening for some malevolent entity to enter the world of matter and draw upon the energies emitted by that disturbance in such a way as to enable it to perpetrate its violence: and should we, bearing in mind that the accounts of these various attacks give the overwhelming impression of an intelligent, discarnate, external agency at work, take the religious component to be the dominant feature of and hence the key to understanding these reported phenomena: or are we to speculate that the phenomena are self-generated (not necessarily with awareness and deliberation aforehand) and are therefore caused by the individual's emotional turbulence which turns energy into action in ways unperceived by the sufferer and little if at all understood by the commentator?

Unfortunately, asking who were those who reported these incidents and who were their audience does not help resolve the difficulties because, with the exception of Eleonore Zugun's reporters and observing audiences who by and large did not share her own religious faith, or at least not to any profound degree, reporters and audiences were at one with the intense religious devotion of the sufferer or focus. Hence their attribution of the phenomena to an external agency they called 'the Devil' is only to be expected. For the moment, therefore, all we can do is observe the development of such patterns of poltergeist-like behaviour, co-existent but not necessarily co-terminal with the general behaviour of those entities taken to be poltergeists, and see whether they turn out to be a feature peculiar to a hostile entity's dealing with deeply religious individuals, or whether emotional disturbance in the individual without the accompaniment of intense religious devotion produces the same level of targeted malevolence.

4

Late Mediaeval Noises and Other Frights, 1323–1484

During the two centuries immediately following Christina's experiences in Stommeln we find few recorded instances of anything like poltergeist behaviour. Indeed, the relative infrequency of what appear to be poltergeist episodes during the late antique and Mediaeval periods, even after one has taken into account the vagaries of manuscript survival and the personal interest or lack of interest of the author in such things, is both frustrating and notable. Between c.1286 and c.1500, for example, Gauld and Cornell record only eight cases and some of these on inspection turn out to be less than convincing as samples of poltergeistery.[1] One in particular is famous, an account given by Jean Gobi, who belonged to a Dominican house in Alais in the south of France. On 20 November 1323, a citizen of Alais died and eight days later his widow was frightened by strange noises in their house, so much so that she sought help from the convent, clearly thinking that the noises were caused by a demon or by the angry spirit of her dead husband. Jean Gobi, along with three other Dominicans, therefore, went along to investigate the matter. 'I went reluctantly,' he says. 'Still, to see whether it was an imposture or some diabolical illusion, I set off.' Bearing in mind the possibility of fraud, they not only searched the dead man's house thoroughly, but also those of his neighbours. Finding nothing, they turned the neighbours out of their homes and installed trustworthy men to keep watch in case someone was playing tricks, and arranged for 'a worthy and elderly woman' to sleep in the same bed as the dead man's wife in order to make sure it was not she who was imitating her husband's voice. Gobi, who had secretly brought with him a consecrated Host in a pyx, and the three other

Dominicans then sat on the dead man's bed, lit their lanterns, and waited. The friars recited prayers for the dead and, sure enough, suddenly the dead man's spirit manifested as an invisible presence which 'advanced towards the bed of the wife and made a noise like the sweeping of a broom'. His widow was very frightened, but confirmed to the brothers that this was indeed her husband, whereupon they began to interrogate him and were told that he was a good spirit, but that at present he was doing penance for the sins he had committed during life, and he begged them to render him aid in the form of prayers and Masses.

At some point during this encounter – by which time the chamber was crowded with people from the town – he showed himself 'in a luminous form'.

A Carmelite in the crowd exclaimed, 'What is the meaning of this appearance? So far you have manifested only through the sound of a voice.'

The spirit replied proudly, 'The light you see is my good angel who, when I have finished my term of penance, will conduct me to the joys of Paradise.'

And this is not all. Two of our friars sent to Alais by the Pope have, along with the chief men of the town and religious of all Orders, questioned the spirit on three different nights in the presence of three hundred people.

One of them said to the spirit, 'I conjure you by the Body of Christ to tell us under what form you are speaking to us.'

Everybody heard the answer, 'Under the form of a dove.'

Then the brother said, 'Prove it.'

The spirit answered, 'Willingly', and at once (it was the hour of cock-crow and there was not a trace of a feather in the house) the whole room was covered with white feathers.[2]

Interesting though this story is, especially in its details, there is no sign that its spirit was a poltergeist, however one may elect to understand the word. But what is worth noting is Gobi's immediate reaction to his first hearing the tale: is it fraud or diabolic illusion? One can tell which way his mind was going from the preparations he set in motion before settling down to await the voice. Each one, apart from his secretly carrying a consecrated Host, was aimed at obviating trickery, and while in this instance these may be examples of scepticism peculiar to Gobi himself, they also chime with the doubts and reservations of others elsewhere, so that we may legitimately say that Mediaeval clerics could be and were highly suspicious of anything which purported to be a manifestation, vocal or visual, from the Otherworld, a suspicion they also brought to magic and its operations.

Something more in keeping with what may be expected of a poltergeist troubled houses near a convent in Eistett near Nuremberg at some point between 1414 and 1418.

> A spirit was in the habit of disturbing many people during the night hours, but did not upset the convent at all from within. It existed in the chaplain's house and was a nuisance to him and to many nearby places by [making the sounds of] crashing about and strife and rumbling, which were not so much loud as annoying. Sometimes it used to beat on the walls; and sometimes, it seemed, the joker would blow the various pipes [played by] actors and take a lot of pleasure in harmless things such as these.[3]

The noises in question were loud: *strepitus* which include clashes, clanking, rumbling, crashes, rattling, clattering – almost any kind of noise which might be called a racket or a din; *stlites* which means 'strife, disputes, quarrels'; and *pulsus* which include beating, striking, and stamping, (cf. *pulsus terrae* = 'earthquake'). The playfulness, by contrast, is somewhat unusual but can be paralleled from elsewhere. A poltergeist arrived in Jabuticabal in Brazil in December 1965, for example, and although it rained down stones on a house in which an eleven-year-old girl, Maria, was living, it seemed to take to the child. She for her part does not appear to have been disconcerted by the lithobolia and began to ask the poltergeist for sweets or, on one occasion, a brooch; and whenever she asked for such things, they would immediately manifest at her feet. This obliging and amicable mood, however, did not last long and the poltergeist became violent, destroying all the crockery in the house and turning against Maria herself who was slapped and bitten and subjected to even worse attacks. It thus exhibited a volatility of behaviour which also seems to be characteristic of these entities.[4]

Not long after the Eistett episode there occurred another, this time in the city of Nuremberg. The story is related by a 'theologian' who is taking part in the dialogue form adopted by Johannes Nider for his book on Christian ethics.

> Almost ten years ago in the city of Nuremberg, a monastery of our [Dominican] order, called St Catharine's, was with immense difficulty reformed by eleven devout reforming nuns sent thither from another reformed place. All the sisters in that monastery had been unwilling to be reformed, and had not a few supporters in the city. So after the place was subject to enclosure according to the rules and the stubborn fragile sex submitted their necks to the yoke of obedience, a demon came into the monastery. At first it used to bother certain nuns [by making] odd

noises during the night. When I heard about it, I was persuaded that [the nuns] should not believe such things were caused by a demon but by cats or dormice or a weakness of the head, since I suspected this was a piece of women's nonsense.

The demon came a second night and held down one of those who had been rebellious (I believe she was the sacristan), who was wanting to ring the bell for Matins, [pressing her] in such a way that one might have thought she would be brought to her grave that very day. In the end, this demon was disturbing the convent day and night in such a fashion that the sisters had to take turns to stay awake and on guard the whole night because none of them dared walk about on her own. But I enjoined private and public devotions on each one of them, preached patience, and frequently persuaded them to settle down in the Lord.[5]

Here again scepticism comes into play, with the 'theologian' waving aside the convent's nocturnal noises as nothing more than women's fancies. He is robust in his dismissal, and yet we may note that the description of the disturbances – presumably derived from the accounts of the nuns themselves, although there is no telling how close to these first-hand witnesses is Nider's account – contains features such as the Old Hag which we have come across before in earlier poltergeist narratives. (Not that the occurrence of the Old Hag in itself warrants a description of the attack as one made by a poltergeist: simply that this Old Hag incident is consistent with others in which there can be little doubt that a poltergeist is involved.) Conditions in the convent at the time, of course, were ripe for exploitation, had anyone been so minded. Nuns who had lived under the older lax régime were likely to have been resentful of the eleven new sisters imported from a convent which had already had its way of life reformed, and these new sisters clearly jarred with the established sorority which was unwilling to be reformed. The newcomers are described as *devotas reformatrices*, and so two opposing psychologies met and were obliged to live with each other under the rules of strict enclosure – no slipping out of the convent, or slipping in of unauthorised visitors. What is more, the established nuns are said to have had *complices* in the city, 'confederates' or 'participants', which may simply suggest passive supporters, but could equally well be applied to active accomplices in some scheme or other. Are we, then, to think that the claimed night-noises (attributed to a demon, as one might expect from the context) represented merely the beginning of a campaign in which the incoming reformed nuns would be blamed for causing or importing demonic activity, a campaign to be assisted by rumours and demonstrations in the city, manufactured and spread by the nuns' accomplices, after which the local bishop would or might remove the reforming nuns in answer to public clamour? We have no idea, of course, because the incident never got that far, dampened as it was by the dismissive scepticism of the 'theologian'.

The temptation to read fraud into a number of these incidents is alluring and should be resisted, or at least considered only along with other possibilities unless, as in the case we have just been discussing, the evidence for preternatural as opposed to natural activity is thin and the opinion of a contemporary recorder or witness is more inclined to doubt than credulity. We have a similar problem with a narrative from fifteenth-century Egypt. A Dominican friar, Felix Fabri (1441/2–1502), went on pilgrimage to the Holy Land (actually for the second time) in 1483–84, and wrote an account of his journey, *Evagatorium in Terrae Sanctae, Arabiae et Egypti Peregrinationem* ('Rambling on a Pilgrimage to the Holy Land, Arabia, and Egypt'), which he abbreviated and translated into German for the better entertainment of his travelling companions. In this version, but not in the fuller Latin text, he included an account of a poltergeist in Cairo. Not far from the Nile, he said, lay a manor house which should have made a pleasant residence, except that no one was willing to live there. Should anyone be misguided enough to attempt it, he used to find that all the household goods would be thrown through the windows and he himself subject to an attack of the Old Hag. Curiously enough, however, each month a sum of money, wrapped in a small piece of cloth, would be deposited in one of the rooms – a sum equivalent to the rent, had rent been paid – and no one knew whence this money had come. Information about all this came from the locals (*die Heyden*), and Fabri says he does not know whether to believe it or not. The Egyptians, he adds, enjoy fantasticalities and are given to magic; but there are many wonderful phenomena spoken of there of which this is merely one.[6]

Here again the author is dubious about his information because of its source, and one has to wonder why he did not include the story in his original narrative. Perhaps it did not come to mind until he was engaged on the abbreviation, or perhaps he did not hear it until then, in which case he would have been hearing it second-hand at least. The alleged poltergeistery is somewhat different from that in the Nuremberg convent – throwing of heavy objects and instances of the Old Hag, not merely noises in the night. D.J.A. Ross, who provides the German text and a brief comment, notes that 'the payment of rent is suspicious, and might seem to point to fraud by some person wishing the house to remain empty, probably for disreputable reasons', but I do not really see why the appearance of money each month in a room should put people off living there. It was surely the general and personal violence which would have done that and if those are to be attributed to fraud, one would have to ask how they were done without the perpetrator's being detected. So if fraud is partly possible, partly unlikely in this episode, what should we make of the following, a story recounted by Girolamo Cardano, who had it from his father, Fazio?

I was brought up, [said Fazio], in the house of Joannes Resta, and therein taught Latin to his three sons: when I left them I supported myself on my own means. It chanced that one of these lads, while I was studying medicine, fell deadly sick, he being now a young man grown, and I was called in to be with the youth, partly for my knowledge of medicine, partly for old friendship's sake. The master of the house happened to be absent; the patient slept in an upper chamber, one of his brothers and I in a lower room, the third brother, Isidore, was not at home. Each of the rooms was next to a turret; turrets being common in that city. When we went to bed on the first night of my visit, I heard a constant knocking on the wall of my room.

'What is that?' I said.

'Don't be afraid, it is only a familiar spirit,' said my companion. 'They call them *follets*; it is harmless enough, and seldom so troublesome as it is now: I don't know what can be the matter with it.'

The young fellow went to sleep, but I was kept awake for a while, wondering and observing. After half an hour of stillness, I felt a thumb press on my head, and a sense of cold. I kept watching; the forefinger, the middle finger, and the rest of the hand were next laid on, the little finger nearly reaching my forehead. The hand was like that of a boy of ten, to guess by the size, and so cold that it was extremely unpleasant. Meantime I was chuckling over my luck in such an opportunity of witnessing a wonder, and I listened eagerly. The hand stole with the ring finger foremost over my face and down my nose, it was slipping into my mouth, and two fingertips had entered, when I threw it off with my right hand, thinking it was uncanny, and not relishing it inside my body. Silence followed and I lay awake, distrusting the spectre more or less. In about half an hour it returned and repeated its former conduct, touching me very lightly, yet very chilly. When it reached my mouth I again drove it away. Though my lips were tightly closed, I felt an extreme icy cold in my teeth. I now got out of bed, thinking this might be a friendly visit from the ghost of the sick lad upstairs, who must have died.

As I went to the door, the thing passed before me, rapping on the walls. When I got to the door, it knocked outside; when I opened the door, it began to knock on the turret. The moon was shining; I went on to see what would happen, but it beat on the other sides of the tower, and, as it always evaded me, I went up to see how my patient was. He was alive, but very weak. As I was speaking to those who

69

stood about his bed, we heard a noise as if the house was falling. In rushed my bedfellow, the brother of the sick lad, half dead with terror.

'When you got up,' he said, 'I felt a cold hand on my back. I thought it was you who wanted to waken me and take me to see my brother, so I pretended to be asleep and lay quiet, supposing that you would go alone when you found me so sound asleep. But when I did not feel you get up, and the cold hand grew to be more than I could bear, I hit out to push your hand away, and felt your place empty – but warm. Then I remembered the *follet*, and ran upstairs as hard as I could put my feet to the ground: never was I in such a fright.'

The sick lad died on the following night.[7]

Three points are worth noting here. First, the manifestation was preceded by knocking on walls and ended with an immense rumbling crash. These noises were not necessarily connected with the hand, and indeed are related as a separate phenomenon attributed to a *folletto*, that is, a mischievous household spirit more closely related to fairies and entities of that kind than to ghosts or demons or poltergeists, if we are to regard this last as a separate and distinct species of preternatural being. Secondly, the cold hand was felt, not seen, and produced no fear in Cardano's father: rather the opposite, since he says he was delighted at the opportunity afforded him of experiencing something extraordinary. It is only when the hand becomes intrusive that he is irritated, but even so he still describes the visit as a 'friendly' one and attributes it to a very recently dead person's ghost. Thirdly, Fazio was not the only person to feel the hand. The brother who shared his bed had a similar experience, thinking first that it was a human agent before becoming frightened and supposing it belonged to the noisy *folletto*. We are therefore left with more than one experience of indeterminate origin. Were the noises made by some species of fairy or ghost or poltergeist, or were they produced by human agency? Was the cold hand that of a fairy or a ghost, or did it belong to a human taking advantage of what may well have been a pitch-black room? But if we posit the latter, we are bound to ask how its owner was able to move about undetected and without any apparent fumbling for the target. Cardano's father does not suggest or hint at trickery. Rather, the tone of his anecdote inclines towards understanding the hand, at least, as that of a ghost, in spite of the fact that the body to whom he imagined it belonged was moribund but not yet dead.

Chuckling with delight at the prospect of undergoing such a test of nerves betokens a temperament of unusual equilibrium. This is not the reaction of others who have experienced something similar. In Pudsey, a market town near Leeds, a young couple, Catherine and Andrew Kirk, was troubled by a poltergeist during the early 1990s. Objects in the house, including furniture, were moved and thrown around, noises both small and loud occurred quite often, and sometimes, when Catherine or Andrew was alone in the house at night, each experienced a kind of presence in the bed. In Catherine's case this amounted to something like the Old Hag and to sensations of being pulled or touched, after which she would find herself covered in bruises. Andrew, on the other hand, thought one of their pets had tried to get onto or into the bed, but on investigation found there was nothing there and that all their cats and dogs were asleep downstairs. Interestingly enough, this presence seems to have manifested itself at least once as a misty blue shape, and a medium consulted by the couple told them there was a ghost in the house, the spirit of a long dead great uncle of theirs.[8] It is not altogether clear, however, why this dead relative should have manifested at this point and to this couple against whom he appears to have entertained no particular animus. He had never lived in the house they were occupying and did not become recognisably visible to either Catherine or Andrew, only to the medium. One may therefore conclude that the likelihood of the poltergeist's being the same entity as the ghost is fairly remote.

If we now ask ourselves who were the recorders of these Mediaeval incidents, and for whom they were writing, we find that three of them were actually Dominicans, although this is no more than a coincidence, since their narratives are separated from one another by many decades and are clearly individual in their tone and content rather than being imitative of each other or earlier sources. There does not yet exist a suggestive pattern to be followed or to influence the content or form of such anecdotes, and so we may be reasonably confident that each incident recorded has probably been received from an oral rather than written sources – at first telling certainly in Cardano's case and probably Fabri's too, although it is always possible that Gobi and Nider read their anecdotes rather than heard them.

Now, although these reported incidents are very sparse in the literature during the fourteenth and fifteenth centuries, one might think it notable that the motives behind their being recorded seem to differ somewhat from those of earlier authors. Constance de Lyon, Rudolf of Fulda, and the biographers of Bishop Caesarius, St Willibrord, and St Godric were intent on providing their readers and audience with stories of moral edification demonstrating the power of God over demons and other entities manifested through His saints. Nider's two anecdotes, however, albeit they are contained in his dialogue between a theologian (himself) and a questioning student, which is designed to discuss and illustrate points of moral and spiritual importance and contains a large number of stories for the purpose of illuminating those points further, do not have the same weight and solemnity as those of the earlier centuries. They divert more than they instruct, as does Fabri's Egyptian narrative included, we should mark, in the shorter version of his pilgrimage account, the version intended for laity to read. His message (if there is one) is 'don't foreigners believe strange things?' and is set in a context of credulity anent wonders and magic. So too, Cardano's retelling of one of his father's stories is clearly meant to entertain rather than preach: it is no accident that it appears in a lengthy work entitled *De rerum varietate* ('The Diversity of Things'), a large collection of empirical observations serving both light and serious purposes.

Rather than interpreting this apparent shift in emphasis as an actual change in perceptions, however – these last examples are far too few in number to warrant such a suggestion – we should regard them as simply another illustration of the Mediaeval eagerness to hear novelties and exotica. If anything characterises those centuries, it is *curiositas*, an appetite for *mira*, 'things to make you astonished'. Popular literature revelled in Otherworld enchantments, whether these consisted of magic, marvels, demonic defeats at the hands of saints, miracles, shape-shifting, monsters, or foreign strangeness, this last usually included in travellers' or pilgrims' tales of their adventures, real, imagined, or exaggerated, in faraway places where one could find pigmies or hermaphrodites or people with dogs' heads instead of human or only one eye.[9] Alive to the almost incredible diversity of God's creation which included realms of non-human beings as well as those which might be discovered and explored here on earth, therefore, the Mediaeval audience was prepared to be amused as well as instructed, and the poltergeist tales we have come across so far answered each of and both these needs.

5
A Growing Infestation, c.1500–1591

Fazio Cardano's experience with an invisible, disembodied hand was unusual but not unique. A few years later, Alessandro Alessandri, a Neapolitan jurist, went to Rome with some friends of his, intending to investigate a house which had long had the reputation of being haunted. They gathered together in one room with plenty of candles and lanterns, and in the middle of the night were rewarded (if that is the right word) with the sight of a spectre which called out to them in a loud voice and threw ornaments round the room. One of the party, bolder than the rest, advanced on it with a light, whereupon it disappeared, although it came back again more than once 'through the door'. This phrase is ambiguous. Was the door open or closed? We cannot tell. The spectre must then have ceased for a while, because several of the company went to bed, leaving Alessandro lying on a couch. But the spectre, now referred to as a 'demon', had slid underneath it and when Alessandro got up, he saw a big black arm appear on the table in front of him. Something – perhaps Alessandro's involuntary cries of alarm – disturbed his remaining companions. The room was dark – how did Alessandro see the arm? – and the servants had to bring torches. But as soon as they arrived, the spectre-demon opened the door, slipped past them, and disappeared.[1]

There are two observations to be made about this. First, the book in which Alessandro included this anecdote seems to have been modelled on the *Noctes Atticae* of Aulus Gellius, who put together his commonplace book in the second century AD. It consists of miscellaneous jottings on any subject which took his interest, along with all kinds of quotations from the extensive reading with which he whiled away his time during long nights he spent on a protracted visit to Athens. Now, this is not to say that Alessandro took his story from Gellius – he did not – but his collection, like that of Gellius, was clearly written for the purpose of diverting those who read it, and so his 'poltergeist' incident falls into the category of amusing rather than instructive tale. Secondly, the story carries many of the hallmarks not so much of a genuine brush with the Otherworld as of an all too human jape. Alessandro and his friends deliberately went to spend the night in a haunted house, and it is perfectly possible that a 'ghost' may have been arranged for their benefit, either by some of the friends themselves or by servants attached to and working in the house. The spectre's passing 'through the door' may suggest non-human ability to treat physical objects as though they were not there, but may also merely mean that the door was open in the first place. Indeed, when servants arrived with torches, the ghost, we are told, did not simply pass through the door but opened it first, and that is surely a distinctively human action. It may seem odd, of course, that no one caught on to the deception, if deception it was, but if any of those present were party to the joke, it would have been easy for him or them to prevent anyone else from laying hands on the 'ghost' or otherwise discovering his human nature.

Even so, it may be asked whether anyone, however credulous or gullible, could be fooled by a ghost solid enough to have a big black arm and the need to open a door before passing through it. The answer appears to be 'yes', or at least 'perhaps'. For one thing, stage performances were accustoming people to the notion of physically solid ghosts and would continue to do so. Between 1560 and 1610, for instance, the English theatre alone provided as many as fifty-one ghosts, a vogue which had its origins in earlier literature: in the eleventh century, for example, Otloh of St Emmeram tells us about a drowned monk who returned from the dead to give a dishonest cellarer a sound flogging, and in the twelfth, according to William of Newburgh, 'one man recounted that he saw a woman's hands sinking deeply in a spirit's flesh, as though that spirit's flesh were rotten and not solid, but spectral', an extraordinary combination of the physical (*caro, putrida*) and non-physical (*non solida, fantastica*). We also know that other spirits, such as Satan, were reported as appearing in the guise of human beings, and that some people played tricks on others by dressing up and pretending to be ghosts.

> Practical jokers have been known to dress up with horns like devils or else to swathe themselves in shrouds and white sheets to frighten simple folk, and thus many a poor person imagines that some demon or ghost has appeared ... A piece of tomfoolery, too, which commends itself mightily to some wags who are on a journey, and arriving at some inn, itch to play sad zany tricks on the other guests,

is that one shall tie neatly a string to the sheets and coverture of a bed whilst the other has already hidden himself underneath it, and then in the night away fly the quilt and blankets and all until you would think a poltergeist was in the room.[2]

Fraud of a similar kind can be seen in two incidents, one from 1507–08, the other from 1534. The first involves Johann Jetzer who, at the age of twenty-three, entered the Dominican house in Berne in 1506. There, after only a year, he began to complain that a long-dead brother of the house was pulling the clothes off his bed at night in order to wake him so that he might ask for Masses to be said for the repose of his soul. These manifestations were followed by banging and rapping throughout the convent buildings, and when the Prior ordered relics to be placed in the room next to Jetzer's in the hope of quietening the spirit, a large stone suddenly fell from the air and doors started to open and close apparently of their own accord. The spirit revealed himself to Jetzer: his face and hands were black, and his ears and nose were missing, the result of violence which had attended his murder a hundred and sixty years before. Impressed by Jetzer's accounts, the Prior had Masses said, but could not resist making use of Jetzer's access to this ghost – and we may note that the 'poltergeist' is here clearly identified as a ghost, not a demon or, indeed, a poltergeist.

Theological controversy involving Franciscans and Dominicans was rife at the time. The two Orders (and other theologians, of course) were disputing whether the Virgin Mary's conception had been immaculate or not, and Jetzer's Prior seized the opportunity to find out whether the Dominican or Franciscan position anent this point was the true one. Jetzer accordingly quizzed his ghost, who admitted ignorance on the subject but agreed to have a letter conveyed to the Virgin so that she could answer for herself. She then came in person to Jetzer's room and said that the Dominicans were right, and when Jetzer asked her to prove she was indeed the Virgin and not an evil spirit, she offered to demonstrate that a consecrated Host was truly her Son's transubstantiated flesh. At this point Jetzer eagerly grabbed the Virgin's hand and was suddenly horrified to discover that the Virgin was actually a brother of the convent and that two angels who had accompanied her were none other than the Prior and Subprior. This farcical episode was followed by others. A statue of the Virgin in the chapel began to weep tears of blood which turned out to be paint; St Bernard of Clairvaux, another saintly visitor, was merely the Prior in disguise; and St Catherine of Siena, whom Jetzer stabbed in the leg with a knife, was the convent's procurator in some kind of drag. This nonsense had gone on long for far too long and in 1508 the authorities stepped in to put an end to it. The four friars who had played the roles of Virgin, saints, and angels were arrested, confessed their fraud, and were executed on 31 May 1509. Jetzer himself was imprisoned but managed to escape two months later. He went on to marry and become a tailor, but he soon found himself in prison yet again in 1512. Released in 1514, he died that same year, and thus ended one of the more peculiar episodes of early sixteenth-century religious controversy.[3]

Was Jetzer, as opposed to his conventual superiors who were clearly guilty of fraud, a knowing participant in their deception? It is actually quite difficult to tell, because his episode falls into two quite distinct parts. The first involves poltergeist-like behaviour which quickly turns out to consist of efforts on the part of the ghost to get itself heard and achieve its objective – the saying of sufficient Masses to free itself from Purgatory. Only then does the human exploitation begin, and we may ask, as we did in the case of Alessandro, why Jetzer did not recognise members of his own convent, whom he saw and to whom he spoke every day, merely because they were wearing theatrical costume. The answer depends upon the quality of expectation, his and ours. We probably do not expect to see ghosts or spirits, nor do we expect them to be solid, corporeal-like figures, dressed, speaking, and behaving as though they were still alive. Jetzer and his contemporaries, however, did and in consequence it may have been (if we are to accept for a moment that he was innocent of collusion in the fraud) that he had been so conditioned by his experience with the ghost that when figures appeared in his room, claiming to be the Virgin or saints or angels, he was willing at first to suspend possible disbelief in favour of his pre-formed expectations.[4] In favour of this notion is his horror and indignation at finding himself deceived. When 'St Bernard of Clairvaux' came to his room, all went well until the time came for the saint to take his leave. He appeared to float out of the window, but something must have aroused Jetzer's suspicions because he gave the figure a shove and it fell into the courtyard, thus revealing itself to be the Prior. Similarly, 'St Catherine of Siena' failed to convince Jetzer that she was genuinely the saint – whether right from the start or at some point during their conversation is not clear – and Jetzer stabbed her in the leg, thereby unmasking the convent's procurator.

But if Jetzer may have been imposed on by others who sought to use what was perhaps his naivety for their own theological ends, can we suggest that the Prior, Subprior, procurator, and lector were engaged, not in deliberate criminal fraud, but in a kind of 'holy deception', such as we have discussed anent the Boxley Rood, in which the *mens rea* which would be necessary to convict them of a criminal act was missing, and an *intentio pia*, a devout intention, was operating and guiding their actions? It seems not. The bishop and the local authorities who tried and condemned these men evidently regarded Jetzer as a miscreant and his Dominican superiors as guilty of heresy, for they were executed by burning, which implies they were seen as culpable heretics and blasphemers – and this by men who would have been essentially no more sceptical about the existence of ghosts and the possibility of their appearance in this world than anyone else at the time.

This willingness to accept the possible reality of interplay between various worlds can be seen in our second example of fraud, that of 1534. In that year the wife of the principal magistrate in Orléans died and left instructions that her funeral should be as simple as possible.

When she was buried in the Franciscan church among her ancestors, [her husband] gave the friars only six pieces of gold, which was less than they expected. Moreover, soon after cutting and selling timber, he refused their request for some of it. Out of revenge they planned to proclaim that his wife was damned, and two Doctors of Theology, one of them a skilful exorcist, arranged the details. They put a young novice in the loft of the church with instructions to make a racket during the hour of evening prayer. After exorcisms had been performed, they asked whether the noise proceeded from a condemned spirit, and the noise started up again. Next they invited the leading citizens [of Orléans] to be present the following night. A series of questions was addressed to the spirit and answered by knocking, which was interpreted to mean that the disturbance was caused by the spirit of the chief magistrate's wife, that she was hopelessly damned for Lutheranism, and that her body must be removed from the church. This was put in writing and the witnesses were asked to sign it, but, out of fear of the chief magistrate, they refused to do so. The friars then removed from the church everything necessary for the celebration of Mass, and refused to say Mass until the church was relieved of its profanation by an heretical body. This brought the bishop's officer to the scene with the request that they perform exorcisms and send people to the loft to see what was going on there; but the friars refused. Then the chief magistrate appealed to the King. The friars pleaded their privileges and exemption, but the King appointed delegates with full powers from the Parlement, and the Chancellor, the Cardinal Legate Du Prat did the same. The friars were brought to Paris, imprisoned, and examined separately, but would confess nothing. But at length the novice, under promise of protection, revealed the whole plot. The friars concerned were then taken back to Orléans and forced to do public penance on the place of execution.[5]

In both stories, then, we find evidence in this kind of story of the poltergeist's being drawn, soon after the reformation had begun, into confessional battles which would begin to tear Europe apart, although it is worthwhile remarking that he was actually not used for such a purpose all that often. Obsessive or possessing demons were much more commonly selected to play the role of mouthpiece for one confessional side or another, perhaps because direct speech, a frequent phenomenon of demonic possession, was likely to have a greater impact on the audience than a series of raps which were more open to both scepticism and misinterpretation. But while his activities could be and sometimes were used to underline a particular religious message, as we shall see later, in general the poltergeist tended to confine himself to the kind of secular mischief-making he had indulged in since late antiquity.

A spirit's rapping to communicate answers is an interesting device which is perhaps more familiar to us from the nineteenth century when, by a curious coincidence, its renewed manifestations were also founded upon fraud. But the notion that a poltergeist has at least some degree of intelligence and is able to respond to questions and requests can be illustrated outwith the bounds of deliberate deception. As far back as the ninth century, people endured not only rapping and lithobolia but also a voice which revealed their embarrassing secrets, and similar examples proliferate into later times. In 1592, for example, there was published in London an anonymous pamphlet, *A True Discourse of Such Strange and Wonderful Accidents as happened in the house of Mr. George Lee of North Acton in the county of Oxford*, relating certain poltergeist incidents which lasted from 29 November 1591 until George Lee's death on 22 May the following year. George was twenty-one years old when the phenomena began. These consisted of 'stones of contrary bigness, some weighing a pound, some two, some three, some four, and some two and twenty pounds, to fall very strangely, or to be violently flung (as it were) through the top or roof of his hall, not knowing how or whence this strange accidents should happen'. Diligent search was made, of course, but no one could find any loose tiles or indeed any aperture whatever through which the stones could have passed. The lithobolia continued throughout Christmas and the period immediately after, causing so much unease that the family was obliged to go and stay with the local minister. Edward Lee, the father, then decided that his daughter and a female servant should go and spend a night or even longer in the house until the phenomena ceased, and after a first abortive visit in which the two girls ran away because they could hear the stones thudding and rattling against the walls, they returned with three workmen for their protection to discover that nothing had changed or ceased, and that stones were continuing to fall as before. Two further visitors, however, William Whing and Richard Hickes, were not so easily frightened and Whing challenged the poltergeist, 'Jack, if thou be a good fellow, fling us down a quoit or two, that my companion and I may go and play at quoits.' Whereupon a thin, broad stone fell in answer to his request and then, upon his asking for others, three more.[6]

More modern instances of the same kind of thing are also common enough. Thus, in 1750, a church minister in Iceland was troubled by a poltergeist which threw stones, wrenched a door off its hinges, and held a conversation with his unfortunate victim, and in 1877 an Irish poltergeist persecuted a widowed farmer and his children by throwing objects, removing a large stone which had been put on top of a Bible to keep it safe, and tearing seventeen pages across, an act which seems reminiscent of earlier poltergeists who showed they would not be controlled by church ceremonies or sacramentals. This poltergeist also rapped and knocked, and when the farmer mentally asked it to rap a certain number of times, it did so, even when the farmer more than once put his hands in his overcoat pockets, stretched open some of his fingers, and asked the poltergeist to knock that particular number. In 1988 an infesting spirit in Cardiff was asked to bring a pen and then a paper clip, and sure enough both fell at the requester's feet; and in Runcorn, when a witness to poltergeist activities remarked, 'I don't think it will throw anything at me', a book was flung at her face, while in answer to a clergyman's suggestion – 'If you can hear me, knock three times' – a dressing table shook violently thrice.[7]

The Orléans friars' use of knocking to convey intelligent answers to questions, then, although fraudulent in this case, is thus merely one example of a well-known poltergeist behaviour and shows the friars' and their audience's awareness of what had become a tradition; and if one asks how the laity come to know such things, the answer must be partly through reading, partly through listening to others' experiences, and partly through experiences of their own, for sparsely though the incidents of poltergeistery are scattered through the historical record up to this point, there are enough of them to indicate that the poltergeist type of entity was by no means a rare phenomenon, even though it may have been an unusual one, and of course it is always possible that there were other incidents connected with hauntings about which we know nothing because they were not recorded. If this is so, it may help to account for the growing number of such manifestations during the sixteenth century and we should also bear in mind that by the time Alessandro had his experience, printing presses had been pouring out books, pamphlets, and illustrated broadsheets for sixty years in a quite remarkable flood which thereby enabled an increasing readership to access narratives full of marvels, along with pictures, and to absorb their information more and more through the medium of the vernacular languages as opposed to Latin.

Such a mixture of tongues, for example, told people about Luther's experiences with and opinion on poltergeists. At one point he identified them with ghosts – 'Wherever poltergeists have appeared as dead souls throughout the world, they have all asked for the Mass' – and at another with demons – 'In times past there were many poltergeists and hobgoblins everywhere. They frightened people into doing whatever they demanded of them.' Nowadays, however, he said, 'our consciences have been set free from all the elements of the world, from the Pope, from Purgatory, and from poltergeists', by which he probably meant Catholic priests, since he extended his remarks about poltergeists in the past to say, 'Today [the Devil] seeks different ways of casting a spell on people and deluding them. This he does through his corporeal poltergeists and factions.'[8] He certainly did not mean that poltergeists in the usual sense of the word no longer existed, and he knew perfectly well what kind of phenomenon characterised such a poltergeist as opposed to a ghost or a demon, because he himself had experienced it and was later approached by a Protestant minister for advice on the subject. Luther's personal encounter with a poltergeist took place in 1521 while he was staying in Wartburg Castle. He had a bag of hazelnuts in his room and suddenly this began to jump around, apparently of its own accord, at one point rising to hit the ceiling. Then his bed began to rattle, and no sooner had he managed to go to sleep than he was woken by the sound of a large number of barrels rolling and tumbling about outwith his room. Investigation showed there was nothing there. A woman who stayed in the same room after Luther had left the castle had a similar experience, and these incidents enabled Sigismund Scheretzius, who recorded them, to observe, 'Certain things [he calls them *lemures*, 'ghosts' and *Poltergeister*] play with household furniture at night. They throw down dishes, loaves, jars, tankards, spoons, and other vessels; they open and close doors; or they wake those who are asleep and fill them with fear; or they pretend to be thieves.'[9]

Seventeen years later, Luther was approached by the minister of a church in Stüpitz, who told him that for the past year Satan had been disturbing the peace of his household at night by making a lot of noise and throwing crockery at his head. The items only just missed and then broke, of course, and the minister heard Satan laughing, although he did not actually see him. Things had now reached a point, he said, when his wife and children wanted to leave the house. Luther's advice was to ignore the pot throwing while commanding Satan to leave the house, and he added that a woman from Magdeburg, who was also troubled by Satan, drove him away by farting at him, although, he warned, 'this example is not always to be followed and is dangerous'.[10]

The hostility shown to the family by the Stüpitz poltergeist is by no means rare. We have come across it in Alcuin's *Life of St Willibrord* and again in the *Annals* of Rudolf of Fulda when the targets of the poltergeist's anger were forced to leave their home and camp out in the fields, and it is sometimes a feature of modern cases, too, as in Port Louis, Mauritius, where a family was plagued by heavy bombardments of stones and other heavy objects both inside and outwith the house for four days in September 1937. Eventually things became so bad that the house was wrecked and the owner sent his wife and children away.[11] Nor is it surprising to find that both Luther and the minister identified their poltergeists as Satan although, as we have seen, Luther himself swithered between accepting that some people had been in the habit of seeing the poltergeist as a ghost, and his personal inclination, implicit but clear enough, to view it as a distinct species, even though his theological instincts led him to understand it as a kind of demon. But with the advent of the Protestant Reformation came a fundamental change in some intellectuals' perception and understanding of ghosts, resulting from their rejection of the Church's teaching on Purgatory; and if it were believed that Purgatory did not exist, the whole notion of ghostly movement between worlds had to be revised. The appearance of ghosts then became the result of trickery by Catholic priests and monks, or because demons were impersonating the spirits of the dead for their own nefarious purposes, or because they were hallucinations emanating from some natural cause. As Ludwig Lavater, a Swiss Protestant minister, put it, 'If it be not a vain persuasion proceeding through weakness of the senses through fear, or some suchlike cause, or if it be not deceit of men, or some natural thing ... it is either a god or evil angel, or some other forewarning sent by God.'[12] In practice, however, many people, perhaps a majority of Protestants continued to see ghosts and experience ghostly visitations much as they had always done, and certainly the poltergeist who should, in theory, have suffered confinement to Heaven or Hell along with spirits of the dead or angelic or demonic entities, went on committing nuisances in the physical world without regard for theological differences of opinion.

But if Luther, at least at one point in his career, seems to have hesitated about how to understand the nature of the poltergeist, no such distinction troubled Erasmus, who, in a letter to Damian von Goes, Treasurer to the King of Portugal, dated 25 July 1533, described the cause of a fire which burned down the Swiss town of Schiltach on 10 April that same year.

> According to statements made by the inhabitants to the Mayor of Freiburg which is eight German miles away, the cause of the fire was said to be as follows. A

demon whistled in a certain part of an inn and the pub landlord, thinking it was a thief, went upstairs but found no one. The whistle was repeated from a higher room, and again the landlord went to look for a thief, but once more found no one. But when the whistle was heard again, this time from the top of the chimney, it occurred to the landlord that it was the work of some demon. He told his family to keep calm and summoned two priests who performed an exorcism. [In answer to their questions, the spirit] replied that he was a demon. Asked what he was doing there, he said he wanted to burn the town to ashes. When [the priests] threatened him with holy things, he said he cared nothing for their threats because one of them was a whoremonger and both of them were thieves. A little later he lifted up into the air a young woman with whom he had been intimate for fourteen years (even though all this time she had regularly been to confession and received the Eucharist) and set her on the chimney pot. He gave her a jar and told her to turn it upside down. This she did, and within an hour the whole town was burned to the ground.[13]

Elements of this story are familiar. Fazio Cardano was led out of his bedroom and into one of the towers of the building by the sound of rapping which retreated as he moved onward; the poltergeist described by Gerard of Wales was not affected by priests' attempts to exorcise him and spoke out loud, revealing embarrassing details about people's private lives; and both Christina of Stommeln and Eustochium of Padua were raised bodily high in the air by their poltergeist entities; the 'demon' described by Alcuin, too, was credited with starting a fire in one of the bedrooms of the house it was infesting and burning the whole house down. Arson, along with lithobolia, is one of the traits most commonly associated with the poltergeist and indeed there are several instances of it throughout the centuries. Modern examples include a New York house eventually destroyed by fire in 1887 after forty or so fires were discovered within a few hours, which could not be traced to human agency; another was burned down in 1895 after a period of some twenty hours during which fires kept breaking out in unexpected places; and in April 1960 the *Los Angeles Times* reported that blazes had broken out in the house of the Lopes family in Georgetown, British Guiana, over a period of three weeks in March and April that same year. Household articles, a book, and some dress material were among the things damaged, and while one of the children was showing a newspaper reporter the tail of his shirt which had been scorched in an earlier fire, it suddenly burst into flames for no apparent reason and from no apparent cause.[14] So we may be tempted to think that an apparent pattern of behaviour can be seen emerging from these disparate hostile actions. Such a pattern, however, is only apparent precisely because the elements which go to make it up are indeed disparate, and so it is actually difficult to say that such and such a set of actions is characteristic of poltergeist behaviour, as opposed to that of other entities. It may be that the presence of one or more of them merely *appears* to be characteristic.

Let us take, for example, a French case cited and discussed by Gauld and Cornell. It was recorded by Adrian de Montelambert in a pamphlet published in 1528 and refers to incidents taking place in the convent of St Pierre in Lyon between 1525 and 1526. Discipline there had been lax until 1516 when the convent was reformed, and during this earlier period Sister Alis, the sacristan, had disposed of some of the convent's valuables in the nearby city. Eight years later she died, and two years after that, in 1526, a young nun, Sister Antoinette, began to experience little raps and knockings which seemed to come from beneath her feet and followed her wherever she went, even in church. Asked what she thought was causing these noises, Sister Antoinette replied that it could be Sister Alis, about whom she had frequently dreamed since the latter's death. Sure enough the spirit, when questioned – in what manner we do not know – confirmed this identification and indicated that it would like to be buried in the abbey. So the body was exhumed and brought there to the accompaniment of yet more frenzied rapping. What followed was a cross between an exorcism and a séance, with the spirit's being asked questions about Purgatory and about the angel who attended her during her periods of release therefrom. At the end of the proceedings, absolution was pronounced by the bishop who was conducting the session and that should have been that. In fact it nearly was, but three days later the rapping had not ceased and at one point Sister Antoinette was raised up into the air and held there for a while. At last, however, after about three weeks, Sister Antoinette thought she caught a glimpse of Sister Alis's ghost in the corner of her room and then, in the early hours of the morning, she was woken by Sister Alis's voice telling her that, as a result of the convent's prayers, her time in Purgatory had been drastically reduced. One more series of powerful blows in the refectory the following day announced the end of the episode. They numbered thirty-three and were taken to mean that Sister Alis had only thirty-three more days to endure in Purgatory before she was finally released.[15]

Apart from Sister Antoinette's involuntary levitation, however, there is nothing here to suggest that the spirit in question must have been a poltergeist rather than a ghost drawing attention to itself by making communicative raps in an effort to get its body honourably re-interred and its own purgatorial term either reduced or cancelled. But it is certainly worth noting that in the 1534 story from Orléans, the 'spirit' also communicated through knocking. It seems that practical jokers, as well as the clerical fraudsters we have met already, were able to latch on to an aspect of certain ghostly phenomena which was well enough known to be recognised by both clergy and layfolk as a legitimate technique for communicating with the Otherworld. By contrast, the 1540s seem to have ushered in a series of poltergeist reports which concentrated on lithobolia as their principal feature. Typical is the following account by Antonio de Torquemada, author of a compilation of observations, anecdotes, and unconsidered trifles much in the manner of Alessandro and, ultimately, of Aulus Gellius.

There was [he says] at Salamanca a married woman whose house was commonly reported to be haunted by this kind of stoning. Hearing this rumour, the mayor of the city resolved to prove whether there was any truth in these constant reports, or whether they were rather inventions of the household servants for the purpose of concealing some misdemeanour; for among these [servants] were two not uncomely girls, and it was suspected they had invented the whole story so that their lovers might have easier access to them. Accordingly, the mayor went to the house at the time when the stoning was said to be most frequent; and with him went no fewer than twenty of the townsmen, some of whom he sent with a light to see whether there was anyone at the top of the house who was throwing stones at the servants in this fashion. They carefully searched every corner and reported that they had found nothing which could cause such a haunting; yet they determined to go down to the basements (to which they came from the dining room) and wait there a little in the hope of discovering anything which might be there. And hardly were they there before a great shower of stones began to fall on them with a loud noise, passing by all their legs, however, without hurting them. So again they sent some [of their number] to see where so heavy a shower of stones could come from; and when everywhere was found empty as before, many of them began to feel convinced that the whole business was actually due to the arts and magic of demons. They were further strengthened in this opinion by the fact that a continuous hail of stones fell about their heads even after they had rushed out of the house in terror. At last, one of [the men], feeling more confident at a safe distance, picked up one of the stones and, having carefully noted its shape and appearance, threw it back at the house, saying, 'If this comes from you, demon, throw it back to me at once.' It was hurled back immediately, though without doing any damage; whereupon they ceased to have the slightest doubt that the matter was just as the woman had first reported.[16]

The initial scepticism expressed by the mayor is something we have come across before; it was implicit in the vocabulary (*illusiones*, *figmenta*) of some of the eighth-, ninth-, and twelfth-century writers and explicit in the case investigated by Jean Gobi. Once again, too, the phenomena were associated with demons, although it is interesting to see that the word 'magic' makes an appearance. This could be taken to suggest that human agency dependent on demonic assistance (that is, witchcraft) was actually responsible for producing the barrage of stones, as in the case from Schiltach reported by Erasmus. Oddly enough, however – and I say 'oddly' because witches were frequently credited with causing hailstones to fall and destroy crops, so why not real stones? – this link between magic and poltergeistery is rare.[17] The poltergeist's willingness to communicate by answering a request is simply another example in the chain we have remarked already, while from an incident in 1560 we learn that not only might a poltergeist take note of what humans said and did, but that his mood could easily and quickly be changed according to their reactions. Nicolas Rémy (*c*.1530–1612), a French advocate and historian with extensive personal experience of witches and witchcraft, wrote that 'within our own memory' a peasant's cottage at the end of the village of Colombiers was infested by a poltergeist (a 'demon') which threw stones at its inhabitants during the night without doing any of them harm. After a while, however, they became so used to his lithobolia that they started to find it amusing and began to sneer at his activities. This annoyed the entity which thereupon changed his tactics and burned the cottage down. 'I chanced to be travelling that way a few days later', adds Rémy, 'and, hearing of this event from the villagers, resolved to go myself and see the ruin so that I could more clearly and authoritatively report the matter to others.'[18]

But, as I said, lithobolia becomes the predominant feature of poltergeist reports during the rest of the sixteenth century. Thus, in 1549 the brother of the cacique of a village in Popyan, Columbia, wanted to convert to Christianity, but 'devils' tried to prevent him partly by frightening the cacique, who also wanted to convert, 'appearing in hideous forms which were visible only to him', while Christians who were present saw only stones falling from the air and heard only whistling. Then the devil turned on the cacique's brother and carried him through the air, an incident again witnessed by Christians who heard the lad calling out and the devils whistling and shouting. 'Sometimes, when the cacique was sitting with a glass of liquor before him, the Christians saw the glass raised up in the air and put down empty; and a short time afterwards the wine was again poured into the cup from the air.' Further physical assaults happened to the cacique while he was being taken to the nearby town for baptism, but the devils started to throw stones and when he arrived at the house in which he was going to stay, the devils began to throw small stones on to the roof and whistle – 'hu, hu, hu!' – an Indian battle cry. The hail of stones, however, did not prevent everyone from going to church, with the devils continuing to throw stones all night and making a noise even inside the church, until the cacique's baptism put an end to the whole affair.[19]

At first glance the author, a Spanish traveller and explorer whose journal written on the spot formed the basis for his later published account, seems to have no particular knowledge of any European tradition of lithobolia. Instead, he identifies the perpetrators of the stone-throwing and levitations and other assaults as demons, quite in the expected way, of course, but also in accord with what one might expect of a Christian traveller of the time in an essentially pagan country, since contemporary Europeans were in the habit of identifying the local deities as evil spirits. But it is interesting that Pedro de Cieza's account observes more than once that where the cacique and his brother saw demons, the Christians saw and heard only the falling stones and the inarticulate noises made by those same demons; but this may point to Pedro's knowing that there were instances in Europe of demons' attacking people in which the demons themselves never appeared in visible form, and manifested their presence only through the throwing of stones and sometimes by noise and physical assault. If this is so, it is another example of Europeans' interpreting events in non-European countries by reference to their own experience, derived either from personal knowledge or from some form of literary tradition.

Elsewhere in South America, in Peru, August 1590 saw the death of a servant-girl, a Peruvian baptised under the name of Catherine. On the night she died, the house was filled with a foetid stench, the brother of the lady of the house was dragged out of bed by his arm, a female servant struck on the shoulder by a stone (so hard that it left a bruise for several days), the horses went mad in the stables, and the dogs raced around barking; a maid who entered the room where Catherine had died had a vase or pot thrown at her by an unseen hand; further afield in the town, tiles and slates were ripped off their roofs and hurled about to the accompaniment of a loud noise; and another maid from the house was dragged a long way by her foot, again by an unseen agent. Two months later, these phenomena were supplemented by other acts of violence – the smashing of a vase, the breaking of a crucifix, and the throwing of a brick which destroyed a table set for dinner – all clearly attributed to the malice of Catherine's ghost which now appeared to a number of people, 'afire from head to foot and girt with a blazing girdle eight or ten fingers wide'. She appeared to deliver a message, and her message was clear and simple. Her last confession had not been complete and because she had concealed a number of her sins, principally those of acts of lust, she had been damned. 'Learn, then, to confess well and to keep no sin back.'[20]

The information comes from a letter sent by a Jesuit missionary as part of his regular communication with his religious superiors back in Europe and is obviously written with an eye to providing suitable illustrative material for a sermon or treatise on the importance of taking confession seriously, an emphasis which had probably been stimulated by the Council of Trent whose canons and decrees noted that 'contrition holds the first place among the acts of the penitent … at all times necessary for obtaining the forgiveness of sins'.[21] This does not mean to say, of course, that the details are necessarily fiction. The narrative does look, however, as though it falls into two distinct parts – that containing the poltergeistery and that containing the appearance of the ghost with her dreadful message – these separate elements being conjoined to form a slightly disjointed whole. Thus, the first gives us information about Catherine's confession and death and the subsequent lithobolia and attendant violences, all of which took place early in August. Then comes 7 October when throwing a vase, destroying a crucifix, hurling a brick, and attempting to suffocate a four-year-old child are charges overtly levelled at Catherine's ghost. The lapse of two months between these episodes may, certainly, have been genuine, but one does ask oneself whether there are not here two distinct groups of phenomena which have been linked by making Catherine's ghost responsible for some of the later poltergeistery, and by identifying a poltergeist as the angry or emotionally disturbed spirit of a dead person, an identification which would be entirely in keeping with the instincts of the period.

Again, we find a Jesuit missionary, this time from Riga in Latvia, reporting that in 1583 an apostate named Ruthenus, who had once belonged to the Church but now refused to return to her, had been suffering from an infestation of spectres and other entities in his house. Tables were moved by unseen hands, bedroom doors torn from their hinges, huge pitch-covered stones thrown from the roof (one of which struck a man on the head and wounded him badly), and a large amount of straw within the house was cut up into tiny pieces. The problem was solved by a simple exorcism and so the underlying message of the anecdote is clear: refusal to acknowledge the Catholic Church as the one true Church brings unpleasant consequences in its wake, which can be ameliorated only by the Church herself.[22] These connections, which Jesuit literature makes between failure to observe due religious practice or belief and the onset of poltergeist activity, can be seen yet again in an anecdote from France.

In the year 1580, one Gilles Blacre had taken the lease of a house in the suburbs of Tours, but repenting of his bargain with the landlord, Pierre Piquet, he endeavoured to prevail upon him to cancel the agreement. Pierre, however, was satisfied with his tenant and his terms and would listen to no compromise. Very shortly afterwards, the rumour was spread all over Tours that the house of Gilles Blacre was haunted. Gilles himself asserted that he genuinely believed his house to be the general rendezvous of all the witches and evil spirits of France. The noise they made was awful and quite prevented him from sleeping. They knocked against the wall, howled in the chimneys, broke the glass in his windows, scattered his pots and pans all over his kitchen, and set his chairs and tables dancing. The whole night through. Crowds of people assembled round the house to hear the mysterious noises; *and the bricks were observed to detach themselves from the wall and fall into the streets upon the heads of those who had not said their Paternoster before coming out in the morning.* These things having continued for some time, Gilles Blacre made his complaint to the Civil Court of Tours, and Pierre Piquet was summoned to show cause why the lease should not be annulled. Poor Pierre could make no defence, and the court unanimously agreed that no lease could hold good under such circumstances, and annulled it accordingly, condemning the unlucky owner to all the expenses of the suit. Pierre appealed to the Parlement of Paris, and after a long examination the Parlement confirmed the lease – 'not', said the judge, 'because it has not been fully and satisfactorily proved that the house is troubled by evil spirits, but that there was an informality in the proceedings before the Civil Court of Tours which rendered its decision null and of no effect'.[23]

At first glance this may look like a case of fraud: Gilles wanted to break his contract and arranging for the house to be haunted was one way of managing it. He could easily have made the noises and created the damage himself, and that might have explained everything satisfactorily. But two things stand in the way of accepting this version, at least in its entirety. First, people standing in the street saw bricks detach themselves from the walls and hit certain individuals. Could Gilles have managed to do this or have it done without someone's noticing the human hand behind it? It is possible, of course, but the risk of discovery would have been very great – people, after all, were not fools and nor were they unobservant – and had fraud been detected, Gilles would have lost his case and incurred heavy penalties. Secondly, the Parlement of Paris (and also, by implication, the Civil Court of Tours) was satisfied that it had been fully proved that the house was indeed occupied by spirits, satisfied presumably because its members had been offered sufficient testimony to allow them to conclude that fraud had not been involved. But it is worth noting that the recipients of blows from the bricks were those who had failed to perform a simple religious observance, and it is possible that this helped to persuade Pierre Le Loyer, with whom this anecdote originates, to include it in his *Discours et Histoires des Spectres*, since the principal aim of this work was to demonstrate, in the face of some people's contrary opinion, that non-material entities really do exist. We may also care to add that the spectacle of bricks' detaching themselves from a wall can be paralleled from elsewhere. 'In Sicily in June, 1910', a Dutch correspondent from Dordrecht reported to the Council of the Society for Psychical Research, 'in full daylight, Mr. Paolo Palmisano saw stones falling slowly without causing any damage, and says that one of them ... detached itself from the wall, and after describing a slow semicircle in the air, deposited itself in the hand of a friend'.[24]

For the rest of the 1580s, reported poltergeist incidents seem to echo this point. They also expend their energies indoors more than without. A simple example, which might amount to nothing more than a mere haunting, can be seen in 1588 in Madrid. One night in July, Doña Prudencia Grilo had gone to bed and extinguished the candles in her room when she noticed that her bed-curtains were beginning to shake as though disturbed by a gust of wind. Her bedroom windows, however, were closed and, somewhat alarmed, Doña Prudencia had her maid light the candles again; whereupon her bed-curtains started to slide along their rails without anyone's touching them. A small shrill noise then drew her attention to a chest of drawers in the corner of the room. It began to shake, then sway, and finally, with one great effort, slid slowly across the floor tiles to the centre of the room, where it stopped.[25]

Such an episode is trivial enough. Far more serious and far more interesting is one which happened in Töttelstädt in Thuringia, for example, a town north-west of Erfurt. A farmer, Hans Schiel, his wife Margareta, and his two sons, Hans (sixteen) and Martin (nine), were suddenly subjected on the night of 28 February 1581 to an outburst of noise all round the bedroom, followed by small clumps of earth which seemed to come out of nowhere from an invisible source, and hit the family as well as the walls and furniture. In fright, the two adults and their boys moved to the lower room of the house, but clods of earth kept on thudding above their heads until early morning. During the next few days these and similar phenomena were witnessed and endured by friends, relatives, and neighbours as well as the family, who had invited the others to see and experience what was going on. Several were struck by earth, and even after Margareta and Martin had gone to stay elsewhere, the attacks continued, this time including stones, one of which was so heavy it split open one of the neighbour's toes and sent him in grave pain from the scene. But he was not the only person to be damaged by these stones, and both the elder and younger Hans were bruised and battered as the poltergeist threw stones from the yard and street, as well as plates, dishes, and spoons – indeed, anything it could lay hands on (so to speak). At first the local priest was not convinced by Hans senior's report of this poltergeist activity, but when he agreed to go to the house after Mass on 5 March, he found himself the object of lumps of earth and stones in such a fashion that he immediately took Hans senior with him to see the bishop in Erfurt to ask for his advice.

The bishop listened and then sent Johann Körner, a canon of Erfurt Cathedral and the subsequent author of a pamphlet which supplies us with information about this case, to investigate. Körner celebrated Mass in the house on a temporary altar, and everything fell silent for nearly five days. But the phenomena broke out once more, only to be suppressed again by exorcism until 14 March when not only the family but also the family's cattle were attacked. Next day soldiers arrived and searched the house thoroughly from top to bottom, but uncovered nothing which would indicate there was a human rather than a non-human agency behind the assaults and damage. Their visit, however, did result in a more protracted period of quiet. Then, at three o'clock in the morning of 27 March, everything started up again. Large stones struck the family, a jar full of milk in a cupboard was smashed, Margareta had her head cut open by a stone, and Hans junior was knocked down by a flying cannonball. Clearly lives were now in danger, and Hans senior quickly persuaded the bishop to organise a long and elaborate series of exorcisms to answer the emergency. Organising these took two days, during which the poltergeist tried to strangle Hans junior and hurled further large stones, along with kitchen utensils, a sharp-pointed axe, and virtually every other movable object within the house. But at last, at 6 p.m. on 30 March, two priests and Father Körner arrived, and between then and 28 April, when the bishop himself came and celebrated Mass inside the house, a series of Masses and exorcisms appeared to weaken the poltergeist's power to do violence, until finally the whole episode was over and peace restored.[26]

The amount of violence perpetrated by this poltergeist is noticeably large and the degree of that violence even larger. Splitting a neighbour's toe, cutting open Margareta's head and knocking her to the ground, and felling Hans junior with a cannonball represent an escalation of brute hostility which culminates in the poltergeist's attempt to strangle young Hans under the cover of darkness. Nor is that all, because when Hans senior and his brothers tried to rescue the boy, they too were attacked in a similar fashion.[27] Hurting people this way or with flying objects is a not uncommon feature of poltergeist disturbances. In 1761, for example, a nurse in the house of one Mr Giles in Bristol was struck by a wineglass which 'rose gradually about a foot perpendicularly from the drawers; then [it] seemed to stand, and thereupon inclined backwards, as if a hand had held it; it was then flung with violence above five feet and struck the nurse on the hip a hard blow. One of the maids to whom the nurse next day showed the bruise said that the place was black and blue.' Less than a month later, on 2 January 1762, Mr Durbin, who, along with others, was an eyewitness to some of the varied incidents of this particular poltergeist episode, observed one of the Giles children, Molly, in the throes of being throttled. 'I saw the flesh at the side of her throat pushed in, whitish as if done with fingers, though I saw none. Her face grew red and blackish presently, as if she was strangled, but without any convulsion or contraction of the muscles.' A poltergeist in Devon at the beginning of the nineteenth century beat the women of the household he was terrorising black and blue; and in 1906, for example, Alfred Wärndorfer was attacked in a smithy in a suburb of Vienna. As he recorded, '[I] was hit on the back of my right hand by an iron screw with great violence, and felt a very intense pain. Some blood came at once, and a swelling was raised, which lasted for several months.'[28] Attempted killing, however, is rare. We have an example from c.738 when the poltergeist described by Alcuin in his life of St Willibrord picked up a child and threw it on the fire; and there is a suggestive moment during a poltergeist disturbance in South Shields in 2006, when an investigator of the phenomena there found that something was pulling very hard on the camera-strap round his neck, as though it were trying to throttle him.[29] But in spite of the observable fact that poltergeist activity which goes on for any length of time appears to become more and more intense with the passage of days or months, that intensity usually peaks and then diminishes to vanishing point before it reaches the point of potential murder. This Töttelstädt incident is therefore unusual.

But we may also say – with Alan Gauld, who reproduces and comments on it – that Father Körner's report appears to be trustworthy. 'For almost every detail of Körner's account numerous parallels can be found, and I rate his honesty and his accuracy quite highly.' Körner was an eyewitness to many of these events, and he was in a position to take statements from the principals involved and from other witnesses, so unless we are going to suggest he was lying either in full or in detail – and it is difficult to believe one can be *mistaken* about lumps of earth, stones, and other objects flying through the air – we should try to have confidence in the veracity of his reporting.

Nevertheless, it will be worthwhile our bearing in mind the attendant context of the episode. Töttelstädt and Erfurt formed a Catholic enclave in what was a predominantly Lutheran state, and the poltergeist outbreak thus occurred within it. Now, there can be no doubt that the Schiel family, their friends, relatives, and neighbours, the exorcising priests, and the bishop interpreted the poltergeist as a demon. This was, as we have seen, standard practice for the period and is confirmed by the Church's use of exorcism to control and expel him. In this interpretation they will have been at one with their Lutheran fellow-citizens, and indeed with practically everyone else in Germany, for the second half of the sixteenth century in particular saw a notable increase among German Protestants especially, whatever their shades of opinion, in the belief that the End Times were coming and that Satan and his servants, demonic and human, had been let loose and were rampaging through the world. From the 1550s onwards a new genre of books known as *Teufelsbucher* ('Devil's Books') poured from Germany's printing presses – nearly quarter of a million according to one count – and helped to convince people not only that Satan's power was growing, but also that he might be encountered anywhere and at any time. (There were reports, for example, that he had been seen 'fluttering around in churches in a long, black robe', looking for all the world like Calvin.) Hence, too, it is not surprising to find that incidents of demonic possession were also multiplying at this same time;[30] so a poltergeist incident, however alarming in its details, will not have constituted an unusual or even rare happening, but rather a common, if particularly frightening and ostentatious, exhibition by the Devil of his being loose in Germany. For Father Körner, however, once the manifestation had finally been laid to rest, the episode may have presented an opportunity to demonstrate to his Catholic flock and Lutheran neighbours that it was the Catholic Church which had the key to defeating Satan, since her exorcisms were successful even against a protracted and vicious outbreak clearly intended to convince people of his power and near-lethal hostility. Hence Father Körner's pamphlet – although he had to go as far away as Köln to get it printed. There were four printing presses in Erfurt, but these, to judge by their booklists, all seem to have been in the hands of Protestants. The effort, and no doubt expense which this would have entailed, however, suggest that he considered it worth his time and trouble, an effort he would probably not have made had his account been no more than the mere recording of a *Wundergeschicht*, wonder tale, for the purpose of diverting a few readers. We should probably see it as much more than that: a shot fired from the Catholic side of the fence in the confessional wars which were then disrupting Germany.

Two years later, in 1583, a similar incident took place with similar results. A priest's house just outwith the city of Würzburg was troubled by a poltergeist's disturbance. Anything movable was thrown violently to the floor, lights were extinguished as soon as they were lit, and beds were dragged away from anyone who tried to lie on them. Many of the servants also found themselves subject to suffocation because of an obstruction in the throat, which sounds like an instance of the Old Hag or possibly an attempt at throttling. The priest called in a colleague who saw a salver hurled against one of the walls, an experience which convinced him that exorcism was required. (One asks oneself why the priest himself had not thought of this.) In consequence, the visitor put on a stole at once, went to the seat of the trouble at the top of the house, and performed 'the usual rites of the Church for putting demons to flight'. These, if we choose to follow the sixteenth-century exorcist Girolamo Menghi, will have involved exhortations to the demon to depart, recitation of the initial verses of St John's Gospel, the Creed, and psalms (such as nos 51 and 70), followed by repeated prayers and further adjurations addressed to the evil spirit.[31] As a result of the priest's efforts, the house was freed from infestation; but the episode ends, significantly, with the priest's speaking to the servants, some of whom at least must have been either Protestants or lapsed Catholics, and urging them 'to throw aside heresy and to expiate their sins by means of a good confession'. Many must have done so, for we are informed that, as a result, 'many were reclaimed from heresy to the Church'.[32]

This story is recorded by Francesco Maria Guazzo, a Barnabite friar, whose *Compendium Maleficarum* ('Summary of Women who Practise Harmful Magic') was written in 1605 and published three years later. It appears in the final section of Book 3, which is devoted to providing examples of divine and supernatural remedies against attacks by demons or witches, and is intended to show the power of holy water in particular, although the episode is resolved by exorcism (which admittedly involves the use of holy water) rather than by holy water alone. This third Book as a whole concentrates on demoniacs and the various ways in which they may be treated, a significant point because Guazzo himself was sent to the German duchy of Jülich-Cleves in 1605 as part of a continuing series of Italian exorcists summoned thither to treat the unfortunate Duke, who was suspected of being possessed by demons.[33] So it looks as though this part of the *Compendium*, at any rate, may have been informed or stimulated by his German experience. The poltergeist incident is thus firmly fixed as the work of a demon (with possible links to witchcraft), although it is notable that Guazzo adds 'or some illusion', even though the notion that the evident violence witnessed and suffered by several individuals was hallucinatory in origin and effect is not pursued.

Finally we may note an incident from Bordeaux, which took place early in 1595. A tenant felt obliged to leave his rented house because a spirit in the form of a small child dressed in white began to trouble him and his servants in a series of hostile acts which seem to have increased in menace in quite a short space of time. The spirit would appear three or four times a week, making everything in the house – furniture and household utensils – shake, and altering its own size from big to small in various ways. In the evening it would draw the bed-curtains (one thinks of the episode in Madrid) and then jump on the stomach of anyone trying to sleep. 'It used to press down on them, close their mouth, prevent them from speaking and breathing' – a typical example of the Old Hag – and 'transport the male and female servants from the bed to the yard, and from the top of the house to the bottom', as well as striking and beating a number of people. The owner of the house, annoyed because of these alleged happenings which would affect the value of her property and her ability to find another tenant, brought the matter to court on the grounds that it was not possible for a house to be infested by spirits. But the court decided against her, saying that the tenant's allegation was entirely 'conformable to the usage and tradition of the Church, the authority of the holy Fathers [of the Church], the conclusion reached by Scholastics, the opinion of philosophers, the decision of legal experts, and the experience of many centuries'.[34]

Here we have themes and experiences relatable to others known and endured by several individuals earlier in the century, and it is noteworthy that the decision of the court came down comprehensively on the side of these phenomena's being real. The word 'demons' had crept into the process at some point, too, whether from the defendant or the judges themselves, and the view that the poltergeist was some kind of evil spirit now seems to have taken root and become a general assumption. What makes this Bordeaux episode somewhat different, of course, is the visibility of the infesting spirit. This can only have served to confirm the expectation that the entity was a demon, since it made no demands for Christian burial or Masses or distribution of alms to the poor, or any of the other requests traditionally associated with the distressed ghost of someone dead and suffering in Purgatory, and appeared to work only mischief. We can think back to the Dagworth incidents of the 1190s when the intrusive spirit appeared to one onlooker as a tiny child wearing a white dress. But here, it will be recalled, there was some doubt over how to interpret the phenomenon: was she a ghost, a fairy, or an illusion? The language used by Ralph of Coggeshall, who recorded it in his chronicle, left the matter open to some degree of doubt. Not so that of the Parlement of Bordeaux as reported by Pierre de Lancre. Its decision was that the allegation that the house in question was troubled and its quiet disturbed by spirits or demons was '*receuable, pertinent, et admissible*'. The law, therefore, had no doubts or hesitations; nor did it encompass in its judgement a wider range of possible explanations for the origin of the phenomena than 'spirits or demons', the 'or' having less the force of an alternative, more the implication 'that is to say'.

The sixteenth century, then, saw an increase in the number of reported instances of what appears to be poltergeist activity, which tended more and more to be reported as that of some kind of demon. Indeed, there may well have been many more such incidents than we know about, for the Jesuit scholar Martín del Rio wrote at the very end of the century that in addition to various other species of apparition there were 'spectres which, at certain times and in certain locations and houses, are accustomed to produce different kinds of disturbances and violent harassments. I shall not give examples of this because it is a very well-known fact.'[35] Whether he meant that it was well known to scholars such as himself because they were well acquainted with the relevant literature, or whether he meant that personal experience of these phenomena was widespread and commonplace is not altogether clear. But certainly more people were recording these incidents, and the amount of material we have on the subject burgeons and then explodes in the following centuries. The geographical spread of these sixteenth-century narratives, however, is more restricted than that of their Mediaeval counterparts. Apart from those narratives noted in South America and Latvia, which we owe to Jesuit missionaries, they come in the main from Germany, German-Swiss cantons, France, Spain, and Italy. We should note, however, that nearly three quarters of them have been transmitted via only two authors, Nicolas Rémy and Francesco Guazzo, each of whom was writing a religiously inspired book about witchcraft and the terrifying contemporary spread of Satan's power; and it is clear from the choice of anecdote, the interest of the recording author and that of his potential readership, and the contexts of most of these incidents that, in contrast to some of the Mediaeval accounts of poltergeists which leaned somewhat in the direction of entertainment, and to others which seemed to illustrate difficulties attendant on separating poltergeist from ghost from demon and from fairy, these sixteenth-century anecdotes, when they were not instances of simple fraud, were being taken seriously and put to use as evidence of truth and validity in the confessional battles convulsing the states of Europe. Hence, of course, the almost invariable identification of the poltergeist as a demon. Del Rio's assumption that it was some kind of ghost, *spectrum*, is a minority opinion.

But it is also worth noting that the sixteenth century saw an increasing number of books written in the vernacular, the shift from Latin being encouraged, for example, in France by an edict of 1539 which made French the official language of administration. Hence we find both Nicholas Rémy and Jean Bodin writing their demonologies in French, while in Spain, Antonio de Torquemada chose to commit his omnium gatherum to Spanish, and ghosts as a general topic for discussion from virtually any point of view were rapidly making their appearance more and more in vernacular texts which were either translations from Latin or original compositions in their own right. A double market was thus available to authors, who clearly took advantage of both, and a growing number of translators made their living by rendering Latin into other tongues in the form of complete translations, digests, and anthologies. The latter two decades of the sixteenth century and the opening decades of the seventeenth were also the high point of witchcraft prosecutions in Europe. This, of course, made almost any discussion about the relationship between human beings and non-human entities (here largely meaning demons) both fascinating and irresistible, although curiously enough in view of the sixteenth century's profound interest in questions of what was illusion and what reality in regard to preternatural phenomena, Mediaeval hints about possible demonic or diabolic illusion anent some poltergeist incidents do not seem to have been followed up by the later demonologists.

Non-human entities were therefore news and topics of conversation whether learned or popular, and as long as witches and witchcraft and demons dominated this type of discourse, poltergeists were likely to be regarded as demons rather than ghosts on the grounds that their violent activity tended to be characteristic of what was expected of the former rather than of the latter. Appropriate steps to take in dealing with poltergeists, therefore, consisted of cleansing the object of their violence by confession and communion, and by employing exorcism to liberate the place which was being infested. With the growth and spread of Protestant confessions in Europe, however, such remedies had either to be adopted or adapted,[36] and the growing, widespread conviction that poltergeist phenomena were caused by or at least involved one or more evil spirits presented everyone with difficulties in knowing how to deal with them, which the following century failed either to address or to resolve.

6

A Species of Witchcraft? 1612

By and large we may say that the sixteenth century had got it fixed in its head that poltergeistery was the work of evil spirits. 'Scholars argue about the sort of pact which enables demons to throw stones and do other things of this kind, which appear to require [the use of] hands and physical implements,' wrote Del Rio, and his reference to a pact confirms that he and the scholars were thinking in terms of demons' operating through the medium of human beings in that manner distinctively known as 'witchcraft'. That such an association carried on well into the seventeenth century can be seen in many later reports of poltergeist phenomena, beginning with one of the best known, which referred to a remarkable series of incidents in the French town of Mâcon between 14 September and 22 December 1612. This regularly appears in modern accounts of poltergeists, but detailed examination of the only account we have, that of François Perreaud, who was the principal target of the hostility, reveals a much more complex set of events than is usually realised.

Mâcon, situated in the south of Bourgogne, had a mixed population of Catholics and Protestants, and it was to one of the Protestant churches there that François Perreaud (1572/77–1659), a Calvinist by doctrine, arrived in 1611 from Buxy, where he had been a pastor since 1603, in answer to an invitation from the Protestants of the town. Perreaud had been a widower with two children, but just before he came to Mâcon he remarried and although his new wife, Anne Farci, would go on to give him several more children, they do not seem to have started their own family when the poltergeist began to trouble them. At first everything appeared to be going well and Perreaud made a number of friends in the community, including a staunch Catholic,

97

François Tornus, a local notary. Their friendship may be taken as a testimony to the character of the two men, who were perhaps able to enjoy the brief lull afforded by these crucial years between the end of the French Wars of Religion and the future Thirty Years' War which devastated many parts of Europe.

Stage 1: Initial Phenomena[1]

On 19 September 1612, however, Perreaud returned home after an absence of five days to find his wife and her maid in a state of great agitation and distress. Anne told him that on the day he left, when she went to bed something caused her bed-curtains to move violently, and this woke her up. Her maid, who was sleeping in the same room, got up at once and asked what was the matter. She looked round but the doors and windows were firmly shut and she did not see anything else to make her suspicious. Nothing more happened on that occasion, but Anne was so nervous that the following night she had the maid sleep next to her in her bed, and as soon as the two women had lain themselves down the coverlet was pulled off them and the maid thrown on to the floor. She picked herself up and went to the door to the kitchen – the kitchen and the main bedroom being adjacent to one another on the ground floor – only to find that it resisted her attempts to open it, as though someone were pressing hard against it. Finding that she could not get out that way, the maid went and fetched a boy who was living in the house at the time, and asked him, without explaining why, so as not to frighten him, to come and open the door: which he did, apparently without difficulty. The maid lit a candle and went into the kitchen, only to find that crockery and other utensils were strewn all over the floor. The same thing happened the next night and the next, the chaos being accompanied by a loud noise, 'like [the noise] one usually makes during a carnival procession, or when one makes a sound to detain bees during summer'.[2]

Perreaud's reactions included at once astonishment and doubt, but he took precautions nevertheless, principally against the possibility that someone was playing a practical joke or trying to intimidate the household. So he searched every corner of the house, locked all the doors, shuttered and barred the windows, and then said evening prayers and went to bed, leaving his wife and the maid sitting by the fire with their distaffs and a lighted lamp on a table for extra illumination. The moment Perreaud was in bed, however, a racket broke out next to the kitchen, including sounds of a dreadful rumbling and knocking against a newly erected partition wall as though made by someone's knuckles, fist, and nails, after which plates and platters were thrown against the partition, and a copper pan and various other small objects were moved from their places. Perreaud got up to investigate, sword in hand, his wife's maid walking in front of him with a lighted candle; but thorough examination of the room proved that no one was hiding there, and so Perreaud went back to bed, only to have the noise break out again. A second search found nothing untoward and in consequence, as Perreaud says in his account of the episode, 'I began to realise that this could be proceeding only from an evil spirit (*un malin esprit*), and so I passed the rest of the night in a state of astonishment which anyone can imagine for himself'.[3]

Stage 2: Conversations

Next day, early in the morning, Perreaud sought the advice of the elders of his church and, significantly, that of his friend François Tornus for reasons which will become clear as the narrative unfolds. All these men then came to keep Perreaud company every evening, either individually or as a group, until midnight or even later. The first few evenings they came, the 'evil spirit' made not a sound or a move, but on 20 November – that is, more than two months after the initial outbursts – 'in the presence of us all, and especially that of Monsieur Tornus', it began to whistle three or four times in succession. At first the sound was very shrill and loud, but then gradually turned into a voice, 'very distinct and understandable, although somewhat husky'. It came from very near Perreaud and his friends, 'about two or three steps away', and sang, 'twenty-two pennies, twenty-two pennies', followed by the word 'Minister, minister', repeated several times. Everyone was taken aback, but Perreaud managed to say, 'Get thee behind me, Satan, the Lord commands you.' This, however, had no effect on the entity which simply went on repeating 'Minister, minister' until Perreaud lost patience and retorted, 'Yes, I am indeed a minister and a servant of the living God before whose majesty you tremble': to which the entity replied, 'I'm not saying otherwise.' It is a notable moment, the transition from repetitive words and phrases (which Perreaud likens to the parroting of a caged bird one teaches to speak) to a coherent retort which indicates that the entity has a mind of its own. Perreaud suspected that the 'evil spirit' was saying 'Minister, minister' just to needle him, and indeed it went on to recite the Our Father, the Apostles' Creed, prayers from Evensong and Matins, and the Ten Commandments, although it always cut them short and omitted certain parts. It also sang part of Psalm 81 in a loud clear voice, and here I think we may see clear evidence of sarcasm in the entity's actions which seem to be saying on the one hand that the sacred texts have no effect upon it, and on the other that exorcism (should Perreaud try it) will also be of no avail. Psalm 81 thanks God for Israel's deliverance from captivity and offers a lament that Israel proved ungrateful for that help. Verses 13 and 14 may be particularly significant.

> Oh that my people had hearkened unto me, and Israel had walked in my ways!
> I should soon have subdued their enemies, and turned my hand against their adversaries.

In the somewhat heated religious atmosphere of the time, which would turn into the Thirty Years' War only six years later, both sides of the confessional divide could have heard these words and applied them to their own advantage and comfort, Perreaud and his church elders one way, François Tornus in another. So which side was the entity mocking?[4]

The change of voice from inarticulacy to intelligibility can be paralleled from other cases. In December 1977, for example, in Enfield a poltergeist which had been troubling a household in the usual noisy, boisterous ways since August began to whistle and bark, sounds which then turned first into a name ('Maurice, Maurice', the name of a man who had just tried to speak to it) and next into intelligent, though obscene, responses to further remarks and questions. The nature of the voice used by Perreaud's entity can also be paralleled with that of the Enfield poltergeist. 'The tape recordings of this spirit', wrote Colin Wilson, 'sound oddly hoarse and breathless, as if the voice is not being produced in the normal way by vocal chords and lungs.'[5] We also find similarities with the behaviour of some earlier poltergeists who spoke and revealed embarrassing details about the private lives of their audience; for after mocking those present in Perreaud's room with its chanting of Psalm 81, the entity said a good many things which could have been true, as well as a number of intimate details about Perreaud's family, including the assertion that Perreaud's father had been poisoned, followed by the name of the poisoner, the place where the alleged murder had been carried out, and the type of poison which had been used. (Unfortunately, we do not know whether these details are to be included among the things 'which could have been true'. Perreaud does not contradict them, so perhaps they were actually true either in whole or in part.)

So far the poltergeist had not behaved in any particular way out of the ordinary, and neither, apart from the accusation of poisoning, had it said anything especially startling. But now, having settled in for the evening, so to speak, it volunteered a piece of information which would have caused Perreaud to prick up his ears. 'He said', wrote Perreaud, 'that he came from the Pays de Vaud.' Now, the Pays de Vaud was notorious – and had been so ever since the latter half of the fifteenth century – for being the scene of many of Europe's most intense episodes of witchcraft. One estimate has 1,700 witches being executed over a period of 150 years (between c.1530 and 1680, when such trials stopped).[6] Perreaud's grandfather, also a Calvinist pastor, had practised his ministry in the Pays de Gex and in the Pays de Vaud, and had been followed in both places by his son, Perreaud's father, who had sought refuge in the latter place after the success of Catholic arms had forced him and his family to seek refuge from the Pays de Gex.[7] Perreaud therefore could not have failed to register the poltergeist's saying it had come from there, and to have had a strong suspicion that this entity was a demon come to carry out witchcraft in some fashion or other, a suspicion which would have entailed his wondering who might be the human agent through whom the demon would operate, since witchcraft by definition meant a league and a pact between humans and evil spirits.

The poltergeist went on to tell stories involving Perreaud's elder brother, who was living in the Pays de Gex. In one it said it had turned up in disguise while the elder Perreaud was dining with another Protestant minister, and was invited to take a drink with them. In another, it recalled an occasion when Perreaud senior was living in the Pays de Vaud and relatives came to visit. They decided to go boating, but on a raft rather than in a boat, and a sudden strong wind rose and overturned the raft, so that it was a wonder they were not all drowned. Both incidents, says Perreaud, did actually happen, so the 'evil spirit' was telling the truth, including its worrying claim that it was responsible for raising the near-fatal wind: for 'we read in the Book of Job that the Devil stirred up sudden whirlwinds which completely overturned the house in which the holy man's children were'.

This particular evening then introduced a series of similar evenings during which the poltergeist conversed with the watchers in like fashion, revealing matters private to individuals who were present. He asked Claude Rapai, a launderer, if he remembered the day some cloth on which he had been working disappeared from where he had put it ('I did that!'), and another launderer, Philibert Guillermin, if he recalled laying out some linen to dry, and being pulled backwards two or three paces by the strings on his doublet: and whether he remembered that, on the following evening, after he had gone to bed in his laundry, having his hat on a peg next to the bed, he woke up with a start because his hat had been thrown in his face ('I did that, too!'). Once again, both incidents were confirmed to be true. Next day the poltergeist revealed that Philibert's brother had come to stay with him and wanted to pay Perreaud a visit, but that Philibert had put him off. It provided details of a quarrel between Jacques Berard and Samuel Dumont, which had led to Berard's beating Dumont so badly that Dumont nearly died. It spoke of a recent serious incident in Mâcon, during which François Chiquard had been wounded by a musket-shot and had been obliged to have one of his legs amputated; and it also informed the company that Philibert Masson and his wife, who had owned the Perreaud house before Perreaud and his family moved in, had quarrelled one day, and that Madame Masson had pushed her husband downstairs and killed him, but had been able to pass off the murder as an accident.[8]

Each of these revelations, says Perreaud, was either acknowledged to be true or believed to be the truth, and thus we see the entity as it were establishing its credentials, but thereby behaving in just such a way as demons were believed to behave, since the ability to report events supposedly hidden or happening elsewhere was one of their peculiar attributes. From uncovering secrets, the poltergeist now turned to blasphemy only to be rebuked by Perreaud; whereupon the poltergeist begged them to send for Father Duchassin, the parish priest of St Etienne (and a Catholic), so that it could make its confession – 'And don't let him forget to bring holy water so that he can exorcise me' – having said which, it suddenly fell silent. The company then wondered why it was that Perreaud's dog, which usually barked at the slightest sound, had not barked at all while the poltergeist was creating so much noise in the house. This was enough to stir the entity into speaking again. 'You're amazed that the dog doesn't bark,' it said. 'That's because I made the sign of the cross over its head.'

Another change of mood took the entity from sarcasm to what Perreaud calls 'banter and buffoonery', during which it told silly stories. For example, it said it happened to be in Geneva on the Day of the Escalade, an annual festival held each December to commemorate the defeat of a surprise attack on the city by the Duke of Savoy in 1602, and jumped down from the city walls into the moat, where the frogs did not succeed in eating it – 'in saying which it rather artlessly imitated the croaking of frogs' – but also observed of the Pays de Vaud that 'it was a region where they grilled sorcerers well', and laughed uproariously. It took particular pleasure in chaffing the chambermaid, calling her at every turn 'Bressande', an allusion to the area from which she came, and mimicking her dialect; and one evening, while she was going up to the attic to get some coal, it said to her, 'You're very brave to come so close to me', made a noise as though it were clapping its hands, and added, 'I'll put you in my bag.'[9] This louche sense of humour also extended to Michel Repai, who used to come to Perreaud's house every evening with his father during this period of harassment, and was not inclined to treat the poltergeist with any respect. Nevertheless, the poltergeist repeated a conversation Michel had had with a friend of his the previous Sunday while they were going to hear a sermon outwith Mâcon. They were wondering whether they could trap it by stretching some fine threads across the room, and the poltergeist now said, in front of the company, 'So do you want to stretch them across now to catch and trap me?' It then went on to imitate the voice of Michel's mother so accurately that Michel was obliged to laugh and say to his father, 'I have to say, it's talking just like Mother.'[10]

Stage 3: Playing Games

On another occasion, the entity announced in a pitiful, weary voice, that it had to go to Chambéry (about 73 miles away) on business, and so it wanted to make its will in case it died on the way there. It begged the chambermaid to go to ask François Tornus's father to act as its solicitor,[11] and meanwhile told the company about his intended legacies to various people present, which they in turn contemptuously rejected. The poltergeist's next game was to pretend to be an entirely different spirit from the one who had been talking to them. This one (it said) was the other spirit's valet who was standing in for him while he was away in Chambéry. Perreaud brushed this aside with some harsh words, but the entity replied quietly and respectfully, and asked Perreaud who he was. Whereupon one of the visitors, Simeon Meissonier, launched himself at the spot from which the voice was coming and thoroughly searched both there and outwith the room, just as others had done often enough before, without finding anything. But he came back into the room, carrying a number of little objects, including a small bottle. The entity started to laugh. 'I've heard for a long time that you're a fool', it said, 'and now I see you really are one to believe I'm in that bottle. If that were so, you would only have to put your finger over the top and I'd be trapped.'[12] Then it turned its attention to a goldsmith, Abraham Lullier, who had just come into the room, and offered to become his apprentice, an offer Lullier rejected with scorn. Whereupon the poltergeist said, 'Well then, if you don't want to teach me to be a goldsmith, Maître Philibert must teach me to be a launderer', and it started to pretend it was a spirit-valet again and offered to leave if they would give it something – anything would do. 'I wouldn't give you my nail-clippings,' retorted Perreaud. 'You're not very charitable,' answered the spirit.

Enough has been said for the moment to give a clear idea of the nature of the Mâconnais poltergeist and its relationship with Perreaud and his friends. It is notable that, from its initial rapping, knocking, and creating mayhem in the kitchen, it settled down into what appears to have been lengthy conversations with the group, an extraordinary experience for the men who turned up night after night to find themselves interacting with a disembodied voice. None of them, it seemed, questioned the veracity of the experience unless, as with Perreaud initially and later Simeon Meissonier, a transient suspicion of trickery caused them to search those places from which the phenomena appeared to emanate. But it may seem odd to us that no one suspected ventriloquism, until we realise the immense effort required in keeping up such a performance with all its varied voices evening after evening, the constant likelihood of discovery with its attendant certainty of prosecution and punishment, not to mention ostracism from the perpetrator's community and its network of support, opportunities for work and thus livelihood, and the psychological and emotional strain deriving from such consequences. More important than this, however, would have been the association made at this period between ventriloquism and demonic possession. Demoniacs frequently spoke in voices other than their own, but this happened when the individual was clearly not his or her usual self, as in the case of William Somers, a young lad apprenticed to a musician, who began to throw fits in October 1597, which were witnessed by a large number of people.

> W. Hunt, baker, of the town of Nottingham, sworn and examined, deposes and says that he did see W. Sommers in his fit lying for dead, to his thinking. In this fit, he heard a voice proceed from the said Sommers. And his lips were closed shut. And he did neither move his lips nor jaws to his understanding. And he continued so speaking for the space of a quarter of an hour. And this deponent further says that, in the same fit, he did see a thing the size of a walnut running in the flesh of the said W. Sommers, about his face, forehead, and eyes, and so run about his face to his ear.[13]

Both considerations I think must therefore lead us to put aside ventriloquism on the part of one or more of the men present in Perreaud's house, although it is a subject to which we shall return later after further discussion of the way the episode developed.

The entity kept on insisting that it was not the one who had been in the house originally, or even the previous evening ('That was one of my pals') and that they were both waiting for their master to come back from Chambéry. Here Perreaud tells us something unexpected. 'I found out, on good authority [de bonne part], that there was a spirit in the house of Monsieur Favre, premier président in Chambery.' This spirit spoke to Favre, told him he had come from Mâcon and had been in Bresse, related a number of details about him and his family, demanded that food such as turkey, partridge, and leveret be prepared for the arrival of its master, burst into profane and ribald songs, and then began to shout in the manner of quack doctors, street conjurors, and huntsmen. So here was yet another 'valet' for the original poltergeist, although its behaviour, and the likelihood that Perreaud found out about it only after talking to someone else after the event, suggests that Favre's spirit and that conversing with Perreaud were actually one and the same. Its sense of humour, however, is not quite the norm for those entities called 'poltergeists'. These usually prefer physical and somewhat ill-natured pranks to verbal play. On 25 February 1949, for example, the *Willesden Chronicle* reported that the American Shoe Stores on Kilburn High Road in London was the scene of a quite dangerous poltergeist which threw heavy furniture as well as smaller objects at people who worked there. One of its 'humorous' tricks was to dye brown shoes black and pour solution into other shoes, or to make shoes disappear, which were then brought into the shop, sometimes weeks later, by customers who had found them outside on the pavement. The South Shields poltergeist of 2006 also enjoyed interfering with mobile telephones, causing them to ring or display 'missed call' when in fact no one had actually made contact at all. Such incidents seem to support Colin Wilson's observation that 'the poltergeist is basically a mad practical joker; the mentality seems to be that of an idiot child'.[14] But this is a long way from the Mâconnais entity which took delight in showing off its verbal dexterity by imitating a wide variety of voices, including some known to the watchers in Perreaud's house. In consequence, one begins to ask how much of this episode was 'poltergeist' and how much something else.

Stage 4: Temptations

What that 'something else' may have been is not altogether clear, but the next stage of its behaviour makes it look more demonic than anything else. 'It then thought up another trick', says Perreaud, '[which was] to tempt us through greed for money – this is why the Devil is called Mammon – by saying there were 6,000 écus concealed in the house, and that if one of us would be willing to come with it and follow it, he would be shown where they were hidden'. That phrase 'and follow it' is ominously reminiscent of Jesus's call to His disciples and therefore also of the Devil's invitation to those who would be his servants in the form of witches. Perreaud picked up the allusion at once and vehemently assured his readers that he did not look for the money, nor did he have it done for him, nor did he allow anyone else to go off and look for it. (The wish to do so, he said, never crossed his mind, although the strength of his assertions makes one think, perhaps unworthily, that the pastor doth protest too much.)[15] Next the entity tried to tempt them by an appeal to their curiosity. If they wanted to see it take some physical form – man, woman, lion, bear, dog, cat – it would oblige them: at which they (probably meaning Perreaud) retorted that, far from wanting to see it in any shape or form, they would be pleased not to hear it again either, and hoped that God would soon deliver them from all the spirit's temptations. This angered the spirit, and both it and Perreaud entered upon heated verbal exchanges. Perreaud said it was cursed and damned to Hell, at which the spirit tried to pretend it was the ghost of a woman who had recently died in the Perreaud's house and had come back to cause them trouble. It then reverted to its poltergeist nature and threatened that when Perreaud went to bed, it would come along, pull off the coverlet, and drag him out of his bed by his feet. Perreaud replied with a verse from Psalm 3, 'I shall lie down and go to sleep, for the Everlasting sustains me' – and the two of them bandied further verses from the New Testament. Then, tiring of Perreaud, the entity turned its anger on someone else, calling him 'stinking goat' and 'hypocrite', and threatening him with violence. 'You pretend to be a brave man here, bringing your sword with you this evening. But are you bold enough to come here without a light? Then we'll see which of the two of us is the braver.'[16]

Another mood-change followed. The entity started to foretell the future, predicting that French Protestants were going to suffer and that they should therefore take precautions, and telling Perreaud that his wife, who was pregnant at this time, would give birth to a daughter. (This caused Perreaud some concern, since he was afraid that his wife would be upset by learning of the prediction and whence it had come. So he advised her to leave the house and go to have the child in safety with her grandmother. Anne, however, refused, saying that this would show a lack of faith in God, who was putting them to the test, and that if they resisted the Devil, the spirit would undoubtedly flee.) As far as Perreaud himself was concerned, said the spirit, he would infallibly die in three years' time. It hoped thereby, observed Perreaud, to make him fall into depression or some other illness of body and mind. By now, however, the entity had run through its tricks and was forced to admit openly that it was quite unable to gain ascendancy over the assembled company because they kept praying and invoking the name of God. Indeed, as Perreaud noted, the entity remained silent during their prayers, but once they finished it started up again. The end of this phase of Perreaud's reporting its behaviour came on 25 November when it announced, laughing as it did so, 'Ha, ha, I shan't speak any more'; and sure enough, from that evening onwards it never said another word.[17]

Stage 5: More Poltergeistery

The entity was fond of teasing Perreaud's chambermaid, and once snatched a candlestick out of her hand, leaving her holding the lighted candle. Very often it would hang her clothes from the top of the bedposts in a room at the front of the house, and add a hat made from long strands of animal hair, the kind of thing usually worn by villagers of Bresse, which was where she came from; and it would frequently attach ropes to the bedposts, weaving in so many tight knots that it was impossible to untie them. Yet the poltergeist itself untied them in a flash. This kind of trick seems to have been a favourite, for it once laced Perreaud's boots into the machine on which he used to wind thread, presumably in his workshop, and Perreaud could not remove them; or it would twist rape in with the thread so that it took a great deal of time and patience to get any work done.

One day, at about one or two o'clock in the afternoon, a friend of Perreaud's, Monsieur Connain, a physician in Mâcon, arrived to see him. Perreaud told him what had been going on and together they went into Perreaud's bedroom at the front of the house, where they found the bedspread, sheets, and pillow strewn all over the floor. They told the chambermaid to re-make the bed and this she did in their presence. But no sooner had this been done than they saw the whole bed disarranged and its furnishing thrown on the floor as before. Perreaud also tells us that he often found some of the books in his study treated in the same fashion, and his clock on the ground, but unbroken; and once, while Perreaud was reading there, the poltergeist imitated the noise of a volley of arquebuses, which sounded as though it was coming from the floor above.[18] It also pretended to be Perreaud's stable-lad and 'groomed' his horse by tying knots in its hair and tail, and putting on its saddle back to front. But for some unexplained reason it took Perreaud, as he says, a long time to realise that the poltergeist frequented the room in which Perreaud slept. One night, however, when Perreaud's visitors had left, the household had gone to bed, and Perreaud had seen to it that the doors and windows of his room were firmly closed, the poltergeist began to whistle softly every so often, 'as though it were afraid of waking us', and rapping, as it were, its knuckles on a box at the side of the bed. Then it started to throw Perreaud's shoes round the room. The chambermaid, who must have been sleeping in the same room as Pereaud and his wife, then had her shoes thrown around; but when the poltergeist took one of them, she seized hold of the other, put it behind the bed-head, and laughed, saying, 'You're not going to have this one, at any rate.'

Imitation of sounds seems to have given the entity much pleasure. It once made a noise under Perreaud's table like that of spinners at their work, and on other occasions it made Perreaud and his friends hear the sound of two little iron bells it had taken from the house. (Perreaud says he recognised their peculiar pitch and went to look for them, but could not find them.) This sound the 'demon' – as Perreaud now starts to call the entity more or less each time he mentions it – caused them to hear not only inside the house, but also in various places in the town and the surrounding countryside as when, one Sunday morning, while Perreaud was about his business with some elders from the church at Vrigny, they all heard these bells ringing close to their ears and from their purses, while Abraham Lullier said he could hear them in his house, too.

Lullier, indeed, at one point became the focus of the poltergeist's attentions and told Perreaud about them one day after dinner. It used to take things and hide them, he said, and when he had looked long and hard for them, it would return them to the place whence it had taken them. No sooner had Lullier recounted this prank than a gold ring on which he had been working (it will be recalled that Lullier was a jeweller), along with the tool which held it, appeared on Lullier's apron; and yet the moment Lullier went to pick it up, he could find neither ring nor grip, even though he searched for half an hour while Perreaud was still there. But as soon as both men turned their attention elsewhere, ring and grip fell out of thin air (*comme de l'air*) on to the apron again. Apports – paranormal movements of an object from one place to another, or the appearance of an object apparently from nowhere – are very commonly associated with poltergeist activity. The Reverend C.L. Tweedale, for example, recorded one on Sunday 13 November 1910.

Mother had sustained a cut on the head, and she, my wife, and I were all in the dining room at 9.20 p.m. We were all close together, mother seated in a chair, self and wife standing. No one else was in the room. My wife was in the act of parting mother's hair with her fingers to examine the cut and I was looking on. At that instant I happened to raise my eyes and I saw something issue from a point close to the ceiling in the corner of the room over the window, and distant from my wife (who had her back to it) three and a quarter yards, and four and a quarter yards from myself, facing it. It shot across the room close to the ceiling and struck the wall over the piano, upon which it then fell, making the strings vibrate, and so on to the floor on which it rolled. I ran and picked it up, and found, to my astonishment, that it was a jar of ointment which mother used specially for cuts and bruises, and which she kept locked up in her wardrobe. The intention was evident, the ointment was for the wound. I saw it come apparently through the wall, near the ceiling, and this with no one within three and a quarter yards of the place. The room is over nine feet high and was brilliantly lighted by a 100 candle-power lamp, and the door and window were shut, the latter fastened, and incapable of being opened from the outside.[19]

One peculiarity of such apports is that while they do not exactly materialise in front of people's eyes, onlookers are never quite sure at what stage the object actually makes its appearance. The Swanland case, reported in the *Proceedings of the Society for Psychical Research* in 1891–92, described the way wood-cuttings in a carpenter's workshop would dance about or rise up to the ceiling whence they would fall on anyone below. An apprentice at the time of the disturbance wrote later to one of the Society's investigators.

Nobody ever saw a missile at the time it started. One would have said that they could not be perceived until they had travelled at least six inches from their starting-point ... The missiles moved only when nobody was looking and when they were least expected. Now and again one of us would watch a piece of wood closely for a good number of minutes and the piece would not budge, but if the observer stopped looking at it, this same piece would jump on us ... We were never able to make sure whether the pieces began their flight invisibly, or whether, on the contrary, they profited by a moment's distraction on our part.[20]

Something very similar, then, was the experience of both Lullier and Perreaud in Lullier's workshop. But the entity had not quite finished with Lullier, for one evening he was working late in his shop and was called out by some of Perreaud's friends as they were passing. They wanted to tell him about the latest incidents they had witnessed in Perreaud's house, and for some reason not explained, the little group went and stood beneath the eaves of another shop nearby. While they were speaking to Lullier, however, the spirit (*l'esprit*) banged two or three times on the eaves, presumably to let them know it was listening to them.[21]

But now, it seems, the entity had run its course, and Perreaud notes its final action which was the most annoying and violent. 'The Devil is always more violent at the end than at the beginning', he observes, 'and he acts then with greater rage, when he is unable to do things any longer'. This final annoyance consisted of the entity's throwing stones, some of them weighing more than two or three pounds, incessantly in every part of the house over a period of ten or twelve hours, from morning until evening, apparently for a number of days. During this time, François Tornus came to the house at about midday and whistled to see if the 'demon' was still there. (Presumably there must have been a lull in the barrage, in spite of Perreaud's 'incessantly', otherwise the entity's presence would have been obvious.) The 'demon' whistled back the same way and then threw a stone at him. It landed at Tornus's feet without doing him any harm, and Tornus decided to try an experiment. He marked the stone with a piece of coal he took from the hearth, and threw it on to the back of a nearby house; but the 'spirit' threw it back immediately – everyone recognised it by the coal mark – and when Tornus picked it up, he found it was hot, 'because it had just come from Hell'.

Each of these phenomena can be paralleled from elsewhere and from other times. Stones fell in Portsmouth, New Hampshire, for example, from mid-June to early September 1684, and in a case from the West Indies in 1934 it was noted that 'stones continued falling for more than a month, day and night'. The stones in Portsmouth were hot 'as if they came out of the fire', and hot stones were reported in Canvey Island in 1709.

> As they were standing in the kitchen, looking towards the back door, the door open and the coast clear, they saw a piece of tile come in of the said door, about two foot from the ground, but very leisurely; and yet so straight, as though it had moved on a line; and then, in a languid manner, after its creeping thus five or six yards in her sight, touching against the gown of one of them (who but the Arch-Juggler could so throw it?) fell down near her feet. The other, who was the maid, ran to catch it up, but let it falling, crying it burnt her; and a little blister, in touching it, was raised on her forefinger. The other person then put the tile into her apron, and carried it over a long field to show it the master and work-folks, who all felt it yet warm.[22]

People have also carried out the experiment of marking stones thrown at them so that they can tell whether an entity is throwing the same ones back. In Sumatra in 1928, Ivan Sanderson was sitting on a verandah after dinner one evening with other dinner guests when they all noticed that small stones kept on appearing out of the darkness and hitting the wall behind them. Apparently this was nothing new. Everyone decided to take a stone and mark it individually with whatever came to hand – chalk, pencil, lipstick – and throw it back into the darkness. This they did on several occasions and almost immediately the stones, up to fifty of them, were returned.[23]

Stage 6: The End of the Episode

Finally, on 22 December, the entity left, and the next day a large poisonous snake was found coming out of the Perreauds' house. Some nail-makers who lived nearby picked it up with their tongs and carried it through the town, shouting, 'Here's the devil which came out of the minister's house!' After this, they took it to an apothecary, who examined it and found it was a real viper – a rare sight in that region. This announcement, says Perreaud, was the reason for news about his demon's being spread around the town, but one can hardly be convinced by this. The disturbances caused by the poltergeist had been going on for some time and had been witnessed, not to mention heard, by several people. It is beyond credulity to accept that they had all been completely silent about the phenomena until this moment. Perhaps what Perreaud meant to say was that hitherto public awareness of the harassments had relied on the verbal reports of those who had been present, while now there appeared (or was taken) to be visual proof of the presence of a demon. We should note, however, that Perreaud himself was not responsible for this parade of the snake. It was his neighbours who caught it and took it round the streets proclaiming they had secured Perreaud's demon, even though their actions were clearly *post eventum*, the poltergeist having departed the previous day, and Perreaud would have found it difficult to follow the men around, contradicting their enthusiasm.

Stage 7: Perreaud's Observations

Perreaud begins by emphasising that the poltergeist had not done him or his property any harm during the length of its activities, nor had it removed anything from the house (he means permanently), not even the little bells 'which it was obliged to leave, as a sign of its departure on the said day, hanging on a nail in the chimney-piece of the room in which it had spent most time'.[24] The episode, however, was used against Perreaud by one Father Marcellin, a Capuchin friar, who heard about it while he was preaching in Mâcon and included references to it in a book of religious controversy he published in Grenoble. Here Marcellin (according to Perreaud's account) drew the conclusion that Perreaud had been communicating with evil spirits (*malins esprits*) – by implication, deliberately – and this Perreaud denies with vehemence. Father Marcellin had obviously been shocked by what he had heard of Perreaud's poltergeist, for he got in touch with both the Lieutenant General of the Bailey of Mâcon and the Bishop to such effect that the Bishop asked François Tornus to explain what had been going on, and sent his own secretary to Perreaud to hear his version of the story.

Having cleared the decks, as it were, by these preliminary remarks, Perreaud now turns to an explanation of those recent events, and 'considering the circumstances of the time, place, and people I was then dealing with', he says, 'it seems to me there are several causes which came together at the same time'. First, he suggests, there are times when devils (*diables*) are allowed to be active, and others when they are not, and clearly Perreaud's experience coincided with one of their active periods: and here he cites a book by Pierre de Lancre, *Le tableau de l'inconstance des demons et malins esprits*, which had just been published and recounts his experiences at a succession of trials for witchcraft in the Pays de Labourd, and another notorious trial, that of Louis Gaufridy, a priest in Marseille, who had been burned for witchcraft in April the previous year.[25] This link with witchcraft is significant and Perreaud goes on to develop it and make it clearer. 'At about the same time, Mâcon's gaols were filled with quite a large number of people, men as well as women, and young people from the village of Chasselas and places round about, who had been accused of witchcraft and were appealing to the Parlement of Paris against their death sentences.' While they were being taken to their appeal, their carriage was stopped by a man who looked like an officer of the law. He asked who they were and where they were being taken, but then recognised one of the prisoners and addressed him by name, using the familiar *tu*. Then he told them all not to worry, because they would come to no harm; and sure enough they all came back acquitted of their charges. Perreaud says no more, but we are obviously meant to infer that the mysterious law-officer was the Devil in disguise and that he was successful in fulfilling his promise to see his alleged servants escape true justice. In fact, there is probably nothing untoward about these acquittals at all, for while the number of trials for witchcraft in the lesser courts was undoubtedly increasing at this time, the Parlement of Paris was releasing many suspects and commuting the majority of death sentences. So the result of the incident reported by Perreaud is entirely in keeping with the way the Parlement was dealing with accused and sentenced witches in the first decade of the seventeenth century.[26]

Here Perreaud embarks on a series of anecdotes, all relating to contemporary Mâcon, intended to provide evidence of what we should call the context of his own poltergeist experience. Each begins with the phrase 'at about this same time' or 'at this same time', by which he says he means 1612. At about this time, then, the young daughter of one of the richest and most important merchant families in Mâcon noticed that her maid, who should have been sleeping in the same room as herself, was frequently absent at night. So she asked the woman where she went. The maid answered with a tale of the witches' Sabbat, which so intrigued the girl that she accompanied the maid on her next visit thither and went through the usual ceremonies of being made a witch. Then suddenly a demon lifted her high in the air and deposited her, 'according to what common gossip has always said', adds Perreaud, 'in the garden of the Capuchin friary'. There she began to cry, thereby attracting the attention of the brothers, who came and found her and asked her who she was and how she came to be there. She told them her tale, and two monks took her home. 'I have always heard a very large number of people swearing to the truth of this story', says Perreaud, 'and I myself have seen the girl several times. I heard she was married, but whether she is still alive or not, I do not know.'

Common gossip was also responsible for the next story, which is about a demon in the shape of a man wearing a red bonnet; 'some time ago' the demon infested a baker's house in Mâcon, appearing by moonlight at the windows, and it was seen by several people, including Abraham Lullier. 'I don't know if this demon is still there', Perreaud admits, 'in spite of the exorcisms and even judicial proceedings taken against it, I presume with the intention of driving it away.' This sounds more like a haunting than a poltergeist disturbance. The opposite, however, might be said of Perreaud's next 'demon' which moved and overturned coffins in the Church of St Etienne in Mâcon, and made so much noise while dong so that it attracted a number of townspeople who came to see what was going on. 'I lived close by and saw them,' says Perreaud. The same happened in the Church of St Alban, and in Marigny-les-Nonnains a widow's house was infested by a poltergeist (*un démon*) which did a lot of harm, such as letting the wine out of the casks in her cellar. It also beat and insulted several people, including a drunken locksmith who came into the house and threatened the spirit, and was chased out very quickly with an andiron. 'In other words', Perreaud adds, 'at the time the demon was in our house, the Devil had been let loose, as these and a number of other similar examples show.'[27]

Perreaud's second explanation for his being harassed by a poltergeist is that when he arrived in Mâcon to begin his ministry, he saw that his church was inconveniently situated for the exercise of his religion and so, on 11 August 1612, he decided to petition the Conseil du Roi for somewhere nearer the town. This, he thought, in all likelihood was the cause of his 'demon's' appearance. He expresses himself here with an interesting clause: 'this demon *was sent* to me out of hatred for that [endeavour]. Perreaud meant both that the poltergeist had been sent by God to test his faith, and that someone else had acted, knowingly or unknowingly, as God's instrument therein. Such a person, of course, would have been a witch. Royal permission, as it happens, was granted for the new establishment, and commissioners arrived in Mâcon to see the King's decision carried out. But Perreaud and the church elders were summoned to attend a meeting with these commissioners on 14 September – this is why he had been away from home when the poltergeist episode started – because the local magistrates and other town worthies were objecting to his choice of location, and doing so with some violence. 'We shall rather eat our walls, our wives, and our children than ever agree to your being established there,' said one, while another warned Perreaud that they had all spoken well of him in the past, but that he should now be careful in case something bad should happen to him. This was the very day (observes Perreaud) on which trouble began to afflict his house, adding significantly that 'the man who threatened me may have been a pupil of someone called César, a known magician who had lived in Mâcon not long before'.

A third explanation, however, comes much closer to home. His wife's chambermaid, the woman from Bresse, was suspected of being a witch (sorcière) and rumour had it that her parents had also been under suspicion of practising witchcraft. Indeed, certain things she had said to Perreaud himself had made him equally suspicious, such as asking him if God would never forgive those who had given themselves to the Evil Spirit, or telling him on one occasion that the poltergeist (ce démon) would not harm two boys who were sleeping in the room next to where it was making a racket. Perreaud also noted the way she and the entity seemed to be on familiar terms, and says that once, when she had complained to the entity that it did not bring her wood for the fire, it gently threw a log at her feet. The friendly relationship between the entity and the maid was evinced further when she pretended she wanted to leave the Perreauds' service and a girl called Philiberte came to take her place. The entity appeared to be angered at the presence of this new girl and beat her all night, even though she was sleeping next to the woman from Bresse. Nor was it satisfied with beating her, for it took the water-jug and poured water over her head; so, not surprisingly, she decided to leave. 'What made me particularly suspicious of the chambermaid', observed Perreaud, 'is that when I was ill during that period, she told me one day that the previous night a tall man clothed in black had appeared to her in the moonlight. He looked like a physician and held a flask in his hand,[28] and had had a conversation with her.'

A fourth explanation lay in the house itself. If what the poltergeist and common gossip said was true, the man who had owned it just before Perreaud arrived had been murdered, and this type of spirit (ces esprits) was accustomed to appear only in houses polluted by murder or something equally dreadful. Witness (says Perreaud) Girolamo Cardano's story about a family in Parma, which used to see an evil spirit (un malin esprit) in the form of an ugly old woman whenever a member of the family died. Apparently it was the ghost of an old woman who had been done to death by her nephews, who then cut up her body and threw the pieces in the latrines. This is a good example of the dilemma over ghosts in Protestantism, which did not allow the appearance of souls from Purgatory, and yet people frequently met apparitions seemingly of the dead in their everyday experience. These, without the doctrine of Purgatory to account for them, therefore became subject to official reinterpretation as hallucinations of one kind or another, trickery (usually by 'Papists'), or demons which were simulating the dead in order to mislead the living observer. Hence people were confused about what to think, although they gradually solved their problem, at least to some extent, by fusing the concepts of 'ghost' and 'demon' with the result that their spectre might be reported as exhibiting behaviour or visual or oral signs appropriate to each and both at one and the same time; and, as Jo Bath has pointed out, the poltergeist may actually provide some of the best examples of this fusion.[29]

Fifthly, however, Perreaud produces the explanation he considers to be the most likely. The woman who had lived in the house before he arrived and who, rumour said, had murdered her husband, had been dispossessed by a court order and therefore hated Perreaud, whom she blamed for depriving her of the property. One day, says Perreaud, she was found within the chimney-breast, invoking the Devil and uttering ritual curses against Perreaud and his family. The hearth was a common focus for magical or counter-magical practices, either when something was buried beneath it or because it was used in a spell to identify a witch. Thus, the *Malleus Maleficarum* says, 'If a cow is deprived of her milk by an act of harmful magic, they hang a pail of milk over the fire and, while pronouncing certain superstitious words clearly and distinctly, beat the pail with a stick. Now, the woman may be striking the pail, but the Devil is transferring all the blows to the witch's back.' (This will make her come to the house and beg to be released from the beating, and so reveal herself.) Pots, too, were commonly buried under thresholds or hearths, perhaps to trap evil spirits, and so-called 'witch bottles' were also buried there as an apotropaic against attacks by harmful magic.[30] Under the circumstances, the woman in Perreaud's house was either a witch or had decided to practise magic on this particular occasion. In either case, she was deeply disturbed by anger and hatred, because when discovered, she burst out that she did not care not only if she were hanged and throttled, but also if she were damned to the depths of Hell, as long as she might be revenged on Perreaud and his family. Not unreasonably, Perreaud reported this to the local authorities, who ordered the women to appear before them. This she did on 22 December, the very day on which the poltergeist activity ceased, and was bound over not to harass Perreaud or his family or his household in the future in any way whatsoever, direct or indirect, on pain of exemplary punishment.

A woman with a bitter grudge who turns to witchcraft to solve her problem and soothe her injured feelings: this is surely the *antidemon* of the title of Perreaud's narrative. *Anti-* is a Greek preposition which, among its various meanings, indicates 'standing in place of'. Hence, an antidemon is someone who takes the place of a demon, and this in Perreaud's eyes is clearly not a trickster – almost from the start he takes his infestation seriously as harassment by some non-human force – but a human being acting as the conduit through whose incantations an evil spirit is enabled to slip from his world into ours and thus cause havoc and distress on behalf of the witch who summoned him. Witches, in fact, may have been at the back of Perreaud's mind at this time, for not only were there the Mâconnais examples he mentions in his story, but others in regions contiguous with Bourgogne. If we have a look at figures of trials for witchcraft in Franche-Comté, for example, during the year of the disturbance and the two previous years, we find 1610: 13; 1611: 5; 1612: 8, and in Neuchâtel, 1610: 7; 1611: 6; 1612: 1, while in Geneva itself, news from which would surely have reached Perreaud through the annual provincial synods, there were 1610: 10; 1611: 4; 1612: 5 – 30, 15, and 14 in all, enough to attract attention and linger somewhere in the memory.[31]

Having thus identified his most likely cause, Perreaud ends his account, although he cannot help tacitly identifying himself with Job, by saying that his recent ordeal had been inflicted upon him by God as a way of testing his faith and resolution. 'To Him, then, be eternal glory, Amen.' So all these are the reasons Perreaud offers to explain why he and his family should have been singled out for 'demonic' attention, and in effect they boil down to an accusation of witchcraft. It was a time when Satan had been let loose; Perreaud had made enemies among some of the important men of the town because of his religion, and one of those men was said to have been the pupil of a local magician; his wife's chambermaid was on suspiciously amicable terms with the invading entity and may even have had at least one conversation with the Devil, who was disguised as a physician at the time; the house in which he and his family were living was haunted; and he had actually caught a woman practising witchcraft in his house with the clear intention of doing him harm. In other words, time and circumstance, both redolent of demonic activity, had combined, with God's permission, to target him, and the poltergeist, no matter what variant guises it cared to employ, was in fact and evil spirit sent to try him.

Such, then, is one of the most detailed accounts we have of a relatively early poltergeist disturbance and it raises a number of different questions: is Perreaud trustworthy as a narrator? Why did he publish this account? Who was his audience? Why did he wait for forty-one years before committing himself to print and what can we usefully say about the nature of his experience? That Perreaud was highly regarded by those who knew him or had dealings with him, even at second hand, may be gauged partly by the willingness of the Catholic François Tornus to testify on his behalf before the Bishop of Mâcon, not to mention the offer of his frequent support during the period of the infestation, and partly by a written testimonial from Robert Boyle, who met him in Geneva in the early 1640s, and another from the pastors and elders of the Protestant churches of Bourgogne, dated 29 October 1651. Boyle's approbation is expressed in a letter he wrote to Pierre du Moulin, a Protestant minister whom he had met in England many years before.

> I must freely confess to you that the powerful inclinations which my course of life and studies hath given me to backwardness of assent, and the many fictions and superstitions, which (as far as I have hitherto observed) are wont to blemish the relations where spirits and witches are concerned, would make me very backwards to contribute anything to your publishing, or any man's believing, a story less strange than this of Monsieur Perreault. But the conversation I had with the pious author during my stay at Geneva, and the present he was pleased to make me of this treatise before it was printed, in a place where I had the opportunity to inquire both after the writer, and after some passages of the book, did at length overcome in me (as to this narrative) all my settled indisposedness to believe strange things.[32]

These favourable sentiments are reiterated in the *approbation* of an earlier provincial synod.

> We, pastors and elders of the reformed churches of the province of Burgundy ... certify to all that Monsieur Perreaud, minister of the holy ministry in this province for the space of fifty years ... in all that time, and in all churches, doing the office of a good pastor and a faithful servant of God, both in doctrine and in life, of which he had an especial testament given him by the church of Mâcon in the last synod of the province ... and he has the like from the church of Thoiry ... to which we add that altogether it has pleased God to bring him into many, and some very extraordinary trials, especially when he served the church in Mâcon; yet the same God has strengthened him with a constant health of his body and

godly tranquillity of mind, and has endued him with virtue to bear and overcome all his afflictions. We therefore beseech the Lord daily to fill his servant with more and more strength in his old age, and that after he has finished his course, he may depart in peace and obtain the crown of glory reserved for those that will persevere faithful to the end.[33]

As a Protestant, of course, Perreaud would have had little choice but to bear his afflictions, since Calvinism provided neither exorcism nor any other ritual remedy in a case of demonic infestation, and once Perreaud had convinced himself that the poltergeist was not the result of trickery or personal illness (common Protestant explanations for any manifestation purporting to be ghostly in nature or behaviour) he was bound, like Job, to thole it with prayer and fasting (which Perreaud does not mention) as his only consolation and resort. Self-identification with Job is by no means rare at this time. Indeed, he had long been held up as a pattern for behaviour under just these circumstances.

Be not dismayed, although thou hear some spirit stir and make a noise for in case he rumble only to make thee afraid care not for him, but let him rumble so long as he will, for if he see thee without fear, he will soon depart from thee ... If the Devil see thou art of a good stomach, and well armed with God's word, he will soon seek after others whom he may mock with fear. But if it please God to exercise thee by the Devil for a certain time, as he did sometime Job, thou must patiently suffer all things which He layeth upon thee, and that willingly for God's commandment's sake. And know thou well, that he cannot thus much hurt, neither thy goods, nor body, nor soul without the permission and sufferance of Almighty God: if God give him leave to plague thy body, think with thyself howsoever it be done, that God hath so done for thy profit and commodity, who also sendeth grievous sicknesses upon other men, by other means and instruments, or else doth exercise them with other kinds of calamities. Be therefore strong and constant in faith.[34]

Perreaud, then, sees himself as a kind of latter-day Job although he does not do so in any self-glorifying way, and neither is there any boasting in his narrative either in connection with his surviving a particular incident or the ordeal as a whole. All in all, therefore, we may concur with Herbert Thurston's assessment: 'I may confess that I have conceived a very good opinion of Monsieur Perreaud's truthfulness and sobriety of judgement.'[35]

The recording and later publication of his narrative, however, were spread over several decades. It seems from Pierre du Moulin's preface to the English translation of *L'antidemon de Mascon* that Perreaud wrote an account of his ordeal soon after it happened so, as Thurston observes, 'it was certainly not a story concocted by an old man in his dotage'. Nevertheless, to all intents and purposes Perreaud contented himself with this private record until 1621 when he told something of it Pierre du Moulin, who was staying with him before they both went to a synod in Alès. Attendances at these synods, indeed, seem to have sparked Perreaud's urge to recount his story, for in 1625 and again in 1626 and 1627 the provincial synod of Bourgogne invited him to submit a written version to the Consistoire in Lyon. It has been suggested that these Calvinist authorities were keen to rebut the Capuchin Father Marcellin, who, it will be remembered, had accused Perreaud in print of being in league with the Devil. Father Marcellin's book had appeared in 1615 and informed its readers that 'Satan runs away and flees before Jesuit Fathers, but he runs after you [Protestants]. The demon which lived for several days in the house and study, and among the books of Monsieur Perreaud, a minister in Mâcon, did housework in a number of different ways.'[36] On the other hand, there is a whole decade between Father Marcellin's passing observation and the synod's first request that Perreaud commit his experience to writing, so one might say that the connection seems to be somewhat tenuous. Dismissing it, however, could turn out to be mistaken, as we shall see in a moment. A more immediate question, perhaps, is why Perreaud did not submit the written account he already had or, if that was too sketchy in its original form, why he did not use it as the basis of a fuller version, as he was bound to do later. (The inadequacy of his existing account, indeed, may well be the reason for the synod's asking him to put pen to paper, because the request of 1627 referred to his 'completing' (*parachever*) his narrative.)

Still he delayed and delayed until the synod of 1631 ran out of patience and decided to censure him for his procrastination, and to threaten him with worse than censure if he did not comply. Even so it took a meeting with the Prince de Condé the following year to rouse him from his torpor. The Prince listened to his story, showed great interest, and urged him to write it down. So at last, it seems, Perreaud complied, for in May 1633 we find the synod of Bourgogne issuing an *approbation* of his work.

We, the undersigned, entrusted by the synod of the reformed and united churches of the province of Bourgogne, to examine a little book containing the account of what happened in the house of Monsieur Perreaud, then minister and inhabitant of Mâcon in the year 1612, having read it in its entirety and carefully scrutinised it, certify that we have found nothing repugnant to piety and charity, and therefore that it may be brought into the light of day.[37]

This version, however, seems to have been still a manuscript, although ten years later, when he met Robert Boyle in Geneva, Perreaud was able to provide him with a copy of the work so that it could be translated into English. But procrastination, it appears, afflicted almost everyone connected with *L'antidemon*, as it became, for another ten years passed before at last Perreaud saw the work in print along with a very much longer companion treatise on demonology which was published in Geneva at the same time – indeed, conjointly with it. A second edition appeared in 1656, and its preface finally explains why Perreaud had pulled himself together and submitted his manuscript for publication. For it seems that Father Marcellin's old accusation that Perreaud was in cahoots with the Devil had succeeded in tainting his name over the years, so putting 'a detailed and absolutely true account', as the title page has it, into the public domain proved to be the only way Perreaud could counter 'the various falsehoods which have been going the rounds'. That these had had an effect is evidenced by Richard Baxter, who observed in 1691 that 'this history of Mascon is denied by some that say they have spoken with some that have been at Mascon and knew nothing of it'. But he defends the integrity of witnesses and other reliable men, and then goes on to ask:

> Could it be counterfeit, and never contradicted in fifty or sixty years (I remember not just the year), that in a city, so many of both religions, for so many months together, might crowd at a certain hour into the room and hear a voice answering their questions, and telling them things far off and to them unknown, and disputing with a Papist officer of the city, and the whirling him oft about, and casting him to the ground, and sending him home distracted: I say, if this and all the rest there written, so attested, be not sufficient evidence, I know not what is.[38]

Doubts, however, seem to have been few, and Perreaud's narrative proved popular in Protestant circles. It was translated into English in 1658, into Dutch in 1665, and into Welsh in 1681, helping to fulfil at least one of the roles Perreaud probably intended for it – offering proof that if God decided to test His faithful severely by allowing Satan to harass them, steadfast trust in Him and unflinching prayer would triumph and the demon would be put to flight by those alone. No need, therefore, for ritual exorcisms such as those used by the 'Papists'.

Perreaud's purpose in writing, then, is clear, but what, if anything, can we say about the nature of his experience? It is perhaps notable for consisting of what appear to be two different phases: (i) identifiably 'poltergeist' behaviour such as knocking, throwing objects, apporting, violence against individuals, and lithobolia; (ii) conversational episodes in which the entity made intelligible and intelligent exchanges with various individuals. Some of these were mocking in tone, others playful or serious or unpleasant. We have already remarked on the practical difficulties in the way of ventriloquism. If one person had been responsible, he would have stood in constant danger of discovery, with serious consequences for himself. He would have had to have been able to speak and understand the Bresse dialect when he was addressing the chambermaid, and had there been more than one ventriloquist, the danger of discovery would have been even greater. Moreover, where does one find one expert ventriloquist in a relatively small community, never mind two; and if ventriloquism be advanced as an explanation of the conversational episodes, it does nothing to account for the 'poltergeist' behaviour. It is perfectly true, of course, that Perreaud had acquired enemies, or at least ill-wishers in Mâcon since his arrival, but to suggest a conspiracy between two or more of them to drive him and his family out of his house, or humiliate him in the eyes of his parishioners, founders upon the practicalities we have just been discussing. Furthermore, driving him away or humiliating him would have been fully effective only if it was known that he had been made a fool of by one or more of the locals, and nowhere in the contemporary references to him or to the event is there the slightest hint that fraud by any of Mâcon's residents had been involved. Only in 1684 do we find such a suggestion in a letter by the Swiss theologian Jean le Clerc to a friend of his.

> A respectable man told me that this [incident] was merely a fable, embellished by the gentleman who had given the public a number of circumstances which fear had made him see; and people have known for a while that it was only a piece of trickery a man carried out in the house of the minister at Mâcon. I don't know if that is true, but I think I am more inclined to believe that than the story Monsieur Perreaud has given us.[39]

This, of course, was written over thirty years after *L'antidemon de Mascon* had first appeared in print, and, while it obviously expresses one man's personal scepticism, it also reflects a deep suspicion of Otherworldly manifestations in general, which had grown in some intellectual quarters during the course of the century. If trickery was indeed used, its mechanics therefore need to be explained, and that is not only somewhat difficult at this remove in time, but also flies in the face of what equally respectable men thought and wrote soon after the events themselves. Our conclusion, then, tentative though it must necessarily be, is that fraud is beyond our capability to propose convincingly in regard to this episode, and that when Perreaud and the other witnesses thought they were being dogged by an evil spirit of some kind, they meant what they said; and what they said was undoubtedly in tune with the circumambient intellectual and emotional expectations of the time.

One further characteristic of Perreaud's narrative is worth noting, because although it had become a feature of sixteenth-century ghost stories in general and poltergeist accounts in particular, the seventeenth century, whether consciously or not, took it further and indeed employed it until it became something of a cliché: namely, the domestication of the ghost or poltergeist. During the Middle Ages and the first half of the sixteenth century, the theatre for a ghost or poltergeist's performances was as likely to be a convent, friary, or monastery as a private house. During the second half of the century, however, this changed and its preferred locus, even among Catholic writers, became the house. Admittedly, this may reflect one's choice of source-material, but in fact such choices do not make all that much difference to the general observation. Protestant concerns, of course, lay behind some of this change. By removing the ghost and the poltergeist – but not the demon, for he continued to be active in religious houses – to the domesticity of hearth and home, Protestants lessened the perceived connections, strong in both past and contemporary Catholic sensibilities, between priests and the dead, and so between the Church and the individual, and therefore drew any sufferer from the attentions of spirit-forms away from institutional and (as they called them) 'superstitious' remedies, and threw each such person upon his or her resources of patience, prayer, and faith. Invasion of the home is, in fact, deeply personal and the spirits' choice of one's house as the preferred venue for their activities thus turned any invasion of its privacy into a battle between the beleaguered soul and (as they were perceived and interpreted) the forces of darkness, a drama in miniature of the conflict between Good and Evil which would take place at the End of Days and which the seventeenth century, like the sixteenth, believed was, if not actually then being waged, at the very least imminent, the clarion call of Satan's liberation having been sounded in their generation.

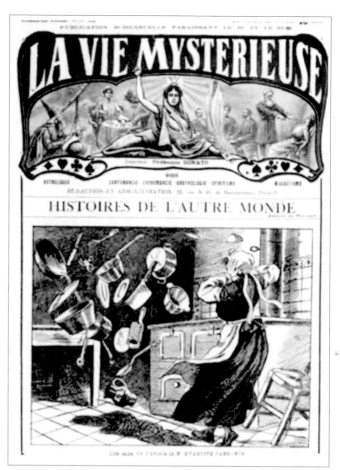

1. A fourteen-year-old domestic servant, Thérèse Selles, experiences a poltergeist. The cover of the French magazine, *La Vie Mystérieuse*, 1911. Author's collection.

2. A poltergeist frightens a priest. Nineteenth-century engraving. Author's collection.

Left: 3. Poltergeists in the nursery. Nineteenth-century painting. Author's collection.

Above: 4. Velitrae, modern Velletri. The Emperor Augustus's nursery in the villa here was reputed to be infested by a poltergeist. From Georg Braun & Franz Hogenburg, *Civitates Orbis Terrarum*, 6 vols, 1572–1617. Vol. 3 (1582). Author's collection.

5. Poland, Slawiecice, Slawentzitz, Ehrenforst. Castle entrance. This castle was the scene of a major poltergeist outbreak in the nineteenth century. Author's collection.

6. Outbreak of lithobolia in a Paris street during the building of a road between the Sorbonne and the Pantheon in 1846. Contemporary engraving. Author's collection.

7

A Type of Demon? 1605–1696

Perreaud's story exemplifies both a doctrinal and a propagandistic approach to the whole topic of spirits typical of the end of the sixteenth and the early part of the seventeenth century in which each side of the confessional divide sought to emphasise the differences between itself and the other, while glossing over the notions they had in common. Thus, Catholics used this kind of literature to emphasise the reality of the spirit world, the community which exists between the living and the dead, and the truth of Purgatory from whose all too real pains the living may liberate the dead by prayer and the sacrifice of the Mass. Protestants, on the other hand, laid stress on the reality of Satan, demonic interference in human lives, and the necessity of faith and prayer to survive their onslaughts. But in an age which increasingly felt the need to demonstrate the realities of the Otherworld as a buttress of faith against attacks by sceptics and (to use the contemporary word) 'atheists',[1] the poltergeist presented a problem. If it could be identified as a ghost or a demon, people, whether Catholic or Protestant, knew where they stood and were able take whatever steps they considered appropriate to deal with it. But what would happen if ghosts were called into question and banished to the realms of superstition or melancholia? Where was the ghost, and with him the poltergeist, to go? The answer seems to have been 'to the land of witchcraft'.

Perreaud, so near the beginning of the new century, had faced his trial the way he was almost bound to do, by reference to hostile magic. Just over fifty years later another Calvinist, this time a weaver in the south-west of Scotland, had experiences which matched those of Mâcon and which seem likewise to have been attributed to witchcraft.[2] It began in the common way of many

126

witchcraft cases. In October or November 1654, a beggar, Alexander Agnew, called at the house of Gilbert Campbell in Glenluce and asked for alms which were refused. He went away promising to do the family a mischief, and not long afterwards they began to suffer strange whistling noises and the violent throwing of stones and clods of peat. Gilbert reported these phenomena to the local minister, but found that they became worse as time went on. 'Not long after, he found often-times his warp and threads cut, as with a pair of scissors, and not only so, but their apparel were cut after the same manner, even while they were wearing them, their coats, bonnets, hose, and shoes, but could not discern how, or by what means.' Eventually the poltergeist was doing so much damage that Gilbert could no longer work and reluctantly sent his children away for their own safety. Peace ensued for a few days, and so the children came back home, all except one called Thomas who was away at the grammar school in Glasgow.[3] The peace continued, but the moment Thomas came home violence broke out again, this time in the form of fires which threatened to burn down the house. Thomas was sent to stay with the minister, but this made no difference, as the family's clothes were still slashed to pieces, peat was still hurled around the house, and turf and straw pulled from the roof.

By this time it was February 1655. On the 12th, members of the family began to hear a voice, and 'from evening until midnight too much vain discourse was kept up with Satan, and many idle and impertinent questions proposed, without due fear of God, that should have been upon their spirits under so rare and extraordinary a trial'. It was not long before the minister heard of this and turned up at Gilbert's house with several other people to find out what was going on; whereupon the poltergeist addressed him with a Latin tag from a schoolboy's grammar and exclaimed, 'You are a dog, sir!' only for the indignant minister to find that there was indeed a dog behind him in the room. Everyone began to pray, but the moment they finished a voice, apparently speaking from underneath the bed and using the local accent, asked if they knew the witches of Glenluce. It named four or five individuals, one of whom was long dead, although (said the poltergeist) 'her spirit is living with us in the world'. Thus, interrupted by silences while the company prayed, the entity sought to needle some of those present: Gilbert, by concentrating its verbal malice on the boy Thomas, who had come back home again from the manse along with the minister, and the minister, by exchanging biblical texts with him until the minister fell into the trap of seeking information by asking whence the spirit came. (It was a trap he had actually foreseen earlier, for he had said to the entity, 'The Lord rebuke thee, Satan, and put thee to silence. We are not to receive information from thee, whatsoever fame any person goes under.')[4]

To the minister's question the entity replied, 'I am an evil spirit, come from the bottomless pit of Hell to vex this house. Satan is my father', and revealed a naked forearm and hand which beat violently upon the floor. It was not long, however, before the entity became bored and started to entertain itself by aiming remarks at individuals in the company. It called one respectable man a witch, appeared to take a pair of scissors to the brim of another man's hat, offered to brain one of the children, and asked a woman present for some food. But when the company prepared to go home, the entity became angry and began to beat the children, and only when it became clear that everyone really was going to leave did it calm down slightly and demand that the candle be put out, roaring in everyone's ears until that was done.

These and similar assaults went on for months, the entity refusing to go on the grounds that it had a 'commission from Christ to harry and vex this family', and in spite of leaving them alone between April and July, in August it renewed its attacks on their food and livelihood with such ferocity that the Campbells were reduced to near-starvation. Now, clearly the Campbells' ordeal was worse and longer – it lasted for two more years, as we know from a private letter – than that endured by the Perreauds, but they have in common not only their poltergeist phenomena, but also the inarticulate noises' becoming an intelligent voice, the exchange of biblical quotations, the parallels with Job (implicit in the Campbells' case), and the connections with witchcraft, more tenuous in Glenluce, but visible in the spirit's pointed references to witches and in the behaviour of Alexander Agnew, whose malice after Gilbert's refusal of alms would have been interpreted at the time as a likely prelude to hostile magic; and as far as both the Perreauds and the Campbells, and their respective neighbours were concerned, their poltergeist was evidently a demon and, even if sent by God to test their faith, was likely to have depended on a witch to help it operate.

Modern times have not been so inclined and have decided upon fraud as a reasonable explanation for the Glenluce incident. Rossell Hope Robbins, commenting on the case, blames young Thomas Campbell and the rest of the Campbell children on a number of flimsy grounds.

a) Thomas was afraid he would be obliged to leave the grammar school in Glasgow and become a weaver like his father.
b) The first words spoken by the entity consisted of a Latin phrase which appeared in a school textbook.
c) After some of those present had conducted a search of the house to see if they could locate the source of the voice, they found nothing, but

one of them suggested it might be emanating from the children.

d) When the entity threatened to brain one of the girls, she answered calmly and continued apparently unruffled with what she was doing.[5]

Hence, Robbins concludes, the whole thing was a device stage-managed by Thomas to make sure he stayed at school in Glasgow. As an explanation this is a touch desperate, and if one is going to suggest, for example, that Thomas was using ventriloquism to create a demonic voice, one will run up against the obvious caveats: is there any evidence that Thomas did or could practise ventriloquism? Would he have been able to keep it up for several hours at a time, and how old was Thomas at this time, because a child's voice would have been easily detectable from the start? Then we have to consider the practicalities of throwing stones and peats, again without detection. What exactly are the mechanics of this and does one expect children to have worked them out? Why did Thomas, if we are to propose that he was indeed the source, continue his campaign until the family was near starvation? Surely that last predicament would have ensured his being recalled from the grammar school to work in the family business rather than encouraging his father to let him stay away from home. As important as any of these reservations, however, is the sense that Robbins's theory springs from a twentieth-century unwillingness or inability to put aside its own impulses to consider what may have been those of Gilbert Campbell and his community. Of course they considered the possibility that someone was playing a trick – so did many people suddenly subjected to domestic turmoil of this kind, as we have seen – but that was neither their first nor their final thought. Their immediate assumption was that the phenomena were being produced by an entity of some kind intruding from the Otherworld, and when their second thought – a note of hesitation, perhaps, rather than outright scepticism – had been satisfied by a thorough search of their surroundings, they reverted to what their instincts told them was the probable and natural cause.

This is not to say, of course, that we should dismiss the possibility of fraud in every case in the seventeenth century. Indeed, the well-known Woodstock episode of 1649 is an example in which fraud is more likely to have been behind the poltergeist phenomena than not. This incident was variously reported at the time, starting with a popular ballad, 'The Woodstock Scuffle', published in the same year as the incident. Other sources include notices in the diary of Thomas Widows, the minister of Woodstock church at the time, and information purporting to come from one of those directly involved. What happened was that the manor house there was captured by Parliamentary troops during the

English Civil War, and after the King met his death in January 1649 the manor, which had been royal property, was confiscated and seven commissioners were sent to arrange its sale. They arrived on 13 October and, after an odd incident with a dog on the 16th, poltergeistery started on the 17th with footsteps and noises coming from a locked room. On the 18th the commissioners' secretary and two servants were distressed by severe jolting movements of their beds; the next night, the candles went out suddenly, wooden plates were thrown around, and one of the men was hit; and on the 20th the same kind of thing happened again. After a quiet night on the 21st, the next night was disturbed. Something pulled the bedclothes off the frightened men and threw bricks around, while a bitch they had brought in for protection set up an unhappy yowl. The 24th and 25th saw much the same performance, and on the 26th broken glass fell around in the room, although the windows were found to be intact. On the 29th lithobolia started for the first time, and people had the impression that a ghost or spirit 'walked majestically through the room and opened and shut the window'. Whatever the spirit may have been, it made itself felt again the next night, waving a warming pan and accompanied by showers of glass and stones and horses' bones. On the nights of the 29th and 31st everyone was subjected to the sound of cannon fire which was loud enough to disturb and alarm the whole neighbourhood. All Hallows, in fact, saw the climax of the affair. Burning pieces of wood were thrown all over the place; stagnant water, along with stones, cast by the pailful over the commissioners' beds; and the windows and bedroom furniture broken or ripped apart. Assuming that all this was the work of the spirit they had seen or sensed before, one of the commissioners spoke up and asked the entity what it wanted. There was no reply: merely silence. But then one of the servants lit a candle and placed it in the doorway of the affected room, only to see a hoof kick the candlestick away. Boldly, the man drew his sword, but it was wrested from him by an unseen hand and used to strike him to the floor, where he lay unconscious. Loud bangs, 'like the broadside of a ship of war', then punctuated the rest of the night while the household and its frightened neighbours sang psalms and offered prayers in an effort to calm their fears and exorcise whatever it was that was causing the trouble.

Such in essence is the generally agreed version of the episode. Variants in the story, usually more colourful, tend to come from Widows's diary and are not really helpful in an assessment of what the commissioners and their servants actually experienced; and the matter is further complicated by 'authentic memoirs' purporting to come from the pen of one Joseph Collins and witnessed by the commissioners themselves. The authenticity of this document, however, which was not mentioned by anyone until 1747 and whose author's existence cannot be traced, must be treated with caution.[6] But the 'memoirs' do call the whole episode into question, pointing out that a few people – servants in the house, for example – with some gunpowder and a concealed trapdoor, could have produced all or most of the phenomena which so alarmed the commissioners; and this is also the conclusion reached by Robert Plot in his *Natural History of Oxfordshire*, published in 1677, which used Widows's diary and the verbal account of one of the commissioners as the basis of its account of the episode. We should bear in mind, too, that Thomas Widows was a Royalist, and exaggerating the separate elements of the incident could have served his purpose in making the commissioners look foolish after the event, although this would have been in the nature of a more or less private satisfaction, for had he been privy to or suspicious of a plot against them, he would not (indeed, given the political circumstances of 1649 onwards, could not) have revealed any trickery, supposing trickery had been used.[7]

A fraud, however, loses its effect once it is known to be a fraud, just as a joke acquires its effect only if it is known to be a joke. Whatever we may think about the Woodstock 'poltergeist', and whatever the doubts raised by some people decades after the event, its impact at the time will have been notable, and the final appearance of a hoof coming out of the darkness to kick over a candlestick will have been sufficient to suggest to susceptible onlookers (of whom, we are told, there were many) that Satan himself was the source of the disturbances, an implication which may have had propaganda value in suggesting that it must have been God who had let loose the Devil upon Parliament's officers, but which would also have confirmed the neighbourhood in any predisposition it may have had to believe in the reality of demonic intrusion into the world, and the efficacy of prayer and psalm-singing as counter-attacks.

The year, of course, is significant. In January the King was executed or murdered (depending on one's point of view), the civil wars which had ravaged Britain since 1642 were over, leaving behind a repressive régime in London, a bewildering variety of religious sects and, ironically, an increasing secularisation as the overriding prestige and authority of the established Church broke down in the face of constant emphases from the new pulpits on neighbourliness and charity and the individual's *personal* search for salvation. Add to this that discoveries in what we should call the natural sciences created among the intellectual classes a notion that Nature presented merely a series of puzzles to be solved and that therefore a 'natural' explanation was available for everything, and we can see why there were many who were fearful of the new 'atheism' and sought on the one hand to counter the old Protestant argument that ghosts, spirits, and apparitions were explainable either as Catholic trickery or physiological imbalance, and on the other to show that such manifestations were real and that therefore the Otherworld was not to be dismantled so easily. The poltergeist might serve this purpose well. People's maintaining they could see an unearthly spirit was one thing, readily dismissed by the usual Protestant arguments involving fraud or demonry. But the wide variety phenomena usually attendant upon poltergeists, and the large numbers of independent witnesses to them, was more difficult to brush aside, and so these entities should have provided apologists of the Otherworld with solid examples and illustrations wherewith their opponents could be more readily defeated – provided, of course, the phenomena were not fraudulent.

The tendency of the seventeenth century, then, as it had been that of the sixteenth, was to diabolise Otherworld entities, whether ghosts or poltergeists, frequently adding elements of magic in the form of witchcraft to account for the presence of the Devil either in or behind the phenomena. Hence, in Rothenburg in 1605, Hans Hoffman, a joiner with a reputation for being able by use of magic to find lost or stolen objects, was asked by David Walther, an important member of Rothenburg's community, to finish and deliver a table started by someone else and left unfinished. Hofman obliged in a remarkably short time, but as soon as the table was delivered, strange noises, it was said, began to resound through Walter's house and it was not long before Hofman was blamed for using spirits to help him complete the table so soon, spirits which then infested the house in which it stood.[8] Noisy spirits are not always poltergeistic, of course, but what we should note is the clear assumption made by Rothenburgers that magic was somehow involved in the manifestation. That is just the connection which had appealed to Perreaud and the people of Mâcon, and we find it again in several cases from the first half of the century. In November 1620, for example, a wealthy man died near the city of Oppenheim, and not long after his funeral people in the house heard rapping against the wall, followed by whistles and groans and a voice raised in lamentation. These rappings were asked to identify their source, and did so, revealing that it was the ghost of the recently deceased man. They continued to disturb people for about six months, after which they ceased, only to break out again several months later. This time the ghost spoke and made known his wishes, which included the saying of three Masses for his soul and the distribution of alms among the poor. Asked why he had come back to haunt his old house, the ghost replied that he was being forced to do so because of hostile magic and maledictions.[9] Hence what is otherwise an ordinary ghost story, ending happily with the granting of the spirit's request and its subsequent departure and silence, is rendered peculiar to its time by this reference to malicious magic.

A variant upon this can be seen in a witchcraft case from 1644, where poltergeistery becomes an attendant feature in an otherwise straightforward magical incident. Patrick Malcolm appeared before the presbytery of Strathbogie on 28 February to answer a charge of raising some kind of disturbance – 'clodding and fearful trouble' – in Alexander Christie's house, which lasted for nearly three weeks. Apparently Patrick wanted 'to commit filthiness' with Alexander's servant and managed to come and stay in Alexander's house while he made his attempt. He asked the woman to give him her left shoe (presumably so that it could act as a focus for love-magic: the request hardly makes sense otherwise), but the woman refused and so the 'clodding' (pelting with missiles) began, continuing until the woman herself was removed, whether dismissed from Alexander's service or merely sent to another house is not made clear.[10] A more obvious poltergeist incident involved Paul Fox, a silk weaver from Plaistow in West Ham near London in 1645. A sword hung in one room of the house where he lodged there. One day 'it came flourishing about the room, flying up and down, no hand touching of it, nor anything but the sword possibly appearing'. Fox grabbed it, took it into the next room, laid it on a bench, came back to the first room and locked the door, in spite of which, however, the sword simply reappeared. Nor was this all. A walking stick hopped upstairs from the kitchen and danced round the table; tiles, brickbats, oyster shells, and pieces of bread whirled round the room and broke the windows; a stone weighing nearly half a hundredweight lifted itself from the yard and tumbled upstairs; and when one bold individual, having observed the commotion from the safety of the street, went into the house, keen to uncover what he took to be trickery, and examined the room at the centre of all this activity, he found nothing – no string or hair which could have pulled or hoisted the flying articles, and no hole or button in any of the walls or ceiling through which such a string or hair could have been fixed or lowered. Even so, on his way downstairs, the investigator was pursued by a 'clatter of chairs and stools and candlesticks and bedstaves'. Once down, he spoke to the landlady and, while he was doing so, witnessed a pipe rise from a side table and fly to the other side of the room. So he came to an interesting, but not unexpected conclusion.

> It was neither the tricks of wags, nor the fancy of a woman, but the mad frolics of witches and demons: which they of the house being fully persuaded of, roasted a bedstaff, upon which an old woman, a suspected witch, came to the house and

was apprehended, but escaped the law. But the house was after so ill haunted in all the rooms, upper and lower, that the house stood empty for a long time after.[11]

A witch was also blamed for an outbreak of poltergeistery in the manor house at Welton in around 1658. Furniture moved about of its own accord or apported from one room to another, bedclothes were removed by unseen hands, food and drink were spoiled, and objects hurled at the window or at onlookers. Stones were thrown all over the house, and on at least one occasion the assembled company was showered with wheat. Witchcraft again was blamed and an old man arrested for causing the disturbance; but although he was convicted and sent to gaol, the harassment did not stop. What happened after that is not recorded.[12] In Youghal in Cork, too, a witchcraft case of 1661 revealed poltergeist activity which was blamed on the defendant. It was deponed that Florence Newton had conceived a grudge against Mary Longdon and had bewitched her by kissing her full and hard upon the lips. Nearly a month later, Mary began to exhibit symptoms of demonic possession, and odd things started to happen both round her and to her. A large number of small stones used to fall on her as she walked, and then vanish; or she would be carried by invisible hands out of her bed to another room, or even to the top of the house; and, in a scene reminiscent of the courthouse in Salem, when Mary finished giving her evidence before the assize at Cork:

Florence Newton peeped at her, as it were betwixt the heads of the bystanders that interposed between her and the said Mary, and lifting up both her hands together, (as they were manacled), cast them in a violent angry motion, (as was observed by W. Aston), towards the said Mary, as if she intended to strike at her if she could have reached her, and said, 'Now she is down'. Upon which the maid fell suddenly down to the ground like a stone, and fell into a most violent fit, that all the people that could come to lay hands on her could scarce hold her, she biting her own arms and shrieking out in a most hideous manner, to the amazement of all the beholders.

It was the evidence of John Pyne, Mary's employer, however, which mentioned poltergeist-like phenomena: lithobolia, a Bible's being struck out of Mary's hand into the middle of the room, and the apporting of two Bibles, laid on her chest to calm her in the midst of a fit, from there to somewhere else. Nicholas Pyne deponed that one evening the door of the prison shook and there was 'a very great noise, as if somebody with bolts and chains had been running up and down the room'. Asked if she knew what caused it, Florence replied that it was her familiar-demon.[13]

Witchcraft thus intruded upon tales and reminiscences of poltergeists during the first half of the century to an extent which is not, perhaps, altogether surprising. European sensibilities anent witches were raw – the most intense period of witch-prosecution ranges from *c.*1580 to *c.*1660 – and so we may expect to find that people were liable to link virtually any unusual manifestation with hostile magic of one form or another, and the ease with which this could be done can be illustrated by an anecdote from one of Montaigne's essays.

> While I was passing through a village two leagues from my house the day before yesterday, I found the place still het up about a miracle which had just failed to be successful and which had entertained the neighbourhood for several months. The adjoining provinces were starting to become excited about it and people of every class were beginning to rush there in great herds. A young man from there had amused himself in his house one night by mimicking the voice of a spirit, without any other intention than that of enjoying a momentary joke. This succeeded a little more than he expected, and to prolong his practical joke as far as possible, he took as his partner a thoroughly stupid, simple-minded village girl. In the end there were three of them, of the same age and similar self-conceit. From sermonising at home they went on to sermonise in public, hiding themselves under the altar of the church, speaking only at night, and forbidding anyone to bring along any light. From words dealing with the conversion of the world and the threat of Judgement Day (because it is under cover of their authority and the respect [they are given] that deception most easily hides itself) they proceeded to some visions, and actions so stupid and ridiculous that one can scarcely find anything as crass in children's games. All the same, if Fortune had been willing to favour them a little, who knows to what extent this buffoonery would have grown? As I write, these poor 'devils' are in prison and will readily pay the penalty for everyone's silliness; and it is quite possible some judge will take his revenge on them for his own. Because it has been exposed, we can easily see what is going on in this case, but in many things of a similar nature, which go beyond what we know about, I am of the opinion that we should be as ready to hold on to our discernment when we dismiss them as when we accept them.[14]

Notice the alliance with trickery. The important thing is not that a few individuals behaved in a manner which, if we are not careful, may lead us to imagine they were some kind of sceptics, but that the hoaxers were able to rely on their community's instinctive impulse to believe in the truth of their spirit.

In addition, whatever Montaigne's attitude towards the credulity of those who were fooled in this particular instance, his judgement is that of caution in the face of untoward happenings. If some can be seen as crude hoaxes, it does not mean to say that others can be tarred with the same brush, or even that because fraud may be detected or suspected in aspects of an incident, the incident as a whole can be dismissed as fraudulent. With this in mind, therefore, let us look briefly at a well-known English example of poltergeistery, the Tedworth episode of 1662–63.[15] In the middle of March 1662, John Mompesson, a local landowner, challenged an itinerant drummer, William Drury, who was making a nuisance of himself by drumming round the streets, and found that the written authority Drury claimed gave him permission to sound his drum had actually been forged. So he had Drury arrested and confiscated his drum, promising it would be returned should Drury's good character be vouched for – a promise he failed, through carelessness, to honour. In consequence, from April onwards his house was plagued by noises – knocking, thumping, drumming – for five nights together, after which there would be peace for three before the racket started up again. The longest period of quiet came when Mrs Mompesson, who was in the last stages of pregnancy, gave birth, and lasted a full three weeks while she recovered. But thereafter the noises returned, louder than before, pursuing the Mompesson children round the house while the entity jolted them in their beds. By this time it was November and furniture, shoes, and other objects began to move apparently of their own accord. But the entity was also showing signs of willingness to communicate with its victims. A servant noticed two floorboards move in the children's bedroom. 'He bid it give him one of them, upon which the board came, (nothing moving it that he saw), within a yard of him. The man added, "Nay, let me have it in my hand", upon which it was shoved quite home to him again, and so up and down, to and fro, at least twenty times together.' One evening, when several people were present in the house, one of them spoke to the poltergeist and said, 'Satan, if the drummer set thee to work, give three knocks and no more.' Three knocks were heard distinctly The man then tested it again, asking for five knocks, which were given; but that was all, and the rest of the night passed in silence.

Sometimes the poltergeist lay heavily upon the servants when they were in bed; sometimes it lifted them up into the air; one servant in particular suffered its attentions, having his bedclothes constantly pulled off him and his shoes thrown at his head; and when the new year arrived, the spirit seemed to redouble its tiresome pranks, harassing one of Mompesson's daughters, throwing a Bible into the ashes in the grate, strewing ashes all over a bedroom and leaving marks therein, such as those of claws or letters or circles. It was at this stage in the disturbance that Joseph Glanvill, to whom we owe this account, went to stay in the house 'on purpose to inquire the truth of those passages [events] of which there was so loud a report'. He was told that the drumming had stopped, but that the children were being annoyed as soon as they went to bed; and sure enough, when Glanvill went to investigate, he heard scratching sounds coming from behind the children's pillow.

> There were two little modest girls in the bed, between 7 and 8 years old, as I guessed. I saw their hands out of the clothes, and they could not contribute to the noise that was behind their heads. They had been used to it, and had still somebody or other in the chamber with them, and therefore seemed not to be much affrighted. I standing at the bed's head thrust my hand behind the bolster, directing it to the place whence the noise seemed to come, whereupon the noise ceased there and was heard in another part of the bed. But when I had taken out my hand, it returned and was heard in the same place as before. I had been told that it would imitate noises, and made trial by scratching several times upon the sheet, as 5 and 7 and 10, which it followed and still stopped at my number. I searched under and behind the bed, turned up the clothes to the bed-cords, grasped the bolster, sounded the wall behind, and made all the search that possibly I could to find if there were any trick, connivance, or common cause of it. The like did my friend, but we could discover nothing, so that I was then verily persuaded, and am so still, that the noise was made by some demon or spirit.[16]

Further witness from Mompesson himself includes mention of a light which came into the children's bedroom one morning, accompanied by a voice which cried out, 'A witch, a witch!' over and over again; some wood stacked in a chimney corner began to move and Mompession, who happened to have a loaded pistol at hand, discharged it at the wood and later found drops of blood on the hearth and on the stairs; and then the entity concentrated its attention on one of the youngest children, only just weaned, and kept it awake night after night. Finally it, or something, revealed itself to Mompesson's servant, appearing at the foot of his bed: 'a great body, with two red and glaring eyes which were for some time fixed upon him, and at length disappeared'. By now over a year had passed since the noises and other harassments began, but even so they continued, distressing as ever. Meanwhile William Drury, whose original grievance against Mompesson was blamed for starting the troubles, had been arrested on a charge of theft, and while he lay imprisoned in Gloucester gaol he had a visitor.

'What news in Wiltshire?' he asked.

The visitor said there was none, but William replied, 'No? Don't you hear of the drumming at a gentleman's house at Tedworth?'

'Yes, I do,' said the visitor.

'Aye,' said the drummer, 'I have plagued him, and he'll never be quiet until he has made me satisfaction for taking away my drum.'

Needless to say, this boast was his undoing because after he had been found guilty of theft at his trial on 21 March 1663 and sentenced to transportation, he managed to escape from the barge which was taking him to the transport ship and was foolish enough to come back to Wiltshire. Mompesson heard about his absconding and quickly had him indicted on another charge under the Witchcraft Act of 1604, for which he was brought to trial on 3 August. William's boast, and the fact that while he had been at liberty he had been travelling the countryside 'to show hocus pocus feats of activity' – either as what we should call a 'conjuror' or as a type of cunning man – combined to make him a figure of deep suspicion to almost everyone concerned; and this probably helps to explain why the grand jury allowed a true bill to go forward to trial and why the petty jury found it difficult to reach a verdict. It did so, however, and William was acquitted, but only just.[17] It was thus not difficult for contemporaries to see witchcraft as a likely explanation for Mompesson's sufferings, as is confirmed by the reaction of a physician called Compton to hearing Mompesson's story. The friend of Glanvill, Mr Hill, who had accompanied him to Tedworth, happened to find himself in company with Compton and, knowing Compton had an interest in occult matters, related the whole thing to him. The physician told him he was sure '[Mompesson's house] was nothing but a rendezvous of witches, and that for a hundred pounds he would undertake to rid the house of all disturbance'; and to prove his credentials, he asked Mr Hill, whom he particularly desired to see. Hill answered he would like to see his wife, who was at home many miles away at the time.

> Upon this, Compton took up a looking-glass that was in the room and, setting it down again, bid my friend look in it, which he did; and there (as he most solemnly and seriously professeth), he saw the exact image of his wife in that habit which she then wore, and working at her needle in such a part of the room, (there represented also), in which and about which time she really was, as he found upon inquiry when he came home.

But if educated opinion saw the hand of witchcraft at work in Tedworth, so too did popular sentiment, picking up on an actual incident from the affair. A ballad by Abraham Miles entitled 'A Wonder of Wonders' appeared in February

1663, prefaced by a woodcut of the sixteenth-century English comedian Richard Tarleton playing a drum and tabor. Its final verse runs:

> So powerful were these motions all
> By Satan sure appointed,
> The chamber floor would rise and fall
> And never a board disjointed.
> Then they heard a shout from on high,
> Three times, 'A witch, a witch!' did cry.
> O wonders, notable wonders,
> Ye never the like did hear.[18]

Glanvill's involvement in this affair is not unexpected. He was an Anglican clergyman who had diverted from his Puritan upbringing to an intellectual position of advocating religious toleration and freedom of thought. In 1664 he became a Fellow of the newly founded Royal Society and fully supported its spirit of empirical inquiry into every kind of topic: hence his turning up at Mompesson's house to investigate the widespread talk of a poltergeist. On one topic, however, he was fully persuaded, partly because of the amount of evidence there appeared to be to support its validity: namely, the existence of witches and the reality of their witchcraft. 'In order to furnish the proof that there have been and are unlawful confederacies with evil spirits', he wrote in an essay addressed to Robert Hunt in 1668, 'by virtue of which the hellish accomplices perform things above their natural powers, I must premise that, this being a matter of fact, is only capable of the evidence of authority and sense: and, by both these, the being of witches and diabolical contracts is most abundantly confirmed.'[19]

Now, this must be appreciated in context, for Glanvill and many of his friends and contemporaries were engaged in looking for ways to reconcile demonology with the principles of an experimental philosophy which had captured the imaginations as well as the minds of the mid-seventeenth century. The recent civil wars and interregnum had helped to create a kind of secularisation in which God certainly had a place, but not the overriding centrality He had been accorded before. Inquiry into the physical world by the methods of close observation and experiment, measurement and inductive reasoning, all of which had been urged by Francis Bacon and refined by René Descartes, promoted the idea of a brave new world which was dominated by Man and of which Man rather than God was the measure. Yet (and it is an important 'yet') for all its apparent endorsement of what has often misleadingly been called 'the scientific revolution', the mechanical philosophy, as it was called at the time, by no means exercised unchallenged sway over people's minds, or even those of the much smaller educated circles. The newly founded Royal Society, for example, owed its inspiration in part to Francis Bacon's fictional 'Solomon's House', envisaged as a kind of research institute 'dedicated to the study of the works and creatures of God', and partly to the actual existence of a circle of friends and correspondents gathered round the figure of Samuel Hartlieb, who promoted Bacon's idea with a mixture of practicality and esotericism. Hartlieb was interested on the one hand in improvements in agriculture, especially fruit husbandry, and on the other in astrology and sympathetic medicine, a combination spanning the natural and occult sciences which was fairly typical of the circles in which he moved.[20]

Glanvill, then, was scarcely a fish out of water as a Fellow of the Royal Society, and indeed a number of his co-Fellows thought very much as he did. Henry More, a personal friend as well as a colleague, believed that witchcraft was not a fantasy but an actual operative force under the control of certain human beings aided by the Devil; Robert Boyle practised alchemy and had been much struck by what he took to be the authenticity of Perreaud's account of the Mâcon poltergeist; and a later Fellow, Robert Plot, was persuaded of the necessity of alchemy to medicine. In fact, as Stuart Clark observes, 'In these years, men who were undoubtedly leading exponents of the new styles of natural philosophy, who championed the Royal Society, and were, some of them, fellows of it, went out of their way to insist on the reality of witchcraft and the importance of demonic activity in the natural world.'[21] What made their approach different from the theologically based explanations and interpretations of the earlier century was that they believed it could and should be studied in just the same way as any other branch of inquiry with a view to providing it with a proper scientific grounding. If this could this be done, it would protect the religious orthodoxies of Anglican theology against those individuals and sects, such as Thomas Hobbes on the one hand and the Quakers on the other, who were seeking to undermine them. Hence the agendum of Glanvill and his colleagues had a practical motive as well as an intellectual dynamism of its own.

Glanvill's assembly of narratives about witches, ghosts, and other apparitions was thus motivated by a scientific impulse: collect data, examine them critically, draw conclusions. The Tedworth episode actually shows this part of Glanvill's body of evidence evolving, since the documents upon which he was able to draw for his account, as well as his personal recollections, produced more than one 'final' version, the best-known (and the one I have used here) appearing in print only after his death. These other documents included Mompesson's letters 'which were sent to the Doctor of the Chair at Oxford, that contained an account of all the remarkable particulars of the whole disturbance', copies of which Mompesson handed over to Glanvill; and here we find the source of one or two individual points which Glanvill incorporated in his narrative. While the poltergeist was annoying one of Mompesson's daughters one night as she lay in bed, 'they' (whoever 'they' were: the text does not specify, but it may refer to her parents or one or two of the servants) tried to thrust at it with a sword, though without success. This strategy may have come out of a conversation Mompesson had had with a colleague, Sir Edward Nicholas, who told him about a similar case in France in which a number of men had slashed the air at random with their swords in the hope of wounding the witch – 'they never could hit her', he wrote of one of his servants in a letter to his cousin, 'by reason of the faculty witches have of passing in the air' – and it may have been the same conversation which caused Mompesson to keep a loaded pistol by him (which, it will be recalled, he discharged at some moving wood in the fireplace and afterwards found drops of blood on the hearth and stairs). Both men, it seems, were convinced that the source of the trouble was a witch who was effecting it invisibly. Hence Sir Edward's further advice that Mompesson should not refer to the plan to have swords and pistol at hand if he were in or near the house, because the witch, invisibly present, would be able to hear him.[22]

Other slight oddities in the narrative include the blue, glimmering lights which appeared in the house in January 1663 'and caused great stiffness in the eyes of those that saw it'. By 'those', in this instance, Glanvill actually meant Mompesson's wife, although the lights did also appear four or five times in the children's bedroom, and seem to have been followed by the sound of footsteps and the rustling of silk. Here we have characteristics more akin to those associated with ghosts, but they would have served to convince the household that the various phenomena – principally auditory and apportative at this time – were being produced by a spirit or demon. Conviction, however, was neither automatic nor immediate in some people, including both Mompesson and Glanvill themselves. In Glanvill's case, we have already seen how suspicious he was of the scratching noises behind the children's bed – mice or rats were common in houses of the period – and how it took concerted efforts on his part and that of his friend to come to the conclusion that trickery was not involved. Many of the visitors to Mompesson's house, too, came and left in a spirit of scepticism.

Last night there came some gentlemen afar off to see this. I admitted them. So they inquired at what time it usually came. It was answered, 'Near about this time'; so they say half an hour longer in expectation. Asked whether it was yet come, the maid said, 'No', whereupon I perceived them to smile. Shortly after, it was told them it was come, whereupon they rose up and ran into the room, so they heard the knocking it usually made. They began to search and very curiously to look whether or no they could discover any secret angles or holes where anybody might be put to make noises to deceive them, but found none. Then they called out, 'Satan, do this and that', and 'Whistle, if thou canst, or let us see whether thou canst tell [count] money, or make chairs dance, as we have heard. Let us see it!' I protest I was afraid at their carriage, and begged of them to be more sober and to withdraw themselves, for there was most to be heard when there was most silence. They were impatient and would not hear me. The spirit kept knocking, but meddled not with any chairs or stools. So I perceived they imagined there was a trick, and one before asked me leave, if they thought fit, to pull up my boards. I told him no, indeed. So when the spirit was silent, they discoursed of it and, I perceived, remained doubtful.

There were two ministers present who both assured them they had seen the motions of the chairs and stools as reported, but because they could not see it, [they] would not believe it, (the Devil was a fool to let them see so much), and began to hold discourses with these two ministers, in which they declared their diffidence [disbelief] of the being of spirits, and so departed with some kind of suspicion that what they heard was only a cheat or a fancy – all but one who seemed to be well satisfied upon a particular observation that he had made – and in their way have reported it to be as before I have said, and not worth regarding, and told it to a person of honour. They were the only persons that ever I observed went away with so much dissatisfaction, and whose carriage was of that nature that I shall be more careful how I admit strangers for the future.[23]

But Glanvill was having none of it. 'It is not to be conceived how tricks could have been put upon so many, so jealous, and so inquisitive persons as were witnesses of them,' he wrote and, in answer to those who had been present when nothing had happened and come away saying the whole thing was nonsense, ''Twas bad logic to conclude in matters of fact from a single negative and such a one against numerous affirmatives, and so affirm that a thing was never done because [it was not done] at such a particular time, and that nobody ever saw what this man or that did not. By the same way of reasoning I may infer that there were never any robberies done on Salisbury Plain, Hounslow

Heath, or the noted places, because I have often travelled all those ways and yet was never robbed.'[24]

The Tedworth case undoubtedly caused a stir, both at the time and later, and Glanvill's account was the object of attack and derision. Samuel Pepys was perhaps the kindest critic when he wrote in his diary on 24 November 1666 that Glanvill's book was 'well writ, in good style, but methinks not very convincing', even though twelve months later when he and his wife lay awake half the night, terrified of noises which they took to come from thieves *or a ghost*, the cause their alarm turned out to be chimney-sweeping in their block of houses;[25] in 1677 John Webster declared the 'strange tricks related by Mr Glanvill' to be merely 'abominable cheats and impostures'; Balthasar Bekker denounced the whole episode in 1694 along with that at Mâcon, saying that both resulted from servants' trickery; John Addison mocked it in a play, *The Drummer: or, The Haunted House* (1716); and Hogarth alluded to it in his print *Credulity, Superstition, and Fanaticism* (1762) by placing a drummer labelled 'Tedworth' on top of a thermometer showing the degrees of raving madness. On the other hand, Increase Mather was happy to include it in his *Essay for the Recording of Remarkable Providences*, along with the remark, 'which was judged by wise men to proceed from conjuration'; and John Beaumont used both Mâcon and Tedworth as two examples among many to criticise Balthasar Bekker's rejection of all such phenomena 'as done by human contrivance'. Beaumont also includes two relevant items of gossip. 'A person lately told me Mr Mompesson owned privately to the late King Charles the Second that all that passed at his house at Tedworth was done by contrivance; and another person has told me it was done by two young women in the house with a design to scare thence Mr Mompesson's mother. This was told them by others and I found them inclined to a belief of it.' Beaumont, however, points out that Mompesson himself denied the rumours of his confession to the King in a letter to Glanvill, and roundly supports Mompesson's integrity in the face of those accusations.[26] Scepticism and cautious belief anent the spirit-world thus locked themselves in dispute among learned circles. Supporters of traditional beliefs, in as much as they were determined to preserve a well-tried philosophy of Nature as well as to modify their approach to the subject matter, saw themselves as redefining those occult operations in Nature whose existence was under threat from an ill-conceived and blanket denial of their reality or validity. Their opponents, largely accepting of a mechanistic philosophy of Nature, which sat uncomfortably (or not at all) with the presence of anomalies, tended to solve their difficulties by dismissing anomalous data as inconsistent with purely material explanations for the working of the observable universe.

Hence the frequent references to 'atheism' which we find in the titles and works of the mechanists' opponents.

It is therefore not unexpected to see English-language writers in particular giving a large number of instances of both ghostly apparitions and poltergeist disturbances as they battled in print either to make their own case heard or decry the other side, even though the danger of fraud, perceived or genuine, was never far away. So, for example, we are told that a 'demon' in the village of Burton in Hertfordshire troubled a family for several months in 1669. Stools and benches were removed overnight from where they had been set and were placed elsewhere; freshly baked loaves disappeared likewise and were found next day hidden in tubs and under linen cloths; cabbages were pulled up during the night and arranged in the form of crosses and fleurs de lys, but no footprints were discovered in the surrounding soil; cheeses, hops, and plates of meat all suffered dispersal within their locked rooms; a roast pig lost all its flesh and only the bones remained; and several cows and a pig died unexpectedly. For some months a pause in the activity ensued, but then it started again with fires in a bedroom and a loft, continuing until one day 'a mow [heap] of pulse and pease was likewise fired in the daytime, and all the grain either burnt or spoiled; and in the middle of the bottom of the mow were found dead burnt coals which, in all the spectators' judgements, could not be conveyed thither but by witchcraft'. It is notable that the pamphlet which describes this episode calls the source of these activities 'the hag', and indeed when the poor tenant of the house reached the end of her tether, a neighbour, John Jones, volunteered to stay there overnight in order to meet and deal with the hag, 'to which end he carried with him a large basket-hilted sword, a mastiff dog, and a lanthorn and candle to burn by him'. No sooner had he gone to bed, however, than he heard a loud knocking at the door and a large number of cats burst into the room, broke the windows, and made a dreadful noise; all of which so terrified both him and his dog that they fled and ran for half a mile.[27]

To our eyes, of course, this particular episode may look somewhat different, in as much as the various incidents of rearrangement and decarnification all took place at night, although they happened in locked rooms 'while the tenant had the keys of the doors in her pocket', and it would have needed no witchcraft to borrow them or have duplicates made (supposing hers were the only set), just as the several fires need not have been started by magic, but simply by lighted candles or coals such as those found beneath the pease. In consequence, we may be entirely justified in suspecting fraud as the source of these ills, just as we may concur with at least one contemporary who regarded 'the devil of Woodstock' as nothing more than a disgruntled, but ingenious, Royalist supporter.[28] Further incidents are recorded from the 1670s: an outbreak of lithobolia in 1670 at Keppoch near Glasgow, which lasted for eight days and seemed to harm no one; a phantom cat, the size of a mastiff, without visible legs, in the house of Edward Pitts in Puddle Dock, London, in 1676, along with some poltergeist phenomena, such as the unexplained opening of doors, the movement of objects, and the lighting of candles; and noises within a house in Dublin in 1678, which pursued a young woman to another house when she tried to escape them in her own. 'Here she continued', says Richard Baxter, 'as long as the owner of that house would bear the resort of people and [the] terror of those sudden and frequent claps.' A third time the young woman moved, but was followed again until, after several nights spent in prayer with the local ministers, who all heard the noises too, she saw something dreadful (we do not know what) and was thereafter freed from any further molestation. The noises had lasted for three months and the experience had made her ill.[29]

From Ewell in Surrey we have yet another episode, dated 1681, overtly linking poltergeistery with witchcraft. Joan Butts had long been under suspicion as a witch. Twice one day in early October she came to the house of Mr Tuers and asked the servant-girl, Elizabeth Burgess, first for some old gloves, which were refused, and then for a pin, which was granted. But about a fortnight later, stones began to fly round the yard in showers, many the size of a man's fist, hitting no one except Elizabeth, to the astonishment of everyone who saw them. Next day Elizabeth complained of severe pains in her back and Mr Tuers, with her permission, put his hand down her dress and pulled out a lump of clay stuck full of pins. Again she complained, and this time the source was some clay stuck full of thorns. The following morning she saw Joan Butts 'sitting amongst the thorns and bushes, bedraggled up to the knees in dew, and looking like one that had lately had converse with some infernal fiend'. They exchanged no words, but the sight seems to have convinced Elizabeth that Joan was the source of her discomforts and so she told Mr Tuers, who quite agreed with her view. That night, poltergeistery broke out once more in the house; andirons were thrown about, so were Elizabeth's clothes, and a bar attached to the street door of the house removed itself and pursued the unfortunate woman upstairs. Three days later it was much the same story, and when Elizabeth tried to escape by going to her mother's house three miles away, she was followed by a great number of stones. Once arrived, she continued to suffer the same kind of hostile attention until her mother, chancing or perhaps intending to meet Joan Butts at the local fair, attacked the old woman and drew blood – a recognised means of counter-magic to undo the effects of a witch's malefice – and there our account stops.

But such instances, while relatively trivial in nature, should not be taken outwith the general context of ghostly apparitions, demonic interferences, and the appearance of prodigies and omens – monstrous births in humans and animals, invasions of mice, three suns seen at once in the sky – so many of which produced ballads, pamphlets, and newspaper articles. These, of course, ensured a wide readership and audience for such things, both answering the prevailing appetite for such material, while creating a bigger one. So to some extent we should perhaps be surprised, not that there is an increasing number of stories about poltergeists during this century, but that there are not many more.[30] Once we reach the second half of the century, however, records of instances of poltergeist activity tend to shift overseas to the various states of New England. European settlers had brought with them many of the traditional ways of thought and practice they had inherited, including the tendency to see many operations of the Devil manifesting themselves through demonry and witchcraft, the result often being that when a poltergeist incident happened, the association of poltergeist and witch was repeated in the New World. So, in December 1679, William Morse of Newbury started to be harassed by a poltergeist which began in the usual fashion by throwing sticks, stones, and other objects, including a cat, within and outwith the house. Things disappeared from their places and reappeared, food was spoiled, and personal attacks made on individuals.

> [Morse and his wife Elizabeth] being laid in their bed with their little boy between them, a great stone (from the floor of the loft) weighing above three pounds was thrown upon the man's stomach, and he turning it down upon the floor, it was once more thrown upon him. A box and a board were likewise thrown upon them all; and a bag of hops was taken out of their chest, wherewith they were beaten till some of the hops were scattered on the floor where the bag was then laid and left. In another evening, when they sat by the fire, the ashes were so whirled at them that they could neither eat their meat nor endure the house. A peel struck the man in the face. An apron hanging by the fire was flung upon it and singed before they could snatch it off. The man being at prayer with his family, a besom gave him a blow on his head behind and fell down before his face.[31]

But it was Morse's grandson who suffered worse than the adults.

> On the 18 of December, he sitting by his grandfather, was hurried into great motions and the man thereupon took him and made him stand between his legs. But the chair danced up and down, and had like to have cast both man and boy

146

into the fire; and the child was afterwards flung about in such a manner as that they feared that his brains would have been beaten out; and in the evening he was tossed as afore, and the man tried the project of holding him, but ineffectually. The lad was soon put to bed and they presently heard a huge noise, and demanded what was the matter? and he answered that his bedstead leaped up and down; and they (the man and his wife) went up, and at first found all quiet. But before they had been there long, they saw the board by his bed trembling by him and the bedclothes flying off him. The latter they laid on immediately, but they were no sooner on than off. So they took him out of his bed for quietness.[32]

As if this were not bad enough, by the end of the month the child was exhibiting signs of demonic possession, rolling about uncontrollably, making animal noises, and eating ash or sticks or yarn. During those intervals when he was able to speak rationally, he said that 'Powell' was making these things happen, 'Powell' being Caleb Powell, a seaman who had called on the Morses, learned of their troubles, and offered to take the boy away with him to afford them some quiet, which indeed happened until the boy returned. Powell had the reputation of being a magician – he claimed to know astrology and astronomy and 'the working of spirits', in other words, how to conjure and control them – but then Elizabeth Morse was also suspected of witchcraft by some in her community who tested their suspicion by nailing a horseshoe to their street door, an apotropaic which prevented Elizabeth from going to visit them, while as soon as it was removed, she came along at once. (Both Elizabeth and Caleb were subsequently tried for witchcraft. Caleb was acquitted, but Elizabeth was found guilty and sentenced to death, although this was later commuted to house arrest.)

Interestingly enough, Caleb blamed John, the grandson, saying overtly that the boy was playing tricks on his grandparents. 'Although he may not have done all [these things], yet [he has done] most of them, for this boy is a young rogue a vile rogue. I have watched him and seen him do things as to come up and down.' This, of course, is entirely possible, although we must bear in mind that this judgement of Caleb's comes from a person who was under suspicion himself and may have wanted to divert attention to someone else. It also rests upon a single occasion on which Caleb (he said) arrived at the Morses' house and looked through a window, to find young John playing tricks while his grandfather was praying, 'and among the rest that he saw him to fling the shoe at the said Morse's head'. But if we allow that this testimony could be true and that much of the demonic possession could have been faked (which is not to say it was), once again practicalities get in the way of our believing that all the stone, article, dust, and dung throwing which went on could have been contrived and carried out by the boy undetected and unsuspected by his grandparents. Let us, for example, take three little incidents which appear to have happened in quick succession.

> While [William Morse] was writing, a dish went out of its place, leapt into the pail, and cast water upon the man, his paper, his table and disappointed his procedure in what he was about. His cap leapt off from his head and on again; and the pot lid leapt off from the pot into the kettle on the fire.

It is difficult to see how John could have manipulated all these objects in such a way as to prevent his grandfather from noticing or suspecting his involvement. Similarly, when he was held fast by his grandfather on 18 December, even if he had been faking his violent convulsions, the fact that his grandfather was making an effort to hold him still by restraining him physically is likely to have made any deliberate attempt on the boy's part to overturn the chair with the weight of them both on it a formidable undertaking, and not one to be managed without grave risk of detection. That John may have egged the pudding, so to speak, from time to time, we may certainly believe; but that he should have manufactured *every* phenomenon is more difficult to accept.

The account of these trials is taken from *An Essay for the Recording of Illustrious Providences* by Increase Mather, and was printed in Boston in 1684. Now, 'providence' had a special meaning for Protestant confessions. It referred both to God's overall intention for the preservation, evolution, and continuance of His created universe according to His fore-ordained laws, and to His particular care for His chosen people whether in general or as individuals. So while miracles had ceased, 'providences' took their place, being special interventions in the normal working of things, foreseen by God as necessary for the working out of His plan for humanity. Accounts of these Protestant miracles and wonders turned into a distinct literary genre which proclaimed God's judgement upon sinners and provided cautionary tales for the improvement of people's consciences. They were, in essence, variations upon the sermon, and their descriptions of prodigies, omens, wonders, and apparitions constituted illustrations of God's mercy towards His people in providing them with both admonition and comfort, in as much as wickedness would always be found out and punished because God's all-seeing eye never winks or sleeps, and the individual's Job-like patience under trial would be rewarded. All this is made clear in a prefatory note by four of his fellow ministers to Cotton Mather's *Memorable Providences*.

The following account will afford to him that shall read with observation, a further clear confirmation that there is both a God and a Devil and witchcraft; that there is no outward affliction but what God may (and sometimes doth) permit Satan to trouble His people withal; that the malice of Satan and his instruments is very great against the children of God; that the clearest Gospel light shining in a place will not keep some from entering hellish contracts with infernal spirits; that prayer is a powerful and effectual remedy against the malicious practices of devils and those in covenant with them; that they who will obtain such mercies of God must pray unto perseverance; that God often gives to His people some apparent encouragements to their faith in prayer, though He does presently [immediately] perfect the deliverance sought for; that God's grace is able to support His children and preserve their grace firm under sorest and continuing troubles; that those who refuse the temptation to use doubtful or diabolical courses to get the assaults of the Devil and his agents removed, choosing to recommend all to God, and rather to endure affliction than to have it removed to His dishonour and the wounding of their own consciences, never had cause to repent of it in the end.[33]

When describing the Morses' trials, Increase Mather shows us the careful distinction he and others were accustomed to draw between demonic activity and what one may call 'popular' magic – the 'doubtful and diabolical courses' referred to above. Suspecting that Elizabeth Morse was a witch (and therefore perhaps guilty of summoning the demon which was troubling the household), one of her neighbours took apples which had come from the Morses' house and placed them on the fire. This (it was said) caused a great deal of disturbance in the neighbours' houses and so confirmed their suspicions. Mather, however, was having none of it and contemptuously dismissed 'the vanity and superstition of their experiments'. 'It is a sport', he added, 'to the devils when they see silly men thus deluded and made fools of by them.' The reality of devils, then, was not in question, only the unorthodox, unapproved means of testing their existence or countering their powers.[34]

Blaming the Devil for incidents such as these stemmed from a consciousness of Satan's ubiquity throughout New England. New Englanders especially regarded themselves as peculiarly susceptible to Satan's influence, partly because they had come to a foreign land inhabited by peoples they were accustomed to regard as Devil-worshippers, and partly because the sermons to which they listened regularly reminded them of Satan's responsibility for sin and suffering and disorder, and of their own unending task to be prepared for diabolic assaults against them. Satan was unrelenting in his malice and therefore, to be prepared, Christians must have a constant awareness both of his aims and of the devices he might use in pursuit of a soul's destruction.[35] Now, Increase Mather and his son Cotton were both Puritan ministers and thus as highly aware of Satan and demonry as any of their flocks – indeed, more so, because they not only preached against him, but compiled 'Providences' awash with examples of his interference in human lives through witchcraft, poltergeistery, and demonic possession, thus to some extent pandering to, and to some extent creating, the febrile atmosphere in which such interests, warnings, and fears were the common currency. To a much greater extent than the Middle Ages had witnessed, this currency was in the hands of the clergy, who took popular gossip, refashioned it, and passed it out again in the form of solemn admonition against the wiles of Satan on the one hand and the follies of superstition on the other.

From such a frame of mind, then, come the prefatory remarks of Cotton Mather to an example of poltergeistery, taken from his *Memorable Providences relating to Witchcrafts and Possessions*, published in 1689.

> Among those judgements of God, which are a great deep, I suppose few are more unfathomable than this, that pious and holy men suffer sometimes by the force of horrid witchcrafts and hellish witches are permitted to break through the hedge which our heavenly father has made about them that seek Him. I suppose the instances of this direful thing are seldom, but that they are not never we can produce very dismal testimony. One, and that no less recent than awful, I shall now offer, and the reader of it will thereby learn, I hope, to work out his own salvation with fear and trembling.[36]

The 'instance' which follows is one of witchcraft, hallucination, and a few poltergeist-like phenomena. In 1684 one Philip Smith, an eminently respectable man in his community of Hadley, failed to satisfy the begging of an old woman, fell ill, and then became delirious. He complained of being pricked with sharp pins and of smelling a strong odour, like musk, in his room; a small pot of medicine was found to be empty, though it had been nearly full; there was scratching at the foot of his bed, and sometimes fire was seen on the bed or on the covering, and 'when the beholders began to discourse of it, it would vanish away'. Something quite large moved in the sick man's bed, which acted as though it were a hand, for on one occasion it pinched a woman who was sitting there and on another the bed shook violently, 'so that [the sick man's] head was often knocked against the post, though he strove to hold it still'. Then at last Philip Smith died, and the second night afterwards various noises were heard in the room where his corpse lay, 'as though there had been a great removing and clattering of stools and chairs'.

Cotton Mather has no hesitation in saying that this death had been caused by witchcraft but, as we can see, the poltergeist elements here are minimal. Similarly, another case he describes, this time at length, is actually one of demonic possession, the possession being attributed to witchcraft,[37] and illustrates the firm conviction in New England that demons were abroad and at work in the region, whether assisted by witches or not. Thus, in June 1682 near Salmon Falls in Maine, Mary Hortado heard a voice saying, 'What are you doing here?' which was followed by something hitting her head so hard that it struck the doorpost. Two or three days later a stone flew through the house and settled in the fireplace before disappearing, and then a frying pan started to ring so loudly that it was heard on the other side of the nearby river. A day or two after that, Mary was struck by a stone and then 'bitten on both arms, black and blue, and one of her breasts [was] scratched. The impressions of the teeth being like [a] man's teeth were plainly seen by many.' These incidents were accompanied by visions or hallucinations: a woman who made as if to strike her, and then the same woman, differently dressed, laughing without making a sound.[38]

By 1692, of course, the Salem witches' trials were convulsing New England, and the two Mathers had become involved, although not quite in the same way. Much of the effect of evidence offered during those trials depended on the bewitched and possessed women's saying they could see and hear the people afflicting them, 'spectral' evidence of which Increase Mather was somewhat suspicious, his father less so. But both men found themselves targets of Robert Calef, a cloth merchant in Boston at the time of the Salem trials, whose book *More Wonders of the Invisible World* was completed in 1697, although opposition to it in Boston meant that Calef had to send the manuscript to England, where the printed version appeared in 1700. Calef bitterly criticised the way in which, as he saw it, the clergy in particular whipped up popular enthusiasm for attributing natural ills to the operation of the Devil though his witches. 'We have seen a bigoted zeal stirring up a blind and most bloody rage,' he warned, adding that both magistrates and ministers had to shoulder the blame because 'they could not but be sensible what a stain and lasting infamy they have brought upon the whole country, to the endangering of the future welfare not only of this but of other places induced by their example, if not to an entailing of the guilt of all the righteous blood that has been by the same means shed, by heathens or Papists etc., upon themselves, whose deeds they have so far justified, occasioning the great dishonour and blasphemy of the name of God, scandalising the heathen, hardening of enemies, and, as a natural effect thereof, to the great increase of atheism'.[39]

Part of his book deals with the case of Margaret Rule, as reported by Cotton Mather. Margaret had become possessed by demons in September 1693 and witchcraft was suspected by some of her neighbours because there lived nearby 'a miserable woman who had been formerly imprisoned on the suspicion of witchcraft, and ... had frequently cured very painful hurts by muttering over them certain charms'. There is little indication of poltergeistery in Margaret's case beyond the unexplained appearance of a white powder on her eyes and cheek, a sudden smell of sulphur throughout the house, and testimony from witnesses that they had seen her invisibly lifted from her bed to the ceiling 'with no assistance from any use of her own arms or hands, or any other part of her body, not so much as her heels touching her bed or resting upon any support whatsoever'.[40] Clearly some people found it difficult to make any clear distinction between demonry and poltergesitery, and we find a similar example in a Hieronymite monastery in Naples in 1696–97. A sixteen-year-old novice was subjected to lithobolia, having his bedclothes pulled off him at night, and being spattered with excrement. Objects were thrown around, too, dishes broken, and bread rolls filled with dung. So far, then, poltergeist behaviour. But the boy also heard voices begging for prayer, and saw figures – a Benedictine monk, a shape dressed in white with a face the colour of flames, and another dressed in black. The demon (as it is now described) held a long conversation with the master of novices, during which he revealed, in an exchange reminiscent of one between Perreaud and his poltergeist, that he was merely doing what God had told him to do, namely, to torment the young novice without ceasing. Sending the boy elsewhere did no good because when he returned to the monastery the phenomena broke out again more violently than before, so violently, in fact, that the ceiling of a room fell down, fortunately without hurt to anyone underneath. Finally it all proved too much for the brethren and the boy was told he ought to renounce all thought of monastic life, whereupon the demon disappeared.[41]

The century thus comes to an end in a state of confusion. Ghosts were commonly reported, demons even more so, especially in cases of obsession or possession, and poltergeists, to judge by the number of reported cases, were increasing their activity, often in connection with charges of witchcraft laid against the imagined source. These, however, might be a double-edged weapon, as in the case of Margaret Hubert from Leicestershire, who was accused of bewitching John Burt in May 1679 with violent knockings, removal of bedclothes, opening of trunks and chests, and affliction of distressing fits on Burt's daughter. Margaret was found guilty and executed, along with two other witches. But in the following year, one Walter Philipson on his deathbed confessed to having engineered the whole thing out of spite, and his body was subsequently hanged in chains. His mistress, Alice Burt, who, he said, had helped him, was executed.[42] It is always possible, of course, to regard his confession as false, a wish to enjoy for a fleeting moment the notoriety which such an admission might bring, but this is not very likely and it is probably more sensible to take the confession as genuine. Such apparent evidences of fraud, of course, proved a gift to scoffers and scorners, and yet, apart from resorting to contemptuous dismissal, opponents of these entities' existence had little to offer the general public by way of explanation for their popularity, an awkwardness which remained common, even among those who meticulously gathered together and related stories of these and similar preternatural events in the following centuries. 'The reader', says Andrew Lang at the end of his account of a poltergeist/ghost/demon/angry spirit episode from Spraiton in Devon in 1682, 'considering the exceeding strangeness of the relation, will observe that we have now reached "great swingeing falsehoods", even if that opinion had not hitherto occurred to his mind. But if he thinks that such stories are no longer told, and even sworn to on Bible oath, he greatly deceives himself.'[43] Such a reader might indeed do such a thing, as the even greater proliferation of evidences, relations, reports, and anecdotes during the eighteenth century was about to demonstrate.

8

No Such Thing as 'Enlightenment', 1703–c.1800

'How much the first view of Paris contradicted the idea I had formed of it,' wrote Rousseau in 1732. 'I had imagined a city as beautiful as it was great of the most imposing appearance, where one would see only the most magnificent streets, palaces of marble and of gold. Coming in through the Faubourg Saint Marceau, I saw only dirty and stinking alleyways, everywhere dirt, poverty, beggars, carters, menders, women selling tea or old hats. All this hit me so forcefully that none of the real magnificence I have seen in Paris since then has been able to erase that first impression.'[1] In a way, this is the eighteenth century in miniature. While indisputable advances in knowledge were made in some of the natural sciences, and Scottish and French philosophers were exercising speculations whose results might be (and were certainly feared to be) the weakening or even the dissolution of traditional certainties – speculations they trumpeted as 'enlightenment' in contrast to the darkness which had permeated earlier centuries – and while technological and environmental changes came helter-skelter, a press restrained only by political censorship grew immensely, and imperial expansion impinged – if only in a distant, hazy manner – on the imaginations of the many, life for the polloi was as brutish and short as ever it had been, and the eternal verities of present comfort and future promise more removed and less meaningful than ever. Caught in the middle of intellectual speculation on the one hand and lower-class ignorance on the other, the new middle classes looked uneasily both ways. While the attraction of the *encyclopédistes*, and David Hume and Gottfried Leibnitz, for example, might be agreeable to some, the campaigns against organised religion, such as those of John Trenchard at the beginning of the century, Voltaire in the middle, and

Baron d'Holbach at the end, were somewhat too stringent, outwith France at least, to be palatable to those who were not similarly inclined in the first place. On the other hand, the emotional excesses of Methodism, Pietism, and other dissenting groups, were equally distasteful and their tendency to fissiparousness unsettling and unattractive. So while aristocracies concentrated on wealth and power, as they always had, and the polloi sought to keep body and soul together, the relatively new and growing bourgeoisie looked for comfort and stability at the same time as nodding nervously in the direction of intellectual innovation. It was a peculiarly angst-informed position in which to find themselves.[2]

This may go a little way to explain why poltergeist experiences reported from the eighteenth century often include details which suggest that the source of the disturbances was seen as some kind of spirit (not necessarily demonic or ghostly) and that verbal communication with its human victims was increasingly felt to be important. Let us look at one or two examples. The first comes from St Maur and is dated 1706. A nobleman, whose name is given merely as M. de S, had gone to bed one night when he heard several loud knocks at his door. His maidservant investigated but found no one. The next night he heard a great blow on the wall. He managed to fall asleep, only to be woken by his bed's crashing into his bedroom wall, something it did again in the presence of his servants after they had dragged it back into place. The next night saw a repetition of the phenomenon, after which M. de S enjoyed one day's respite. But on the 26th, noises resumed, this time in the kitchen, beginning in the morning and going on until the afternoon. At about six o'clock, M. de S went into his study and watched in fright as his bedroom door shut and bolted itself while cupboard doors behind him swung open. It was then that M. de S heard a voice 'which came from a corner of the closet and seemed to him to be about a foot above his head'. The voice apparently gave him instructions, ordering him to do something (the account does not say what), and allowing him a fortnight in which to do it. Everything then fell silent for the permitted two weeks, the entity returning only once more to give several raps against a wall and an immense blow upon a window: and there the disturbance ended.

The story comes from an anonymous report actually written by one Monsieur Poupart, a canon of the Church of St Maur near Paris, and printed at the end of Augustin Calmet's *Traité sur les apparitions des esprits*, first published in 1746. Poupart was of the opinion that this entire episode must have been a hoax perpetrated by M. de S with a view to amusing himself at the expense of his domestics. Personal fear is easily counterfeited, he says, raps and bangs and blows could have been produced by natural means, and the bed could easily have been moved by M. de S if it had been on castors and running across a well-polished wooden floor. Apparently much of this was the opinion of M. de S's father, too. But 'could' and 'might have' themselves indicate speculation rather than fact and they work with equal effect the other way round. The episode 'could have been' entirely factual and M. de S 'may have' reported his experiences accurately. It depends on whether one is prepared to accept the possibility that spirits of some kind exist and have the ability to interact with the world of matter – precisely the bone of contention between educated individuals in France at this particular time, as Calmet points out in his preliminary remarks to his inclusion of Poupart's essay in his treatise.[3]

To be fair to Poupart, Calmet does lay himself open to criticism, as his fellow Benedictine Ildefonse Cathelinot observes: 'when one reads Dom Calmet's book, one is convinced that, while there is a small number of apparitions which are real, there is a huge number which are false and fictional'. In other words, Calmet lacked discrimination in his recording spirit-narratives.[4] Nevertheless, what we have to bear in mind is that Calmet's intention was to put together overwhelming evidence for the existence of spirits in answer to the doubts and dismissals of some of his contemporaries.

The great number of authors who have written upon the apparitions of angels, demons, and disembodied souls is not unknown to me; and I do not presume sufficiently on my own capacity to believe that I shall succeed better in it than they have done, and that I shall transcend their knowledge and their discoveries. I am perfectly sensible that I expose myself to criticism, and perhaps to the mockery of many readers, who regard this matter as done with, and settled in the minds of philosophers, learned men, and many theologians. I must not reckon either on the approbation of the people, whose want of discernment prevents their being competent judges of this same. My aim is not to foment superstition, nor feed the vain curiosity of visionaries, and those who believe without examination everything that is related to them as soon as they find therein anything marvellous and supernatural. I write only for reasonable and unprejudiced minds, which examine things seriously and coolly. I speak but for those who assent even to known truth only after mature reflection, who know how to doubt of what is uncertain, to suspend their judgement on what is doubtful, and to deny what is manifestly false. As for pretended freethinkers, who reject everything in order to distinguish themselves, and to place themselves above the common herd, I leave them in their elevated sphere; they will think of this work as they may consider proper, and as it is not calculated for them, will probably not take the trouble to read it.[5]

Once again, therefore, we find ourselves in the middle of the same kind of intellectual argument as exercised the previous century, although here the terms have changed somewhat. Instead of one theologically based view of the spirit-world against another, we have a defence of that world in the face of those who would deny both its existence and that of religion itself, or at least of organised religion such as had been dominant in Europe since the reign of Tiberius. In this battle, Calmet's poltergeist stands out as curiously old-fashioned. The poltergeistery begins as a set of self-contained phenomena apparently expressing nothing but themselves; but as soon as the voice is heard, we realise they have actually been precursors of this moment and that here, in the presence of this spirit, lies the point of the narrative. One calls the spirit an old-fashioned manifestation because it is clearly modelled on the Mediaeval ghost which makes itself known in order to have a wrong righted or a neglected corpse properly buried, and although M. de S's spirit never calls itself a ghost and the details of its request of M. de S are never revealed, the parallel with a spirit from Purgatory is perfectly clear.

But if we now leave France and turn to Scotland in 1707, we find that the identification of a poltergeist as a ghost is made overtly. At the beginning of September, James Cowan was staying with James Short, minister of Drysdale in Annandale, and while he was there he heard local rumour that a house not far away was being haunted. Neither Cowan nor Short believed this, but were curious enough to pursue the gossip further. So they visited James Murray, the minister of St Mungo's, who told them that the story of the haunting was perfectly true. He had heard it from Mr Johnston, the owner of the house, himself. Apparently a week previously, Johnston's daughter was in the cowshed, milking one of the cows, and happened to look at the end of the stable where the horse was standing.

> She observed a tall man to start up and appear, all on a sudden, hard beside the manger, which filled her with great horror and consternation. Yes, as she said, she had enough presence of mind as to think and say within herself, 'Through the Lord's help, I shall see whether this be a fancy or not'. And, accordingly, she took a steady look of him and narrowly remarked everything about him; and told that he was almost all naked, except that he had a white nightcap on his head, a white sheet about his shoulders, and white socks on his legs. He had red hair, and [she] observed that his feet were very big.[6] He presently comes up to her, lifts the bowl of milk which she had set down at her side, carries it to the other end of the house, and lays it down beneath the manger. He comes back again to her, stretches out his hand, and claps her cheek, and after that makes a great many odd faces,

gaping and staring upon her and grasping at her with his hand; at which she fell into a swoon and there lay till her mother, thinking what kept her so long, came in to the stable and found her lying almost dead.

Since that day, said Johnston, the house had been troubled by lithobolia and the sudden disappearance of clothes, sometimes from people's very hands, and their reappearance next day or thereafter, thrown upon walls and hedges. Not long after they heard this account, Short and Cowan met a recent visitor to Johnston's house, who told them that he and some other gentlemen had been looking at the beehives, then continued walking for two or three minutes before turning back only to find all the hives overturned and lying on their sides. The house, he added, was especially disturbed at night by loud banging and by the sound of the pewter vessels in the kitchen being thrown to the floor, although next morning they were all found in good order again. Several men had been taking turns to keep watch in the house during the night, and each of them had been subjected to more or less the same experiences. Moreover, Johnston's daughter had become a target for the entity which pulled her by the foot when she was in bed, removed the bedclothes, and beat her severely, thereby preventing her from getting any sleep; and one day, 'a servant man that belonged to the family, as he was at his work in the field, happened to say to the rest of his neighbours that were shearing with him, "Lord be thanked, the ghost has not troubled us this last night!" He had no sooner spoken this word than he got a severe pelt on the back with a stone thrown at him from some invisible hand, which they all observed to rebound off his back on the ground; and some of them took it up.'[7]

Here, of course, it is easy enough to separate the apparition in the cowshed from the rest of the anecdote and explain it as a local or travelling daftie who happened to have been disturbed by the daughter's coming to milk the cow (although if he had been local, he would surely have been recognised), or as someone having a joke at the young woman's expense, although one must ask in that case how he would have known she was going to be in the cowshed at that time, since it was not her regular hour to be there at all. 'Rationalising' the apparition, however, does nothing to explain its context. The people on the spot, none of whom can be regarded as a superstitious peasant, interpreted the figure as a ghost and clearly connected its appearance with the poltergeistery which followed: and that is what is important for our purposes. The reason for their doing so is possibly to be found in the title of the book which reports their experiences, *Analecta: or, Materials for a History of Remarkable Providences.* Robert Wodrow, who committed them to paper, was the son of the Professor of Divinity at Glasgow University and himself a minister at Eastwood parish church near Glasgow. His religious sympathies were roundly Presbyterian – he had published a sympathetic history of the Covenanters in 1721–22 – and with 'Remarkable Providences' we are once again in the same field as that cultivated by Increase and Cotton Mather. The slightly twee title (*Analecta* = 'Collector of Crumbs') describes well enough what Wodrow was about – assembling anecdotal information intended to illustrate the workings of divine providence in people's everyday lives – and it is worth noting that in the story we have just reviewed, he is careful to emphasise the respectability and reliability of the witnesses to the incident. James Murray is a Presbyterian minister; Mr Johnston a heritor, that is, a member of the local gentry responsible, among other things, for the maintenance of justice and the appointment and salary of the local minister; and the witnesses (apart from the servant in the field) are all described as 'gentlemen', with the implications of probity which that entailed. We are not told directly that the initial doubters, James Cowan and James Short, the minister, were convinced by what they were told concerning the ghost-cum-poltergeist, or rather, by the quality of the witnesses who were telling them about it, but we are almost certainly meant to infer that they were, otherwise the anecdote would lose something of its flavour and purpose, as well as running counter to the tendency of the collection as a whole.

Other clergy elsewhere reported poltergeist experiences, some with the addition of evidence pointing to a vocal spirit, others without. An eminent Lutheran professor of theology, Dr Schuppart, and his family were harassed for six years from 1703 to 1708 in Pfedelbach. Stones were repeatedly thrown through his study window, his wife was struck noisily with blows from an unseen hand (although they did not hurt her much), and he himself was physically attacked. 'Often', he wrote, 'I have been for four weeks together without taking off my clothes. It has struck me in the face, it has pricked me with pins, it has even bitten me so that both rows of teeth could be distinguished. The two big fangs stood out plainly and they were as sharp as pins.' All this he took most seriously – there does not seem to have been any suspicion in his mind of a hoax or human mischief – and reported his ordeal fully on solemn oath to a Lutheran theological academy. In May 1713, a physician, Berthold Gerstmann, began to suffer from episodes of lithobolia, damage to glass and porcelain apparatus in his laboratory, the transport of large quantities of faeces from the garden lavatory into the house, and the unaccountable disappearance of domestic and personal objects. The Gerstmann father and eldest son tried to defend themselves and their property by slashing the air with their swords, but this merely provoked the entity, which continued to harass them until 2

June when it ripped the clothes belonging to Gerstmann's youngest son and then suddenly found a voice, crying out, 'The end! The end today! The end of mischief! The end of stench!' The Gerstmanns were devout Evangelicals and the account of their trial, derived from a diary kept by one of their sons, was endorsed by a Lutheran minister. These German diarists and memorialists seem to have been particularly meticulous in recording their experiences. Yet another was Jeremias Heinisch, minister at Gröben from 1714 to 1736, who suffered poltergeist attacks for several weeks during the summer of 1718, largely lithobolia and the apportation of various objects.[8]

But one of the best-known such episodes during the eighteenth century is that which troubled the Wesley family while they were living in Epworth rectory. It took place between December 1716 and January 1717 and began with groans and then with knocking during the night. Next it developed into the sounds of people walking and running up and down the stairs, a cascade of coins, and breaking bottles and so continued with variations for nearly a month. Samuel Wesley senior clearly assumed, on the strength of groaning repeated more than once, that he was dealing with a ghost, and asked the entity to identify itself, but received no reply. So much we learn initially from a letter to Samuel Wesley junior in London from his mother. He replied cautiously, asking the obvious questions about the involvement of servants or four-footed creatures, and the exact circumstances in which the family either heard or sensed the phenomena, at the same time reserving to himself the possibility that there may indeed have been spirits at work. His mother answered quickly.

> Though I am not one of those that will believe nothing supernatural, but am rather inclined to think there would be frequent intercourse between good spirits and us, did not our lapse into sensuality prevent it, yet I was a great while e'er I could credit anything of what the children and servants reported concerning the noises they heard in several parts of our house. Nay, after I had heard them myself, I was willing to persuade myself and them that it was only rats or weasels that disturbed us, and having been formerly troubled with rats which were frighted away by sounding a horn, I caused a horn to be procured and made them blow it all over the house. But from that night they began to blow, the noises were more loud and distinct, both day and night, than before, and that night we rose and went down, I was entirely convinced that it was beyond the power of any human creature to make such strange and various noises.[9]

Young Samuel received further information from one of his sisters, who also wrote of various kinds of noise, including one 'as if a great piece of sounding metal was thrown down on the outside of our chamber', and she later remarked that 'something walked beside my bedside, like a man in a long nightgown'. This is interesting phraseology. Why did Susannah think it was a man rather than a woman? The sounds made by their night attire would have been very much the same, so did she see or half-see some kind of apparition? Indeed, she ended her letter with a reference to the something's making 'its personal appearance', but while Samuel expressed himself concerned about this in his reply, he asked particularly about the circumstances attendant upon the knocking rather than anything else. His sister Emilia, however, also mentioned such a sight. 'There came down the stairs behind [sister Hetty] something like a man in a loose nightgown trailing after him, which made her fly rather than run to me in the nursery'. Her parents' reaction upon being told of this is worth noting. Samuel merely smiled, 'imputing it to us or our lovers', while Mrs Wesley, as she had written to son Samuel, 'firmly believed it to be rats, and sent for a horn to blow them away'. This comes from an undated letter, but as Emilia refers to the noises' having lasted for a month already, we must assume that Samuel and his wife preserved a degree of dubiety anent the source of at least some of the phenomena well into the period of the disturbance.[10]

One can see why Wesley *père* and *mère* hesitated to accept at face value everything Emilia said, for she went on to tell Samuel junior that she believed the whole thing arose from witchcraft. Apparently, twelve months before, there had been a disturbance in a nearby town, which Emilia at any rate asserted was caused by witches and her father had recently spent several Sundays preaching against cunning folk who were popular in the neighbourhood. Moreover, a headless badger had been seen under her sister's bed and a white rabbit in the kitchen, 'which seems likely to be some witch'. Now, Emilia was aged twenty-five or twenty-six at the time; in consequence, we are not listening to a child's fantasising. So this, and her reporting that there were magical practitioners active in the area, must act as a reminder of how deeply embedded was belief in the Otherworld outwith the small circles of educated élites. Samuel Wesley's journal recorded all these phenomena, along with one of his own, namely, 'I have been thrice pushed by an invisible power, once against the corner of my desk in the study, a second time against the door of my matted chamber, a third time against the right side of the frame of my study door, as I was going in'; and he also noted that knocking occurred whenever he said prayers for George I and the Prince of Wales – which is why some of the family in jest called the entity a Jacobite – while John Wesley reported further, in a summary of all the phenomena, that whenever anyone wanted to go from one room to another, the latch of the room to which he or she went was lifted up before a finger touched it.[11]

The family sent further accounts ten years later to John Wesley, none of which added anything substantial to their previous reports, but a letter from the rector of Haxley, a nearby village, to John tells us that Samuel Wesley senior asked him to come to Epworth 'to conjure', adding, 'I knew not what he meant till some of your sisters told me what had happened, and that I was sent for to sit up.' Normally 'conjuring' would imply either the use of magic to counter the entity's actions (a proposed use highly implausible in this case) or of exorcism, provision for which was, in theory at least, still made in the Anglican Church. It is therefore interesting to find that Wesley seems to have used this word and that it was not understood by the Reverend Hoole. (Perhaps Hoole genuinely did not know what Wesley meant, or perhaps he was too astonished to believe his ears that a modern Protestant clergyman would be advocating 'Romish' practices.) But Hoole does say that Wesley spoke to the entity 'and said he believed it was the Devil', which would make sense of any reference to exorcism. On the other hand, John Wesley's account, published in the *Arminian Magazine* in October, November, and December 1784, mentions that his father had said to the poltergeist, 'If thou art the spirit of my [dead] son Samuel, I pray, knock three knocks and no more.' The answer, unfortunately, was silence.[12]

As far as later commentators were concerned, the Epworth incident was simply a fraud perpetrated by one of the Wesley children, Mehetabel (Hetty) being the favoured choice on the grounds that 'Old Jeffrey', as the family christened the 'poltergeist', used to follow her round the rectory. But this derives from the theory that poltergeists' activity is centred upon children, especially troubled teenagers, who either provide the psychic energy for the entities to use (if one accepts that a separate entity is involved) or who unconsciously expel forms of energy from themselves, which manifest in the disturbances described by other people. However, whether the theory is valid as a whole or in part – and one should perhaps note that teenagers or younger children are by no means invariably present in poltergeist narratives – it is of no account if poltergeist phenomena are going to be attributed to trickery. Hetty's involvement was also raised by J. Arthur Hill, only to be dismissed as unlikely. Hetty, he wrote, 'had the singular wit of trembling in a sound sleep', and he raised a possible explanation that 'the trembling was due to suppressed laughter at the puzzledom of her parents and sisters, who were sometimes kept up nearly all night, and had broken sleep for two months: or to the muscular effort involved in pulling a string which somehow made distant raps'.[13]

That 'somehow' betrays the flimsiness of the speculation. Hetty would certainly not have slept alone. The Wesleys had nineteen children, space would have been precious, and single bedrooms for each impossible; in any case, it was entirely usual, even in smaller households, for offspring to double up at night. So Hetty would have had constant witnesses or would-be witnesses of such a string. How did she fit it up to be invisible? Since the noises happened outwith the room – and not only hers, but others in the house – are we to suppose she drilled a hole in the wall or wainscot or door through which to pass her string? Did she do this for every room in the house outside which noises were heard? How did she do all this, and pull the string, undetected? 'Somehow' explains nothing and is merely a vacant gesture in the direction of a pseudo-rationalism which has nothing coherent to offer in this case. Sacheverell Sitwell is even vaguer. Epworth, he says, was an isolated place, children have vivid imaginations or exaggerate, and 'there can be no doubt whatever that the actual poltergeist was one of the children of the family', although no reason is offered for this flat assertion. He hints at ventriloquism and at collusion between the mother, Susannah Wesley, and Hetty – not actual conspiracy, but something more intangible.

> It is possible that it may have been the mother and daughter together who were responsible for these extraordinary happenings. Not as deliberate accomplices, but in subconscious intention, working in with each other, without surface knowledge, and with nothing approaching planning or discussion, to the perfecting of these mediumistic pranks. Their subconscious intelligence, their souls, for this is one meaning of that word, had, therefore, if this were true, a definite, but dumb, contract between them. And such a compact almost presupposes a third person who drew up the terms, and for whose benefit it was put to work. The contracting of this silent alliance must have had a go-between, or a power whom both parties implicitly obeyed. For, in its workings, it was a treaty of mutual balance; neither mother nor daughter, it is evident, would do anything to invalidate the tricks or wonders of their cherished master.

What Sitwell means by his 'cherished master' is to be found (if anything believable is to be found in the midst of this gobbledegook) in what he calls 'the mysteries of puberty' – his theory is thus a variant upon the theme of the neurotic or troubled teenager – and he builds a picture of this third party as more or less an entity in and of itself, the principal difference between this and earlier 'demons' being that Sitwell's 'cherished master' has nothing of the supernatural about him.

> Some outer thing is really inhabiting a human body and imparting to it powers of deceit of which only a half, or, it may be, none of its normal intelligence at

all is aware. But, as well, it has often powers which cannot be explained away as mere trickery or sleight of hand. And it has always, and in every case, a devilish ingenuity that is entirely different from the naughtiness or mischief of any ordinary child. The bias is never directed towards doing something funny or amusing; it is always meant to instil terror. It is the dark background to the mind upon which it preys.[14]

All this, however, begs the question of whether the Epworth entity – let us put aside as unhelpful the possibility of fraud – was actually a poltergeist at all. The principal disturbances endured by the Wesleys were rappings and knockings, none of which displayed any conscious effort at communication; the sound of breaking glass on one occasion proved to be merely a sound and not an indication of actual damage; the apparition was entirely consistent with that of a ghost rather than a poltergeist; and the appearance of a badger at one point and a rabbit at another are really neither here nor there. The indications are, in fact, that Samuel Wesley's initial disposition to wonder whether or not the entity was a ghost fit the circumstances rather better. But whether we take one view or the other, we may note that the immediate reaction of both adults and children was to be suspicious, and that only after they had tested their suspicions by searching diligently for any natural or fraudulent cause of the noises did they allow themselves to be persuaded that the source must be preternatural.

This caution may have sprung from a well of personal inclination, but it is also likely to have owed something to the febrile atmosphere which is noticeable not just in England but in France as well during these early years of the new century. Political autocracy seemed to be in the ascendant, and yet revolution of one kind or another bubbled, and not always beneath the surface. Warfare cost millions of whatever was the national currency, and speculative adventure in lands abroad swallowed even more, mostly with devastating effects on the economy at home. Anti-clericalism battered the walls of the national Churches and, by and large, made them more withdrawn and inward-looking, to the detriment of their flocks, while the growth of towns brought extra problems, especially for the poor, which the established Churches struggled to address with any degree of achievement. Among the educated classes, too, there was a fashion for 'sentiment', which increasingly meant a willingness to indulge emotional reaction at the expense of rational response, and did nothing to lessen a fevered pace of living which flirted and then fell in love with the Uncanny, the Grotesque, the Sublime, the Picturesque – a whole range of phantasmagoria hitherto kept under some kind of control and in some degree of proportion by the very Churches whose authority was now under attack. Throughout it all stalked the Devil. For Catholics and Anglicans and dissenting confessions of all kinds preached a world beset by evil, in which the Devil was ever-present, driving people first to despair and then to suicide, either physical or spiritual or, sometimes, both. Their preaching, however, was often met with anti-clerical scorn. As Lady Sarah Cowper observed, 'The sinners of this age are grown impudent and appear with a whore's forehead, forsaken of all modesty, turning the world of God itself and the most serious manners of religion into raillery. Such clamorous sins are almost come to be the garb and fashion, and to be accounted the wit and gallantry of these times.' Thus, for example, Henry Sacheverell, a High Church Anglican much opposed to the political revolution of 1688–89 in England, was cartooned as a fanatical windbag, not to be taken seriously.

> To draw him to perfection, I here present him in his full length, that the public and such as are the inverse of monsters, may not lose an inch of him, though black. Like a lobster be indeed his natural or original colour; yet to show him truly, he should be printed in crimson or bloody colours. For he is [like] Apostles or Church dragoons, that, instead of waging war with the Devil, is always found a charge against his own brethren – which he manages with such High Church fury and immoderate zeal, that woe to the poor Dissenter or moderate Churchman that comes within the reach of his flaming sword. 'Danger' and 'the Church' are two great words with him, of which happy doctrine he is so brimful that he is a mere speaking trumpet, and may with a favourable wind sometimes, when he is deeply elevated on the subject, he is heard as far as Saint Germain. Yet for all his zeal, 'tis thought that if the faggots were clapped to his arse, he'd hardly die a martyr for that Church he makes such a noise of.[15]

Perhaps we may take the trial and conviction of Jane Wenham in 1712 for 'conversing familiarly with the Devil in the shape of a cat' as symbolic of the split personality of the period. The trial judge clearly thought the charges against Jane were nonsense. But the jury did not and convicted her, swayed partly by her own confession (not obtained by torture) that she had shape-changed into a cat and in that form tormented a girl called Anne Thorn, and partly by her inability to recite the Lord's Prayer in full, balking at the sentence 'Lead us not into temptation, but deliver us from evil'. Several clergy and a justice of the peace, Sir Henry Chauncy, along with his son Arthur, were also persuaded of her guilt, so the hurdles of class and education cannot be said to have played a part in shaping the views of the various people concerned.

Nevertheless, and in spite of the guilty verdict, Jane was reprieved, but not before her case had been taken up and put to propagandistic use by the Whigs and Tories.

The haunted psyche of the period, then, provides the context for the reports of poltergeist activity which fascinated the century, many of them, it will be noticed, written by clergymen (such as Dr Schuppert or Samuel Wesley or Augustin Calmet or Robert Wodrow) who had what one might call a professional interest in the subject. A printed sheet, anonymous but likely to have been produced by a minister or at least one of the godly, appeared in 1718, relating to 'spirits that trouble the minister's house of Kinross'. Mr McGill and his family found that their spoons and knives disappeared only to turn up amid the straw in their barn, pins kept on appearing in their food, and their household sheets and personal clothes were ripped and slashed. 'A stone thrown down the chimney wambled a space in the floor, and then took a flight out at the window. Also there was thrown in the fire the minister's Bible, which would not burn; but a plate and two silver spoons thrown in, melted immediately.' These activities were attributed to evils spirits – not surprising given the ecclesiastical context and the minor miracle of the Bible's preservation, like Daniel, in the fiery furnace. In the same year, between June and September, we learn from a Lutheran minister, Jeremias Heinisch, that he suffered the attentions of what the pamphlet account of his experiences calls '*eines insgemein sogennanten Kobolds*', a so-called goblin. Stones rained upon the roof of a cowshed and were thrown through windows from the outside in and from the inside out, and on one occasion it looked as though a large stone was about to fall on the minister's head from a height. But it diverted its path at the last moment and succeeded only in frightening one of the servants.[16]

Herr Heinisch's pamphlet describing the episode was published at Jena in 1723, and its lengthy title includes the interesting phrase 'an attempt to test how the truth can be discovered'. Clearly, then, although the report was written to inform his ecclesiastical superiors, Heinisch's motives in putting pen to paper were similar, in their way, to those of Augustin Calmet, who compiled his collection of narratives with what we might call the prevailing 'scientific' end in view. To this extent, both clergymen were operating within a relatively new mental framework, the inclination to treat manifestations of the Otherworld as though they were tokens of a potentially pathological state of mind in individuals or groups of individuals, rather than genuine appearances or intrusions of other realities into the world of matter. Hence the treatment of personal experience or the records of the experiences of others, which were slowly turning into data whose contribution was less and less to a revelation of the working of God in the created universe through created but non-physical entities, and more and more to a speculation that the created universe alone, including the human mind, was responsible in one way or another for all such phenomena.

Not all clerical reports were affected by this, of course. Some were made, or appear to have been made, simply for the sake of recording a set of disturbing experiences. Thus, in Norway, one minister noted apparent poltergeistery lasting for ten months between 1722 and 1723, which included strange noises, throwing plates, extinguishing the fire, lifting up the roof of a house, and a childish voice which merely repeated what was said to it. Another, writing in c.1730, recorded loud knockings which seemed to leave club marks on the walls of the house, fire scattered on the floor while the family was asleep, and rocks thrown into rooms. Other reports, however, were motivated by specific aims. Father Charles-Louis Richard, a Dominican preacher and theologian, for example, published his 'Dissertation on Possession of the Body and the Infestation of Houses by Demons' in 1746, in which he included an account of a house in Amiens troubled by ghostly noises and subject to movements of furniture he described as 'dancing' along with personal attacks on individuals, which were enough to leave them bruised, all of which had been going on since 1732. But the point of his publication was not so much the anecdote for the anecdote's sake as to furnish a contribution to his defence of religion against the *encyclopédistes*, and, rather than representing a silent acquiescence in the methods of the new 'scientific' approach to eliciting explanations from accumulated material, his book is closer to a continuation of the previous century's outright battles between established religious orthodoxy and speculative, unorthodox inquiry.[17] Equally traditional in outlook is an extraordinary case of demonic possession and witchcraft in the Premonstratensian convent of Unterzell, near Würzburg, in 1746. The sub-prioress of the community, Maria Renata Sänger, was accused of bewitching one of the sisters, Cecilia Pistorini, causing her intense physical pains, and of sending demons to possess several of the other nuns in the midst of their reciting the Divine Office. Her confession after her arrest revealed remarkable details of devil-worship and acts of hostile magic; and for these she was tried, found guilty, and beheaded, her body then being burned in a public square. The 'poltergeist' elements of this tale amount to animal noises, shadowy figures, movements of furniture, and the overturning of a huge chest too heavy for more than one man to lift – pretty standard poltergeist stuff, but here clearly associated with demonic rather than any other kind of activity.[18]

But if the clergy, however traditional or contemporary in their mode of thinking, were keen to inform the public that spirits were not only real but active in the world of matter, they might, unless they were careful, find themselves open to the dangers of overeagerness and credulity and thereby to the trap of fraud. Perhaps the best-known example of this is the Cock Lane hoax which diverted, entertained, and annoyed London from January 1760 until February 1762.[19] In brief, William Kent, a somewhat naïve individual, moved to London from the country with Fanny, a woman he pretended was his wife. She was actually the sister of his first wife, who had died not long before, but as canon law forbade him to wed his sister-in-law and public decency demanded they marry or live apart, William and Fanny decided to masquerade as a married couple in London, far away from their scandalised relatives. At first they lodged in Cock Lane, a seedy thoroughfare not far from St Paul's Cathedral, in a house owned by Richard Parsons, a parish clerk and alcoholic with a family of his own. It was not long, however, before strange noises began to disturb the household, scratchings and knockings whose source could not be determined. William and Fanny decided to move elsewhere. Fanny was pregnant, William had been foolish enough to lend Parsons money, and he had let slip that he and Fanny were not actually married – an admission which Parsons stored up for possible future use – so their situation in the house was turning fraught. The move was made, but Fanny caught smallpox and died, and Parsons, who had conceived a hatred for William after being asked to repay the money he had borrowed, looked for ways to avenge himself for what he regarded as William's blackguardly attitude towards him.

The weird noises continued to disturb the Parsons' house and were joined at one point by a ghost, seen one night by the landlord of Parsons's local pub, a man of excessive nervousness with an immense fear of anything which smacked of the supernatural. Invited to be a witness to the scratchings and rappings, he reluctantly came to the house, only to run away upon being told they were produced by the ghost of William's first wife, who was angry at his seduction of her sister. As he was leaving, however, the landlord saw a white figure 'seemingly covered in a sheet', which brushed past him and ran upstairs, a sight which terrified him, as he reported, still full of nerves, to the judge and jury who examined him two years later. The hauntings now burgeoned into a public menace. More and more people flocked to Parsons's house and into the bedroom where his daughters were supposedly sleeping through the constant racket, first of the 'poltergeist's' knocking and scratching, and secondly of the excited crowds who had turned up for the divertissement. But the sheer numbers and excitement also attracted the attention of the authorities, who had had experience only a few years previously of the London mob's enthusiasm for weirdness and mystery, and were therefore nervous of anything which might set it off again, especially as the newspapers were beginning to take such an interest in the phenomena that a circulation war started and reports of what was happening in Cock Lane became wilder and more lurid as successive weeks rolled by.

There were two factors which added fuel to the flames. One was the 'poltergeist's new accusation, constantly repeated via rappings in answer to direct questions, that William Kent had actually murdered Fanny in her last illness by lacing her drinks with poison, so that he could get his hands on her not unsubstantial money, and that the ghost was now not William's first wife, but Fanny herself, demanding justice from beyond the grave. (William had not, in fact, murdered her at all, but in the days before forensic science, both guilt and innocence in these and similar cases were more difficult to prove.) Secondly, the churches became involved, in the persons of John Moore, an Anglican clergyman but a Methodist sympathiser, and Stephen Aldrich, another Anglican minister, but one who disliked both Methodism and the supernatural. The Methodist movement stemmed from the religious activity of John and Charles Wesley in 1738 and quickly found favour with the working poor, who were largely neglected by the state Church, and who responded to the emotional conviction with which John Wesley in particular spread his message about the evils of materialism and the desirability of personal salvation through self-discipline and prayer. 'Catch on fire with enthusiasm', he said at one point, 'and people will come from miles to watch you burn.' The Anglican establishment, both ecclesiastical and secular, disliked this appeal to the emotions, which characterised early Methodist gatherings – 'enthusiasm' they called it, and thus 'enthusiasm' in certain mouths became both a dirty word and a rallying cry to defend the established order – and, fairly or not, early Methodists were credited with a strong belief in all aspects of the supernatural, following, it was maintained, where John Wesley himself had led.

The English in general, and indeed most of the men of learning in Europe, have given up all accounts of witches and apparitions as mere old wives' fables. I am sorry for it, and I willingly take this opportunity of entering my solemn protest against this violent compliment which so many that believe the Bible pay to those who do not believe it. I owe them no such service. I take knowledge that these are at the bottom of the outcry which has been raised, and with such insolence spread through the land, in direct opposition, not only to the Bible, but to the suffrage of the wisest and the best of men in all ages and nations. They well know (whether

Christians know it or not) that the giving up of witchcraft is in effect giving up the Bible. With my latest breath I will bear testimony against giving up to infidels one great proof of the invisible world: I mean that of witchcraft and apparitions, confirmed by the testimony of all ages.[20]

John Moore, a young man in his late twenties, first came across the Cock Lane 'poltergeist' in December 1761, and from then until February 1762 he remained more or less convinced that the noises in the Parsons' house did indeed emanate from the late Fanny Kent's unhappy spirit and that her revelation that she had been murdered by William was simple truth. I say 'more or less convinced' because as evidence mounted that the phenomena were fraudulent and were being produced by one of Parsons's daughters, Elizabeth (known as 'Betty'), Moore found himself in an increasingly awkward position. If the episode turned out to be a hoax, he would look a fool and, in addition, bring his Methodist sympathies into further disrepute. Moreover, if the 'poltergeist' were false, so too were its accusations of murder, levelled against William Kent, and that outcome would bring Moore within the purview of the law and ruin both his character and his career. So he stuck to his support for the Parsons as long as he could, until arrest and imprisonment cured him of his intransigence.

Meanwhile, Stephen Aldrich had been pursuing his intention to expose Parsons and his daughter, while London divided itself between the *bien pensants* who agreed with him and the mob, well titillated by its own inclinations and a deluge of newspaper reports, which did not. The end of the affair – arrest and conviction for many of the principals, including Moore and one of his main supporters, and vindication for William Kent and Stephen Aldrich – indicated once again the gulf that appeared to exist between those who were prepared to accept the reality of the Otherworld and its manifestations, and those who were not. Both parties included the educated class. Thus, Joseph Addison expressed himself highly dubious: 'When I consider the question whether there are such persons in the world as those we call witches, my mind is divided between the two opposite opinions; or rather (to speak my thoughts freely) I believe in general that there is and has been such a thing as witchcraft, but at the same time can give no credit to any particular instance of it'; while William Blackstone, famous for his systematic description of and commentary on English law, tentatively agreed with Wesley. 'To deny the possibility, nay, the actual existence of witchcraft and sorcery, is at once flatly to contradict the revealed word of God in various passages both of the Old and New Testament, and the thing itself is a truth to which every nation in the world hath, in its turn, borne testimony by either example seemingly well attested or by prohibitory laws, which at least suppose the possibility of a commerce with evil spirits.'[21] But what the Cock Lane episode also illustrated was the appetite for marvels, wonders, and astonishment which pervaded the reading public and made people eager, almost regardless of their personal beliefs, to read any account, true, false, or dubious, of preternatural happenings in their midst.

Much of this eagerness was satisfied via private letters and cheap pamphlets. A poltergeist disturbance in the village of Sandfeldt in the Duchy of Mecklenburg-Schwerin from 26 January to 30 March 1722, for example, was recorded by Heinrich Hänell, an estate manager, on the instructions of his employer, and his words were quickly published under the title 'Curious and Truthful Report or "Diary" of a Ghost and Poltergeist'. Hänell had witnessed many of the phenomena himself, as well as gathering information from twenty-seven other witnesses whose names are attached to his account. Many of the incidents can be paralleled from elsewhere, although they also have their individual characteristics. On 14 February, for example, the entity started throwing things around early in the morning, its violence increasing in intensity to the extent that by the time Hans and Katharina Dunckelmann, the objects of its attention, went to confession in the afternoon, people were afraid that everything in the house would be destroyed. There was, however, one lighter moment. A wooden box for keeping meat was torn from the kitchen ceiling and thrown violently to the floor where it burst open, revealing its contents – a tasty goose. A cat seized hold of it and ran off, pursued by the family children, who succeeded in rescuing what was clearly intended to be a human dinner. But less amusingly, on 4 March one of the young girls was in the garden and heard a voice say 'Lend me a jug.' She did so and a little later her mother, who was in the kitchen, heard the voice from the garden say 'Cheers!' as though in acknowledgement of a toast, and then the jug was thrown back through the window, full of faeces.[22]

Another diary of poltergeist activity is that of William Dyer, an accountant from Bristol, which was later published in pamphlet form by a friend of his, Henry Durbin. Reports also appeared in the local newspapers and caused quite a sensation at the time. Now, Dyer was a Pietist, belonging to a broad movement within Protestantism which emphasised personal and private devotion and practical Christianity, and was thus more closely aligned by religious temperament with the Methodist confession than with the Anglican Church. It seems that between November 1761 and December 1762, the landlord of the Lamb Inn and his family were subjected to rappings and scratchings, particularly at night. These were then perceived to be attempts at intelligible communication, and in answer to questions put by Henry Durbin and others, revealed that the source was a spirit doing the bidding of a local witch who had a grudge against Mr Giles, the landlord, and was revenging herself by having her spirit torment his children. An attempt at exorcism was carried out by a Methodist-trained curate and had a brief temporary effect; counter-magic was also tried by the family at the suggestion of a cunning woman, but its effect was inconclusive, and then Giles's younger daughter began to see visions of a witch. Giles himself caught sight of something similar in May, but not long after fell sick and died, his death being attributed by Dyer not to natural, but to preternatural causes, a conclusion not altogether at odds with his religious faith, although actually Dyer was not entirely convinced by every aspect of the case.

However, just as the Dunckelmanns had been troubled by a ghost and a poltergeist (or a poltergeist which acted partly like itself and partly like a ghost), the Giles family had to endure more than scratching and rapping; for quite early in the disturbance, heavy objects were moved, overturned, and thrown, and the children were pricked with pins and bitten upon the neck and hand. One particularly notable event happened on 5 January 1762.

> I went up, and the nurse went up to show me where the great knockings were last night, by the children's bed. On my left hand was a sash window. About three feet from the window was a case of drawers, [and] on the drawers stood a wine glass which I saw glitter in the sun, and was astonished to see it rise from the drawers without hands. It rose gradually about a foot, perpendicularly from the drawers. Then the glass seemed to stand, and thereupon inclined backwards, as if a hand had held it. It was then flung with violence about five feet and struck the nurse on the hip a hard blow, so that I heard it give a loud report … There was no person near the drawers when it rose. The children were standing by me, who saw it and ran to the other end of the room, fearing it would be flung at them, as things generally were. I was so amazed at it that I said, 'Do I see what I see?' I then thought I would examine the glass, whether there were any wires or hairs tied to it. I then took up the glass from the floor and found no wires nor anything else. But the glass was quite whole, except that the foot of it was broken, as if pincers had pinched it all round. This was about nine in the morning, clear daylight, close by a sash window.[23]

There were, of course, sceptics as well as believers. London was being fascinated, to an extent which worried the authorities, by the Cock Lane ghost and its final exposure as a hoax will not have been unknown to the larger country. But

Bristol was divided, partly because some people accepted the current notion that witches and ghouls and demons were mere superstition, partly because others were by no means so sure and noted that efforts to prove imposture in the Giles affair came to nothing, and partly because Bristol found itself at the beginning of a new religious convulsion involving Trinitarians and Unitarians, a disagreement which may have informed some of the questions put to the 'poltergeist', whose answers appeared not only to support belief in angels and demons, but also the doctrine of Trinitarianism. Suspicion that the whole affair was merely a hoax did not disappear under the additional burden of belief in witchcraft, which acceptance of the reality of the episode clearly demanded. But while there was enough scepticism to make Durbin reluctant to publish his version of events until they had long been over, there was also sufficient acknowledgement of Dyer's personal probity – not to mention many people's willingness to accept such incidents as validation of the reading of biblical texts which gave substance to the existence of the Otherworld – to make the Giles' long-lasting disturbance an important touchstone of contemporary attitudes towards non-materialistic explanations of Nature and people's understanding of what that explanation entailed for their personal experience of it.[24]

These pamphlet accounts reached wide audiences, not perhaps as widely as newspapers, which were actually rather expensive, but widely enough to make their intended impact, even though they were often battling against a press which was as willing to dismiss the very notion of the Otherworld as it was ready to make cash from people's eagerness to be told stories based on the Otherworld's existence. 'The ridiculous notion of witches and witchcraft still prevails amongst the lower sort of people,' sneered the *Reading Mercury* on 15 March 1773, while on 16 March 1790 the *Leeds Intelligencer* reported an incident which, expressed as it was in a similar supercilious fashion, nevertheless bore witness to the sway the Otherworld still exercised over those outwith the magic circle of would-be *bien pensants*.

A carrier, between Aldstone and Penrith, lately had some goods stolen out of his wagon. In order to detect the thief, he made a pilgrimage to Rumbles Moor near Skipton in Craven, to consult the wise man who resides there, and who, having received the carrier's offering, dismissed him with the consolatory assurance that if the thief did not restore the property before a certain day – 'it should be the worse for him!' The carrier's reports of these oracular words had a wonderful and, as it happened, a beneficial effect on his neighbours ... They having wisdom enough to know that in order to effect this, the wise man must inevitable raise the Devil, and the Devil, through vexation, would most probably raise the wind, they loaded the thatched roofs of their houses with harrows, etc. which prevented the fatal consequences of a violent hurricane that came on in the night, and was felt in most parts of the kingdom. There can be no doubt that this circumstance will add considerably to the high opinion already entertained of the wise Robin of Rumbles Moor.[25]

To this larger group were addressed Hänell's and Durbin's pamphlets, and another in 1772 on what the anonymous author calls 'the astonishing transactions at Stockwell, in the county of Surrey'. Clearly there had been a recent spate of such accounts, because the author begins with a disclaimer: 'the events [to be described] are of so strange and singular a nature, that we cannot be at all surprised the public should be doubtful of the truth of them, *more especially as there has been too many impositions of this sort*'.[26] The probity of witnesses having been asserted, the story then begins. In essence, it is a tale of noises, broken glass and crockery, objects falling from shelves or being apported, furniture tumbling about, and a possible attempt at fire-raising when a lantern fell and spilled its oil on the floor, followed by the basket of coals' being upset and the rolling of the coals round the room. All this happened in the house of an elderly woman, Mrs Golding, and in the frequent presence of her twenty-year-old maid, Ann Robinson, very recently come into her employment. Ann remained remarkably calm throughout the whole episode. 'With uncommon coolness of temper, [she] advised her mistress not to be alarmed or uneasy, as she said these things could not be helped. Thus she argued as if they were common occurrences which must happen in every family', a reaction which led both Mrs Golding and her niece's husband 'to think she was not altogether so unconcerned as she appeared to be' – that is to say, they suspected she was involved either in producing the phenomena or being the focus of them. (One is reminded to some extent of the Perreauds' maid and her amicable relationship with their poltergeist.) Certainly it seems to have been true that when Ann was away from the house, the disturbances ceased. But blame for them (if we can talk of 'blame' in these circumstances) was attached, not to Ann but to Mrs Golding herself by Richard Fowler, 'an honest, industrious, and sober man' who lived almost opposite Mrs Golding's niece and with whom Mrs Golding and her maid had sought refuge from their afflictions, only to bring those afflictions with them. Fowler therefore

desired she would quit his house, but first begged her to consider within herself, for her own and the public sake, whether or not she had not been guilty of some atrocious crime, for which Providence was determined to pursue her on this side

174

the grave. For he could not help thinking she was the object that was to be made an example to posterity by the all-seeing eye of Providence for crimes which but too often none but that Providence can penetrate, and by such means as these bring to light. Thus was this poor gentlewoman's measure of affliction complete, not only to have undergone all which has been related, but to have added to it the character of a bad and wicked woman, when till this time she was esteemed as a most deserving person.[27]

This notion that ghostly or poltergeist affliction may be the result of some sin, perhaps not immediately connected with the disturbances of those involved, can be seen again in an episode reported in a series of private letters from 1771 and further narratives written for the benefit of the children of the woman most concerned.[28] Mary Jervis married William Ricketts in 1757, and when he went away on business to the West Indies in 1769, Mary chose to stay at home in Hampshire with their three young children. From 1765 there had been evidence of unexplained phenomena in the new house into which they had all moved in January that year: a ghostly figure, groans, rustling silk, and slamming doors. The noises continued, but thorough investigation could not account for them, and in a letter to her husband, Mary confessed, 'you know how much the notion of haunted houses is exploded, and how careful any man would be of asserting it, and in that I think them right. As for myself, I am not ashamed to pronounce that it must proceed from a supernatural cause.' Even so, a reward was posted, on the assumption that the whole thing was a hoax.

Whereas some evil disposed person or persons have for several months frequently made divers kinds of noises in the mansion house occupied by Mrs. Ricketts at Hinton Ampner, this is to give notice that if any person or persons will discover the author or authors thereof to me, such person or persons shall receive a reward of fifty guineas, to be paid on the conviction of the offenders: or if any person concerned in making such noises will discover his or her accomplice or accomplices therein, such person shall be pardoned and be entitled to the same reward, to be paid on conviction of the offender.

September 20, 1771.   John Sainsbury

The inducement, however, produced nothing and the noises continued regardless. According to Mary's own memorandum to her children, written in 1772, there had been sightings of more than one ghost, and the knockings and bangings were often accompanied by articulate sounds of a female voice, answered by two male voices. No matter how often members of the household switched rooms and sat up late at night in hope of catching out the sources of annoyance, not a thing nor a person was uncovered, and the family pets, a cat and a dog, began to give evidence of being much afraid, their fear being evidence, commonly found elsewhere, that a paranormal presence had made itself felt to their heightened sensibilities. Indeed, so frightening had been the whole household's extended experience that Mary Ricketts left the house and never returned. It was occupied by another family, but they too left after a year and the place was left deserted.

Now, as we remarked, the Stockwell affair raised the question of whether or not Mrs Golding was being punished for some sin or offence she had forgotten or wanted to keep secret. Similarly, the servants in Mary Ricketts's house, while acknowledging that she was a fine woman and a good employer, nevertheless wondered about the cause of the noises.

> Lucy said, 'God knows whether these noises were not in consequence of their sins.'
>
> [Martha Jervis] replied, 'What did you suppose they were guilty of?'
>
> She said, 'God knows whether she had a child and killed it, but I cannot say. It is not for us to suspect them, God knows.'
>
> She spoke of Mrs Ricketts in the highest terms and with many tears; said she did so much good in the neighbourhood that is was very unlikely any should seek to drive her away, above all, her servants, who loved her and were in perfect harmony with each other.[29]

The 'she' here refers not to Mary Ricketts, but to an earlier housekeeper, Sarah Parfait, who, according to this speculative gossip, may have had an illegitimate child by her then employer. So whether the servants were suggesting that the ghost of that employer was trying to drive Mary Ricketts out of the house – why would he? – or that some of Mary's own servants were trying to do so by manufacturing the phenomena – why should they want to do either? – one cannot be altogether sure. What is interesting from our point of view is the servants' apparent acceptance of the reality of ghosts, and the link they made between haunting and previous sin.[30]

But while clergymen and private individuals were keen to put on record their experiences, whether first- or second-hand, of ghostly visits and poltergeist-like disturbances, secular 'men of science' were no less eager to do the same. John Beaumont, for example, a surgeon with a particular bent for geology, and a Fellow of the Royal Society since 1685, issued a detailed discussion of 'spirits, apparitions, witchcrafts, and other magical practices' in 1704, with a view to refuting the Dutch clergyman Balthasar Bekker, who had attacked belief in magic, witchcraft, and demonic possession in his *Die Betoverde Weereld* ('The World Bewitched') in 1691, and had proved a potent influence ever since, especially in France and Germany. Beamont noted that 'last year' (i.e. 1704), at Butley near Glastonbury, a Mr Pope, whose teenage son was subject to fits and to the sight and sound of spirits during those fits, suffered the loss of his house and ox-stall and heaps of wheat from an unexplained fire, just as had been foretold by his son's visionary spirits; 'and stones were seen to come in at the windows in the daytime, no man perceiving from what hand they came'. Now of course this sounds like possible arson with stone-throwing attached, as Beaumont himself acknowledges: 'If any man can make out that all these things were done by trick and contrivance, as some say they were, they may do well to satisfy the world of it.'[31] Not, perhaps, the most convincing example he could have chosen. Somewhat better would have been a series of incidents on Canvey Island in 1709. An isolated farmhouse there was plagued by unaccountable noises and the violent opening and shutting of doors. A local cunning man was called in to exorcise what was commonly supposed to be the ghost of the previous owner – notice the resort to magic rather than the Church – but his efforts were unsuccessful and the ghost of a woman was heard, loud noises continued, and the spectre of the dead owner 'having on a grey coat such as he was used to wear in his life-time' was seen more than once. Then poltergeist-like behaviour began to happen. A dead chicken was hurled into the hall, loud knocking and rattling followed, and glass kept being smashed.

Thus far it would not be difficult to attribute some of these phenomena to natural (that is, human) causes, although some of the glass-breaking would have been difficult to achieve by such means. One episode, however, selected by Gauld and Cornell as especially peculiar, casts doubt on the notion that it could have been perpetrated by a hoaxer or maliciously intentioned individual.

Two of the company, standing in the kitchen, the others in the hall and elsewhere, they saw a stone with some dirt and straws upon it, the bigness of a turkey egg, come as from the crevice of the fore door, which as the door was close shut, one could not thrust a small hazelnut through. I say, come 'as from', not 'in' of the crevice because one of the persons who was not above half a yard from it, and looking that way, discerned it not till 'twas an inch within side (so that how it came there we have no account), but closely observing its progress afterwards clearly saw it to take a kind of half circle, but so slow as though its motion had proceeded from a regular piece of clockwork: and then gently, as if let down by a spring, descend to the ground about a foot and a half from the said crevice. This stone was also hot, and being presently taken up by the person next to it in her apron, she called Mr Lord who, with the other company, came, and all feeling it, found it too hot to grasp in the hand. Mr Lord then said, 'Consider this stone. This is enough to convince anyone. For besides the amazing circumstance how it came in, and its being hot, this straw and dirt upon it, could not be in the form you see it had it been heated by a material fire.'[32]

The disturbances ended the next day with the appearance of one of the ghosts, the man with the grey coat, who so terrified the young maidservant who had been working in the house that she fell into a fit and vomited blood for two or three hours.

These episodes involving spirits of some kind as well as poltergeist-like phenomena are especially common during the first half of the century. In 1710 Anne Haltridge, a widow living on Islandmagee, a peninsula on the east coast of Antrim, had stones and turf thrown at her bed. The bedclothes were pulled off too, but a careful search revealed no obvious cause. Then, three months later, in December, she was visited by a spirit in the form of a twelve-year-old boy who was able to speak, because he had a conversation with one of the servants, and was also able to wield a sword, break windows, and make away with a turkey-cock. (Was this just a mischievous child? If so, what was he doing in Mrs Haltridge's house and where had he come from? Islandmagee was quite an isolated place at the time and he was not a local, otherwise people would have recognised him.) His importance to the anecdote is that everyone took him to be a spirit, not a human, for which there must have been some reason. Adults are not stupid and do not mistake real children for non-human entities unless there is something about the child which makes them doubt their immediate senses. So the people of Islandmagee were not altogether surprised when, in the course of his mischief-making, this child prophesied Mrs Haltridge's imminent death, and the family suffered further distressing signs until the middle of February 1711 when suddenly Mrs Haltridge complained of a violent pain, as though a knife had been stuck in her back. A week later she was dead, and the prophecy had been fulfilled. After the funeral, a young woman by the name of Mary Dunbar came to sit with Mrs Haltridge's daughter-in-law and was told the local gossip that the cause of Mrs Haltridge's death had been malicious witchcraft. Signs that the house was still infested with something untoward then appeared in the form of clothes' being scattered through the rooms and an apron tied up with a number of magical knots. Whereupon Mary Dunbar fell into a fit and declared she was being tormented by three women, and then by seven or eight whose names she gave. A trial for witchcraft followed, at the end of which one of the two judges made it clear he was sceptical of the whole business, while the other made it equally plain he believed it to be true. The jury agreed and brought in a verdict of guilty.[33]

One of the features of these cases, however, is the doubt which attends many of their circumstances, especially anent the noises. Rustling, tapping, and sometimes banging can be accounted for entirely naturally – although in acknowledging this, we must be careful to avoid the alluring phrase 'must have been' – and so the noises, like some incidents of stone-throwing and glass-breaking, need to be considered in relation to natural events or a malicious prank before we include them in the category 'beyond the ordinary' or 'inexplicable'. A very good example of this is the noisy poltergeist of Cambridge Castle, experienced by Simon Ockley in the spring of 1718. Ockley was Professor of Arabic in the university and at the time had been put in prison for debt. Over a period of about three weeks he heard tapping, banging, rustling, thumping, whistling, and the sound of inarticulate voices. 'I cannot yet be persuaded that he is a ludicrous [playful] spirit', Ockley wrote to a friend, 'nor the soul of any person deceased. At present I take him to be a malignant evil genius [spirit] of the same sort I met with in Hand Alley, for the sounds and his manner are very much the same. I believe he would speak but cannot.'[34] Any such noises in a large, rambling edifice such as a castle may be explained away, if that is what one wishes to do, although it is worth noting that it has been suggested that spirit noises, while perhaps resembling those made by natural means, are actually different in quality. 'Spirit sounds are usually of a peculiar character. They have an intensity and a character of their own, and, notwithstanding their great variety, can hardly be mistaken, so that they are not easily confused with common noises, such as the creaking of wood, the crackling of a fire, or the ticking of a clock. Spirit raps are clear and sharp, sometimes soft and light.'[35] What is interesting here is that a highly educated man did not turn to natural explanation but, having dismissed the idea that the source of his noises might be a kind of goblin or a ghost, decided upon an evil spirit as a possible explanation partly, at any rate, because he had had a similar experience before and in a different place. It is also interesting that Ockley had the impression the entity was trying to speak intelligibly. John and Anne Spencer have observed that 'poltergeists do not seem to come with well-developed voices, but have to nurture them, usually from small noises and whistles'; so it may be that Ockley's impression is understandable.

The eighteenth century, then, exhibits the kind of split personality illustrated by Rousseau's comment on Paris: there is a fine outward show of rationalism, scepticism, caution, and disbelief from the smaller, more privileged sections of society, frequently tempered by some degree of credulity and adherence to traditional modes of thought, and the more widespread continuance of belief in and acceptance of those traditions, though often modified by reluctance to credit what was seen and heard, or reported as seen and heard. Outright doubters were not yet in the majority – perhaps they never would be, if modern surveys of people's attitudes towards ghosts, for example, can be trusted – and there was certainly a growing willingness among the educated, not only to fight religious battles with the help of evidence drawn from stories about ghosts, poltergeists, demons, and spirits of all kinds, but also to use these stories in a relatively detached frame of mind as raw data in the larger business of inquiring into the composition, working, and potentiality of created Nature. The invention of the magic lantern and similar devices not only enthralled and frightened audiences in Paris, London, and elsewhere: it also showed how ghostly apparitions might be manufactured and thus vividly strengthened the growing tendency of the period to suggest or hope that a natural explanation might be found for everything. Indeed, it helped substantially to transform what had hitherto been the serious arts of the occult sciences into mere entertainment, banishing them from the scholar's study and laboratory to public places of amusement, and thus degrading their seriousness in the eyes and minds of the paying audience. But phantom-creating devices raised a very old question, too, one which had troubled the Middle Ages and been the subject of heated discussion in the late Renaissance: are ghosts, poltergeists, demons, and their activities real or apparent? Do they exist 'out there' or only in the minds of those who experience them?

Terry Castle asks the question and develops its implications. 'Promoters like Robertson and Philipstal prefaced their shows with popular rationalist arguments: real spectres did not exist, they said; supposed apparitions were merely "l'effet bizarre de l'imagination". Nonetheless, the phantoms they subsequently produced had a strangely objective presence. They floated before the eye just like real ghosts, and in a crazy way they *were* real ghosts. That is to say, they were not mere effects of imagination: they were indisputably there; one saw them as clearly as any other object of sense.'[36] Sir Walter Scott, too, latches on to one aspect of this question when he notes the impression skilled conjurors might have on their audiences, and the part played by an individual's stubborn vanity in not wanting to admit he or she has been duped and is therefore more open to reiterating his or her belief in the reality of seemingly paranormal experiences.

Invisible beings will appear less surprising if we consider the common feats of jugglers, or professors of legerdemain, and recollect that it is only the frequent exhibition of such powers which reconciles us to them as matters of course, although they are wonders at which in our fathers' time men would have cried out either sorcery or miracles. The spectator also, who has been himself duped, makes no very respectable appearance when convicted of his error; and thence, if too candid to add to the evidence of supernatural agency, is yet unwilling to stand convicted by cross-examination of having been imposed on, and unconsciously becomes disposed rather to colour more highly than the truth than acquiesce in an explanation resting on his having been too hasty a believer. Very often, too, the detection depends upon the combination of certain circumstances, which, apprehended, necessarily explain the whole story.[37]

In fact, however, the way forward for ghost, poltergeist, demon, and spirit detection and explanation would not lie in going up the cul-de-sac of fraud or theatrical illusion. Rather, it would turn away from the possibility of multiple worlds or universes and venture into the realm of Madness, where hallucination, self-deception, and persuasive imagination governed perception and distorted reality, or into that of the inner Mind, whose wayward behaviours and intricate, winding paths would provide almost endless opportunities for ever more detailed exploration and apparent conquest, matching those endeavours already in progress to dissect, map, record, and conquer the physical world.[38]

9

The Gradgrind Century, 1806–1899

The reality of ghosts and spirits was not in question for many in the nineteenth century, and speculation on the subject would have been considered a waste of time, indeed, worse than waste: a profligate and unnecessary expenditure of one's time on balderdash. Facts, facts, facts were what interested Charles Dickens's Mr Gradgrind, and his bluff, one might almost say brutal, approach to education and, by extension, to the conduct of life in general may be taken as typical of such a strand of thought in the new technology-dominated era. 'It may be laid down as a general maxim', wrote Charles Ollier, one of the period's influential publishers and editors, 'that anyone who thinks he has seen a ghost, may take the vision as a symptom that his bodily health is deranged. Let him, therefore, seek medical advice, and, ten to one, the spectre will no more haunt him. To see a ghost is, ipso facto, to be a subject for the physician.' Not that Ollier attributed ghosts entirely to mental illness, despite his significant use of the word 'deranged'.

> The delusions of ghost-craft [he added] arise from a variety of causes. Some of them are accidental and natural, such as visual deceptions, when 'the eyes are made the fools of the other senses', of which nearly every human being must have had experience. Others are brought about by morbific agency, not a few by imposture and confederacy, more by fear, and many by the wilfulness of credulity in ghost-seers themselves … Such preposterous deceptions would not arise were human beings, when in their infancy, carefully protected from the inoculation of superstitious ideas. That which is impressed on the brain in childhood can hardly ever be effaced. In after years reason may contradict it, but there it remains

indelibly fixed on the sensorium, and in moments of moral or physical debility, its power becomes dominant ... The absurdity, how great soever, becomes part and parcel of his moral being. The tree must grow as the twig is bent.[1]

The search for explanations of Otherworld manifestations, which would, in effect, explain them away, and the Otherworld along with them, proceeded apace as technological innovation captured the hearts and minds of the nineteenth century, and discoveries in the realms of the natural sciences at once increased the size and complexity of the created universe, while suggesting, if only by implication, that this was in fact the only universe and that other modes of existence were delusional and fantastic. A weighty new faith was thus being created, whose priests would entertain no deviation from or questioning of their creed. But while the physical benefits streaming from the good works of this creed were undeniable and attracted many into the ranks of its followers, the prospect of a godless universe – what Tennyson called 'the faithless coldness of the times' – also repelled and left many others gloomy with an incoherent sense of loss and lack of direction.

One can hear their voice in Tennyson's *In Memoriam*:

I trust I have not wasted breath:
I think we are not wholly brain,
Magnetic mockeries ...
(Canto 120)

My own dim life should teach me this,
That life shall live for evermore,
Else earth is darkness at the core,
And dust and ashes all that is;
(Canto 34)

The determination to find some way back to a connection with the dead, and hence to a renewal of confidence that this life and this universe are not the only ones, but that others, different and better in kind, not only exist but may be contacted, informs the Poet Laureate's plangent expressions of loss and abandonment.

If e'er when faith had fall'n asleep,
I heard a voice 'believe no more'
And heard an ever-breaking shore

That tumbled in the Godless deep;

A warmth within the breast would melt
The freezing reason's colder part,
And like a man in wrath the heart
Stood up and answered, 'I have felt.'
(Canto 124)

I held it truth, with him who sings
To one clear harp in divers tones,
That men may rise on stepping-stones
Of their dead selves to higher things.
(Canto 1)

Tennyson was writing these verses between 1833, when the death of his friend Arthur Hallam inspired the poem, and 1850, when the revised and expanded work was published. Within these years, the old rakish, libertine monarchy in Britain had given way to the more sedate and serious rule of Victoria, while in France, Germany, and Italy, the period 1830–48 was a time of instability, revolutions, and conservative backlash. Change and uncertainty seemed to have invaded almost every aspect of human life; but curiously enough the stream of reports about poltergeist activity (not to mention haunting in general) decreased not an iota and, indeed, presented a kind of consistency to any interested audience, because poltergeists continued to disturb, annoy, and attack in very much the same ways as they had ever done. So what makes them interesting at this stage is not their almost invariable lithobolia, or destruction of windows and crockery, and moving of heavy objects, nor indeed their slight variations on the theme of mischief-making, but the separate and local peculiarities attendant on their behaviour; and here we shall see certain changes as the century wears on.

During the early years, ghosts or spirits are frequently blamed for the poltergeists' disturbances. In November 1806, for example, Augustus Hahn, a councillor in the service of Prince Hohenloe, was staying in the castle of Slawensik in what is now Poland with an old friend, Karl Kern. For three days nothing untoward happened, but then the two were bombarded by pieces of lime plaster from the ceiling, loud noises, and flying objects, mostly small. Two Bavarian officers who came to stay later were equally frightened; but what made the incident somewhat different from the usual was Kern's seeing a ghost in the bedroom mirror, which he described as a white female figure. 'She was in front of his own image, which he distinctly saw behind her. At first he could not believe his eyes. He thought it must be fancy … but when he saw that the eyes of the figure moved and looked into his, a shudder had seized him and he had turned away.' He was able to give further details. 'The features of the apparition were very old, but not gloomy or morose; the expression indeed was rather that of indifference; but the face was very pale, and the head was wrapped in a cloth which left only the features visible.' Who she was or could have been was never resolved, even though years later, when the castle had been damaged by lightning, a skeleton was discovered among the rubble. It was, however, the skeleton of a man and so nothing to do with the case. The solemn lady, however, was not the only ghost. Kern also saw a white dog following Hahn as he came back to the castle one day, but Hahn said he himself had seen nothing, although he had heard the sound of a dog's paws on the ground behind him. But the oddest incident involved Kern's servant, a steady middle-aged man, who was chatting to his master one evening when he saw a jug of beer rise from the table, pour its contents into a glass, and then put itself back on the table, while an invisible hand lifted the glass and an invisible mouth emptied it, after which the glass was replaced on the table. No beer was found on the floor afterwards. (Clearly both Kern and his man had looked for it.) These events, wrote Hahn in 1808, happened exactly as he saw and heard them. 'From beginning to end I observed them with the most entire self-possession. I had no fear, nor the slightest tendency to it. Yet the whole thing remains to me perfectly inexplicable.'

Of course people did make suggestions. Kern, they said, was 'a dexterous juggler, who contrived to throw dust in the eyes of his friend'; or Hahn and Kern were drunk every evening and therefore saw nothing but their own imaginings. Both these suggestions Hahn repudiates and they are, in fact, quite inadequate to explain the phenomena, as Gauld and Cornell observe anent this and several other cases. But people also mentioned 'goblins' and both Hahn and Kern joked that the castle must be haunted, having become so used to the phenomena after suffering them for several weeks that they felt able to treat them with a degree of lightness.[2] Ghosts, however, rather than goblins or demons were the preferred nineteenth-century explanations for weird or unaccustomed noises and sights. So we find that a ghost also appears in a case from Iceland in 1807. A boat belonging to the minister of Garpsdal was smashed, his front door broken, the doors of the village sheep-houses damaged, and various other breakages within the minister's house done with increasing vehemence. Most of this happened in broad daylight and was accompanied by the sight of a woman whom everyone took to be a spirit. A female apparition also appeared in the English village of Sampford Peverell in 1810, accompanied by strange noises, and these noises continued in the house of one John Chave. If someone went upstairs and stamped on the floor, the stamping was repeated and might well follow people about. Two women were badly assaulted during the night 'by an invisible agency … These blows left great soreness and visible marks.' A large iron candlestick was thrown at John's head, and a sword 'which they had placed near them on the foot of the bed, with a large folio Testament placed on it, was thrown violently against the wall, seven feet away'. The sword lay on the ground, and then hovered in mid-air before falling to the floor again. Ghostly footsteps were heard by the local minister, Caleb Cotton, who published a pamphlet on this episode later the same year, and he was quite convinced, in the face of protestations by the landlord who had rented the house to John Chave that the noises were fabricated, that the incident was not a hoax. 'If these nocturnal and diurnal visitations are the effect of a plot', he observed, 'the agents are marvellously secret and indefatigable. It has been going on more than three years; and if it be the result of human machination, there must be more than sixty persons concerned in it.' A reward of £250, he added, had been offered to anyone who could uncover such a conspiracy, and after nearly two years no one had come forward.[3]

In 1817 it was a witch who made an appearance in a poltergeist case. This is the 'Bell Witch' affair and it took place on a farm in Tennessee where John Bell lived with his wife Lucy and their nine children. The poltergeist concerned began its disturbance with knocks and scrapings, but these soon graduated to loud noises, and lithobolia, pulling of bedclothes, and physical assault followed not long after. It seemed as though the entity was concentrating much of its hostile attention on one of the children, twelve-year-old Betsy, and it was also developing a voice which eventually turned from throttled gasps into articulate sentences spoken in not one, but a variety of voices. In one, it said it was a disturbed and unhappy spirit, but then identified itself as a dead Indian, a witch called Kate Batts, and four of the witch's attendant spirits, and under this guise began to persecute John Bell to such an extent that 'she' made him seriously ill. For three years 'she' persisted, and then John Bell died, and after lingering for another twelve months 'she' finally disappeared in a cloud of smoke from the chimney, with the promise, 'I am going and will be gone for seven years. Goodbye to all!'[4]

The degree of malice exhibited by the Bells' poltergeist is somewhat unusual and makes one think that in a Catholic environment it could well have been attributed to a demon rather than a witch. Certainly this is so in the case of St Jean-Marie-Baptiste Vianney, the curé d'Ars. Ars was a small village near Lyon during the nineteenth century, and its curé at the time a man of remarkable faith and steadfastness in the performance of his priestly office. He was someone of complete personal integrity, and therefore when he tells us about the molestations to which he was subjected by some kind of hostile entity, we may take it he was telling the truth without exaggeration or modification of any kind.[5] His troubles began in the winter of 1824. Noises, banging, ripping of bed-curtains: these were standard poltergeist-like manifestations. The noises were very loud. André Verchère, the village wheelwright, accepted the curé's invitation to spend a night in the presbytery and later deposed that 'I was unable to sleep. At about one o'clock I heard a violent shaking of the handle and lock of the front door. At the same time heavy blows were struck, as if with a club, against the same door, whilst within the presbytery there was a terrific din, like the rumbling of several carts. I seized my gun and rushed to the window, which I threw open. I looked out but saw nothing. For nearly a quarter of an hour the house shook.' Other visitors, however, heard nothing. 1824, however, was not the first time the presbytery had been the focus of these attentions. Monsieur Vianney's sister stayed there briefly in 1820, and later told the Procès de l'Ordinaire for her brother's canonisation that 'a tremendous noise was produced apparently close to my bed, as if five or six men had been striking heavy blows upon the table or the cupboard. I was terrified and got up. I had strength enough to light a lamp, when I discovered that everything was in perfect order. I said to myself, "I must have been dreaming." So I returned to bed, but no sooner had I lain down than the noises began again.' Various other people also heard dreadful noises in 1832 and in 1838, and indeed they were still audible four years after that. So it appears that Monsieur Vianney suffered over a very long period of time from something specifically aiming its hostility in his direction. The curé, however, bore it all with patience and although he jokingly called this entity *le grappin* ('the grappling hook'), he knew he meant a demon or the Devil himself.[6]

What these accounts have in common, apart from their poltergeistery, is clerical involvement, either as the object of mischief or reporters of it, or both, and people's acceptance that the disturbances emanated from the Otherworld, features which at first glance suggest these accounts could just as well have been written in the sixteenth or seventeenth centuries. Scepticism there was, of course, and self-doubt, but we have noted these reactions in cases from the earlier centuries too, so there is nothing in either of these reservations to suggest that the incidents were taking place in the 1800s, as opposed to earlier decades. For the first half of the century, however, Europe was convulsed either by war or by revolution, while industrialisation was making or at least contributing to profound changes in demography, and individual events such as the great cholera epidemic of 1832 which swept through Europe, killing thousands in its progress, joined hands with war in creating an atmosphere redolent of fear, loss, and abandonment. It is expressed (once again) by Tennyson's *In Memoriam*.

> Are God and Nature then at strife,
> That Nature lends such evil dreams?
> So careful of the type she seems,
> So careless of the single life …
>
> 'So careful of the type?' but no.
> From scarped cliff and quarried stone
> She cries, 'A thousand types are gone:
> I care for nothing, all shall go …'
> (Cantos 55, 56)

In such a frame of mind, people were eager to cling on to what they knew, and to have reassurance that, however dire and short this life might be, their consciousness of being a live individual was not subject, like the body, to decay, but went on, pressed ahead onwards and (they might hope) upwards, as the teachings of their various religious faiths assured them was the case. Such, for example, is the interpretation placed on events in Willington Mill by Edmund Procter, son of Joseph Procter, in 1842. He was reporting certain incidents, based on his father's detailed diary, which had taken place in the family home over a decade and more during the 1830s, including a wide variety of noises – heavy footsteps, mallet beats, voices, whistling, knocking, and the ringing of a handbell – and the appearance of ghostly figures, 'a transparent white female figure in a window in the second storey of the house', and a man 'who went to the window, threw up the sash, put it down again, and then walked out; he had light or grey hair and no hat on'. (The transparency of the female figure is interesting, as it is reminiscent of the phantasmagoria created by magic lanterns in drawing-rooms and theatres.)[7] Joseph Procter, a Quaker by religious confession, clearly came to think that the poltergeist-like and ghostly disturbances emanated from an evil spirit – he says so more than once – and Edmund in later years attended a séance led by a Newcastle medium in the house, which turned out to have mixed results.

> The séance [he wrote] was not without incidents well understood by those acquainted with such proceedings, and which it would be useless at the moment

to describe to those who are not, but absolutely futile as to establishing any communication with the alleged spirit or spirits supposed to haunt or to have formerly haunted the premises.

Nevertheless, he expressed the hope that his father's experiences would serve 'as an argument tending to establish the continued existence of the individual after death'.

> Monsieur Renan, in one of the very last of his charming pages, troubled with doubts as to a future existence, whilst smiling at the superstition of the old-fashioned and orthodox Hell, exclaims how glad he would be to be sure even of Hell, a hypothesis so preferable to annihilation. In the same way, may we not justifiably postulate this: that if we can prove the existence of spirits of a low or inferior order, then faith, analogy, and evolution, if not logic and conviction, can claim those of a progressive, a high and superior order? Is it not rational to suppose that the more debased and the most unhappy have the greatest facility in giving tangible proof of their existence, under certain conditions imperfectly understood; whilst the purer and nobler souls find intercourse painful or impossible, but are yet occasionally able to achieve it in those picturesque and beneficent instances where their visitation is recorded, not only in the Old and New Testaments, but scattered all through literature; cases which possibly the many may still deride, but which others cherish as indications of the divine and proofs of immortality?[8]

With such a strong desire to prove there was such a thing as life after death, and to prove it in such a way as to silence both scoffers and doubters, came the possibility that genuine hoaxers and pranksters would undermine any case for the defence and provide those same scoffers and doubters with an excuse to dismiss any and every anecdote involving preternatural activity, especially if it came from an isolated house or peasant community outwith the comfortable certainties of middle-class urban life. We have such an example from Scotland. It comes from Charles MacKay's *Extraordinary Popular Delusions and Madness of Crowds*, first published in 1841. MacKay was a journalist and songwriter who worked in Glasgow and London, before becoming editor of the *Illustrated London News* in 1852. He has a fine way of pouring scorn on any explanation of apparently preternatural events, other than one which would appeal to Gradgrind's convictions. The incident itself took place in a farmhouse in Baldarroch, Aberdeenshire, and involved the customary lithobolia, flying household articles, knocking, and broken windows. 'The whole neighbourhood was a scene of alarm; and not only the vulgar, but persons of education, respectable farmers, within a circle of twenty miles, expressed their belief in the supernatural character of these events, and offered up devout prayers to be preserved from the machinations of the Evil One.' Others, whom MacKay calls 'some sensible and educated people', blamed gypsies or beggars or the villagers of Baldarroch who 'carried on this deception themselves, for some reason or other, which was not very clear to anybody'. Indeed not, and that is an unconvincing and somewhat desperate attempt to avoid a non-natural explanation. Fortunately for all concerned, however, including MacKay's narrative, two female servants later confessed to having caused the whole thing and 'they were no sooner in the county gaol than the noises ceased'.

It is noteworthy that MacKay lays stress on the sceptics' being educated, for this – and we have come across it before – is his solution to what he regards as the lamentable superstition of the 'vulgar', that is, the common people.

> Lawyers, by blotting from the statute-book the absurd or sanguinary enactments of their predecessors, have made one step towards reaching the people. It is to be hoped that the day is not far distant when lawgivers will teach the people by some more direct means, and prevent the recurrence of delusions like these, and many worse, which might be cited, by securing to every child born within their dominions an education in accordance with the advancing state of civilisation. If ghosts and witches are not yet altogether exploded, it is the fault, not so much of the ignorant people, as of the law and the government that have neglected to enlighten them.[9]

But we have also seen that education, state-sponsored or not, did not necessarily cure people of their insistence on being prepared to envision worlds and universes other than this one, and their intransigence was given a mighty boost by the arrival of new systems for communicating with the dead. One says 'new', although in fact they were not new at all. Contacting the spirit-world and receiving intelligible and intelligent replies had been going on for a long time, as the exchange of knocks and raps with poltergeists has already illustrated. What was new about the recent arrival was its organisation into a system, and from a system into a new mode of religious apprehension. *Ex America semper aliquid novi* (to adapt Pliny the Elder), and so during the night of 29 March 1848, the year of revolutions in Europe, the Fox family from Hydesville, New York, began to hear distinct knocks, and out of that experience came a series of communications with the unknown as the Fox sisters began to rap or to clap their hands rhythmically and were imitated by the unseen source in their midst. On 1 April the family invited its neighbours in to hear the knocking and participate in questioning the entity who revealed that it was the spirit of a young pedlar who had been murdered some five years earlier and buried in the cellar of the house; but digging there uncovered only a few bones and teeth, no skeleton. Naturally, these events caused a great deal of talk (some of it ill-natured enough to suggest that the whole thing was a hoax), and so the family consulted Isaac Post, a Quaker from Rochester, who suggested assigning a letter of the alphabet to a particular number of knocks. This would enable conversation to take place, and sure enough, spirit-conversations quickly multiplied, and it was not long before the spirit proposed the Foxes should give public demonstrations of the phenomena – which indeed they did.

New York soon took to these mass séances, and from New York they spread to other northern states. Belief that the phenomena were genuine was general and new mediums, mainly young women, holding private séances for a small number of people, started to develop the initially simple procedure into something more elaborate, more theatrical, and more religious. Church hymns were sung in preparation, lighting was dimmed, and participants held each other's hands as they sat round a table. Thus, out of a fairly standard poltergeist incident came a movement referred to as 'table-rapping' and 'spiritualism', which spread rapidly from the American states to Britain, so rapidly, in fact, that by the 1850s a wave of American mediums had arrived and were soon occupied in spreading via their demonstrations the consoling message that life continued after death and that bereavement was no more than a temporary parting of the ways.[10]

So did this newly heightened atmosphere favourable to believers in the Otherworld and irritating to the scoffers have any discernible effect on reports of poltergeist activity? The answer is yes and no. Reports increased in number, but they had been increasing ever since the sixteenth century, so that was nothing new. Did the content of those reports change? On the whole, no. If we look at one or two examples, we shall see that the components of a poltergeist disturbance remained the same as ever, with only differences in detail to distinguish it from the rest. In 1850 in Stratford, Connecticut, Eliakim Phelps, a Presbyterian minister with an active interest in the paranormal, accepted a visitor's invitation to contact spirits through rapping, an experiment which turned out to be successful. Unfortunately, however, their attempts seem to have disturbed some kind of entity because, when the family returned home from church on 10 March, they found their furniture scattered about, and their clothing rearranged into human-like shapes, mainly female, engaged in an act of worship, with Bibles in front of them, open at significant verses. From then on, for the next eighteen months, objects were thrown, glass broken, furnishings damaged, letters dropped from the ceiling, and chairs moved, apparently of their own accord. On one occasion, one of Eliakim's sons, aged about eleven, was carried through the air, and on another, his clothes were cut to ribbons. Meanwhile the raps continued, via which Eliakim was informed that the poltergeist was a dead Frenchman, lately a clerk in a firm of local solicitors, who was in Hell because he had cheated a client during life. All these and other phenomena were witnessed by people outwith the Phelps family, and published in the form of newspaper interviews, articles, and a book, *Mysteries: or, Glimpses of the Supernatural*. Eliakim himself was clearly confused by his experiences, telling the author of that book that (a) he had never seen a spirit, (b) he was satisfied the phenomena were genuine and not children's tricks, as reported in some newspapers, (c) he placed no value upon any of the spirit-messages, and (d) if they came from spirits, they were evil spirits.[11]

Colin Wilson observes that Eliakim 'made a mistake in attracting the attention of spirits to his home by holding the séance. They discovered that there were two excellent mediums in the house.'[12] He means the Phelps' children and, of course, if we acknowledge the source of the phenomena as a spirit, not human, he may well be right, although it is worth remarking here, anent the common explanation of poltergeistery which ties it to adolescents, that adults are as capable of being excellent mediums as youngsters, and of being just as neurotic or psychically disturbed, if that is what is to be taken as a requisite in persons acting as the focus of poltergeist activity. What is curious about this episode, however, is the arrangement of the Phelps' clothes into what were said to be realistic human figures at prayer, and the appearance of writing on paper. Apparently, Eliakim was alone in his study one day, turned away from his desk for a moment, and turned back to find that a blank sheet of paper now had 'Very nice paper and nice ink for the Devil' written on it, and that the ink was still wet. Poltergeists do write messages. In 1848 in Amherst, Nova Scotia, for example, Esther Cox was the target of what seemed to be a psychic attack, and at one point, writing appeared on the wall above her bed: 'Esther, you are mine to kill'. And the poltergeist in South Shields in 2006 left more than one on a doodle-board belonging to the son of the family.[13] Nevertheless, such written communications are not common, and the bizarre arrangement of clothes is most unusual. It is not, however, unique, for there is another example of it from Fives, near Lille, in June and July 1865. A newspaper report informed its readers that for the past fortnight houses in the Rue du Prieuré had been struck by a hail of missiles, and that a second phase of disturbance had seen it concentrate on one particular house. There, money fell into the yard, furniture moved, a pair of sabots began to dance, candlesticks fell from their places, and a servant-girl was attacked and beaten.

> One afternoon Madame X [as the lady of the house is designated] went out with one of her friends after examining the whole house and noticing all in order. The door was carefully locked, and nobody could enter. On coming back, Mme. X found on her bed a large figure of 8 traced out with stockings and socks which had been in a chest of drawers. In the evening, with her husband, her nephew, and a lodger, the whole party in the house, she visited all the rooms. Next morning, on going up to the room formerly occupied by the servant, she found a curious figure traced on the bed with hats, and on the lower stairs a dozen steps covered with her husband's, nephew's, and lodger's overcoats stretched out and surmounted by a hat … In the afternoon a circle was found on Monsieur M's bed, formed of clothes, and in the attic a similar design made with a rolled-up hooded cloak and a game basket. All these facts are attested by persons of the house, who are of a settled, calm, and deliberate character. It is all the less explicable as the neighbourhood is well inhabited and a close watch has been kept for three weeks.[14]

Camille Flammarion, who reproduces this report, dismisses the idea that these oddities might have been done by mischievous children or spirits of the dead, but offers instead the feeblest of possibilities. 'We think quite naturally of electrical phenomena, such as lightning, but with a certain rudimentary intention.' In other words, he is at a loss to explain things. What is perhaps most notable about the arrangement of clothes in the Phelps case is the evident mockery of religion, and this is certainly a feature of several poltergeist cases. We have seen already that exorcism was not always effective against these entities, and it continues to be uncertain during the nineteenth century whether religious rituals or artefacts will prevail against them. An episode in Austria in 1818 saw lithobolia, broken windows, and objects thrown, but while two lighted candles standing on each side of a crucifix were cast to the floor, the crucifix itself suffered no such interference. On the other hand, three exorcisms were unsuccessful in dealing with a poltergeist in the Ukraine in 1853, and in the end the house in question, along with four neighbouring cottages, was burned to the ground. In 1867 a house in Labastide-Paumès in the Haute Garonne was troubled every night for two weeks by loud noises, the movement of objects, rappings, and footsteps in the kitchen. Professor Salières, the person at the centre of these disturbances, consulted the local priest, who told him that the house was very old and probably had not been blessed for a long time. 'If the noise comes again', he said, 'I shall go there and bless it, and since a prayer to God is often heard, perhaps you will hear nothing more.' Sure enough, the prayer worked and the noise was not heard again. By contrast, however, in St Thomas's Mount near Madras in c.1872, in addition to all the usual manifestations, when Thomas Cronan took down a crucifix from the wall, placed it on a chest of drawers, and said, 'I defy anything to touch this cross', the crucifix was picked up and thrown at his back as he was leaving the room. Nor did a priest's blessing the house make any difference to the poltergeist activities within.[15]

To an extent, therefore, some poltergeists were still being treated as though they were demons rather than ghosts, and although many incidents contained rappings as part of their disturbance, not many reports of them seem to show the human sufferers turning to those rappings as a way of communicating with the troublesome entity. There is one referring to a house in Scott's Lane, Port Glasgow, in 1864. Knocks were heard there for a period of two weeks and attracted large crowds in a manner somewhat reminiscent of Cock Lane, with the police taking an interest in preserving order and keeping the peace. Hence one Andrew Glendinning from Port Glasgow suggested to Sergeant James MacDonald that the matter should be investigated further, clearly with a view to exposing it as a fraud.

> The knockings commenced about nine o'clock, and continued for more than an hour. The first sounds were similar to what is made by scratching on rough boards; then knocking, as if made with a heavy hammer, on the floor, under the bed, which was situated immediately above the outer stair. Sergeant MacDonald and I took a candle and went below the bed, exactly over the spot where the sounds were proceeding from. Mr Fegan stood in front of the bed. J.F. Anstruther, Esq., and a number of persons were in the room besides the constable. Being informed that the knocks had been given as affirmative or negative answers to questions, we asked a good many questions, requesting that three knocks be given for yes, and one for no. The knocks were rapid and loud, and were often given before the question was quite finished. During any pause in the question, the knocks seemed to beat to the air, 'There is nae luck about the house'. I whistled that tune, and the knocks became still louder and accompanied my measure. I whistled other airs, 'Let us gang to Kelvin Grove, bonnie lassie, oh'; 'Scots wha hae wi' Wallace bled', etc. etc. and, beginning always with the second line, they kept exact time. We asked some questions in a low tone – quite a whisper – our position being such that no one could see our lips moving, so as to guess the nature of our questions;

but it made no difference in regard to the knocks As ten o'clock struck on the town clock, each stroke seemed supplemented by a sound in the wall, above the bed. We got a pickaxe, and tore up part of the flooring at the spot where the knocking was going on. The sounds shifted position for a little, but at times they were the same as if a person were hammering heavily on the edge of the hole we had made in the floor.

We examined minutely the floor, walls, ceiling, etc., and we got the children (who were asleep) out of the bed, and lifted aside the bedclothes, mattress, bed bottom, and, in short, did everything we could think of to discover if possible, the cause of the knockings. Others (amongst whom were police constables and the superintendant) examined the lobby, staircase, and cellars. They likewise tried, by knocking on various places, to produce similar sounds, but without the slightest success.[16]

This report bears witness to the lengths people were prepared to go to satisfy their assumption that paranormal events were bound to rise from natural causes, but also shows that while the table-rapping or spiritualist movements rapidly gaining ground in public consciousness and interest during this period were having a notable effect on many of the public's views about life after death and the active involvement of spirits of the dead in the world of matter, poltergeists as opposed to other spirit forms (if that is what they were) were not really included in the new wave of cautious and not so cautious enthusiasm for spirits. Even the publication of Darwin's *Origin of Species* in 1859 and the growing interest in the religions and philosophies of India, typified by Edwin Arnold's poem *The Light of Asia* (1879) and Max Müller's translations of sacred Sanskrit texts which introduced British readers to the notions of karma and reincarnation – both of which had profound effects on speculation about what the afterlife might be like and what was its place in the grand scheme of things – did not have any impact on interpretations of the poltergeist experience. Evolution of souls, which became a favoured way of expressing the reason for the existence of an afterlife and the notion of 'progress' – a favourite word in the vocabulary of the century's *bien pensants* – did not touch explanations of the poltergeist, which continued to veer between trickery, electrical currents, and 'unconscious cerebration' on the one hand, and ghosts on the other, this latter being quite at odds with the prevailing Gradgrindery of academic and scientific circles.

One problem, of course, had been growing ever since the eighteenth century and that is that the sciences were rapidly turning into highly specialised intellectual disciplines more and more demarcated the one from the other, which meant that scientists were increasingly retiring into their specialisms and so distinguishing themselves as professional observers, recorders, and theoreticians from the amateurs in their fields and, above all, from members of the general public.[17] This withdrawal of their phylacteries, too, tended to make scientists dogmatic about what was and what was not believable, a certainty they were successful in communicating to many public organs. 'The requirements of our age', observed *Fraser's Magazine*, 'as to the amount and quality of the evidence necessary to produce credibility differ so widely from that which satisfied our forefathers, that the change is producing a silent revolution in history, science, and even theology.'[18] With this in mind, Spiritualists in particular were keen to demonstrate, according to these new standards of expectation, that life after death and the spirit-world were not personal fantasies or hallucinations, but realities which could be proved in the same kind of way as any other scientific proposition. 'For those who are following spiritualism as a means and not an end', said Basil Wilberforce, a clergyman, to a Church Congress at Newcastle in 1881, 'contend warmly that it does not seek to undermine religion, or to render obsolete the teachings of Christ: that, on the other hand, it furnishes illustrations and rational proof of them, such as can be gained from no other source; that its manifestations will supply deists and atheists with positive demonstration of a life after death.'[19]

Hence in the following year, a number of interested parties got together and founded the Society for Psychical Research, which was formally constituted on 20 February 1882 in London. The Society's pedigree was impressive. It started with the Cambridge Ghost Club of 1851, which attracted the interest of a number of notable academics, and was followed by an informal group led by Henry Sidgwick, Professor of Moral Philosophy at Cambridge; Edmund Gurney, a gifted psychical researcher; and Frederick Myers, a Fellow of Trinity College and then for thirty years inspector of schools in Cambridge and a close friend of Sidgwick. It was also influenced by the experimental work of the London Dialectical Society which declared that 'the phenomena of spiritualism [were] worthy of more serious attention and careful investigation than they had until then received'. With these antecedents, then, we find that the aims of the SPR were quite broad in scope, and committees were set up with the following aims in view.

1.   An examination of the nature and extent of any influence which may be exerted by one mind upon another, apart from any generally recognised mode of perception.

2.   The study of hypnotism, and the forms of so-called mesmeric trance, with

its alleged insensibility to pain; clairvoyance and other allied phenomena.

3.   A critical revision of Reichenbach's researches with certain organisations called 'sensitive', and an inquiry whether such organisations possess any power of perception beyond a highly exalted sensibility of the recognised sensory organs.

4.   A careful investigation of any reports, resting on strong testimony, regarding apparitions at the moment of death, or otherwise, or regarding disturbances in houses reputed to be haunted.

5.   An inquiry into the various physical phenomena commonly called Spiritualistic; with an attempt to discover their causes and general laws.

6.   The collection and collation of existing materials bearing on the history of these subjects.[20]

For the first time in the West, then, poltergeists were going to be investigated and perhaps explained in a systematic way, a way which did not depend on the Christian religion, and by investigators who were not necessarily or personally bound by any particular adherence to orthodox Christianity. As Sidgwick wrote in a different context, but with sentiments generally applicable to the mindset expected of those investigators, 'What was fixed and unalterable and accepted by us all was the necessity and duty of examining the evidence for historical Christianity with strict scientific impartiality, placing ourselves as far as possible outside traditional sentiments and opinions, and endeavouring to weigh the pros and cons on all theological questions as a duly instructed rational being from another planet.'[21]

Theories then burgeoned. On the whole they fell into two broad categories: those which turned outward to look for causes in the physical environment in which poltergeist phenomena were experienced, and those which turned inward to look for those causes in hitherto unknown or unappreciated powers of the human mind. Both, of course, linked the causes to the material universe, partly because that is what the investigators understood by the 'scientific' method, and partly because only by adhering to that scientific method would their results prove acceptable to the scientific community and thus help to bridge the gap between science and religion, which many among both communities as well as among the public at large found so distressing. The SPR was going to find its task difficult in the face of some scientists' intransigence. 'I make a point', wrote Lord Kelvin, 'of repudiating any appearance of a tendency to accept this miserable superstition of animal magnetism, table-turning, Spiritualism, mesmerism, clairvoyance, and raps. There is no mystical sixth sense. Clairvoyance and the rest are the result of malobservation, with a touch of voluntary self-deception, acting upon simple and trusting souls.'[22]

But this was also the age of Unconscious Cerebration, the Unconscious Mind, the Subconscious, and Empathy, which were being explored by scientists such as Franz Brentano in his *Psychologie vom Empirischen Standpunkte* ('Psychology from an Empirical Standpoint'), published in 1874, and Theodor Lipps in his *Grundtatsachen des Seelenlebens* ('Elementary Facts of the Inner Life'), published in 1883. In France, too, Charles Richet, Professor of Physiology in the Faculty of Medicine in Paris, published studies on multiple personality, and experimented with cryptesthesia and materialisation, becoming satisfied that ridicule and dismissal were not sufficient or adequate reactions to either psychical research or some of the results it was producing;[23] and in Russia, Alexander Aksakov, a translator and journalist who helped organise some of the earliest séances there, coined the term *telekinesis* in 1890 to refer to the ability of the mind to move objects without the mediating assistance of any known physical energy. There was, therefore, a willingness in some intellectual circles to investigate psychic phenomena in a spirit of disinterestedness running counter to that of much of the scientific establishment of the day. Yet in spite of this, such investigations were marginalised by the Establishment, which was determined to emphasise the absolute reign of matter and the uniqueness of the universe in its material manifestation.

Given these polarities among the intellectuals of the day, it is not altogether surprising that reports of poltergeistery tended to rely upon attributing to it solutions which lay at one end or the other of the explanatory spectrum. So when a poltergeist started to steal food, clothing, and valuables from the house of a Mr Chang in Shangtung Province in 1883, and cause destructive fires to break out, it was assumed to be a demon, and indeed expressed itself in Christian terms when it was threatened with exorcism. This was recorded by John Nevius, a missionary, who, as he says, 'brought with me to China a strong conviction that a belief in demons, and communications with spiritual beings belongs exclusively to a barbarous and superstitious age, and at present can consist only with mental weakness and want of culture', and lived to change his mind, to the extent that he concludes that 'modern science furnishes no substitute for the theory of "demon-possession" which still stands as the only "genuine", "rational", "philosophical" and consistent theory for accounting for a certain class of established fact'.[24]

On the other hand, participants in these incidents might find themselves on trial for fraud, or subjected to scientific experiments designed to show that the whole thing was owing to natural causes. So, in 1889 charges were brought against a young lad, Karl Wolter, alleging that he had broken six panes of glass in the windows of a Herr Neumann, by throwing stones and other missiles at them. The house in question was in a hamlet not far from Berlin, and rumours that the damage, along with knocks, banging, and flying objects, had been caused by a poltergeist (*Spuk* in the records) reached the ears of Spiritualists in the city, who retained an advocate to defend the accused. Several witnesses gave their accounts of the phenomena, including a Lutheran pastor, who was convinced of the *Spuk*'s reality, and one of Karl's schoolmasters, who testified that the boy was an expert at throwing a ball. The defence pleaded that here were forces at work, which were not yet properly known by science, but the judge took the view that if science did not recognise these forces, they could not be advanced in explanation. So Karl was sentenced to a total of six weeks' imprisonment, upheld when the case was referred to a court of appeal.[25] Twenty-two years previously in Boston, Massachusetts, an unfortunate Irish girl, Mary Carrick, who was employed as a servant, found herself involved in poltergeist phenomena which terrified her and alarmed the family for whom she was working. Not only were there noises which followed her from room to room, but a heavy table with a nine-year-old child on top of it lifted itself from the floor, and other objects moved of their own accord about her. One of the principal witnesses to all this, a Mr H.A. Willis, had the notion that electricity lay behind these manifestations, and so he tried insulating Mary's bed, the kitchen table, and her usual chair, and the phenomena ceased at once. For two days, 28 and 29 August, Mary was sent away and nothing happened; but when she came back, everything started again and Mary's health, which had been undermined by her prolonged exposure to poltergeistery, collapsed completely and she was removed to an asylum. Once again, however, the phenomena ceased the moment she had her first hysterical fit.[26]

The testing of phenomena, poltergeist or other, followed closely in the wake of the Spiritualist movement. William Crookes, for example, a Fellow of the Royal Society and one of nineteenth-century Britain's outstanding scientists, investigated Daniel Douglas Home, one of the best-known and most extraordinary mediums of the second half of the century. Crookes began from the standpoint that the phenomena he was going to witness would probably be clever tricks, and so he took great care in setting up a laboratory in his own home, in which he could carry out procedures to ensure that Home had no opportunity to prepare things beforehand, and to render trickery as far as he could impossible. Two independent witnesses, William Higgins, an astronomer, and Edward Cox, a former MP, and a laboratory assistant were present at the trials. Home arrived and at once the tests began. During the first an accordion trapped within a cage beneath a table began to play and then to float about, without Home's hands moving from their initial position, a position chosen to make sure he could neither play the instrument nor lift it up. The second was more complex and involved a three-foot-long board, one end of which rested on a table while the other was attached to a spring-balance hanging down from above. Home's fingers rested lightly on the table end and no amount of pushing from him would affect the balance. Yet the far end of the board did oscillate, noticeably, its movements recorded by the balance, and when Crookes stood on top of the board where Home had been, and jumped up and down upon it, his violent efforts could still not move the other end of the board to anything like the extent achieved by Home, whose hands and feet had been under close scrutiny all the time. Crookes's conclusions were straightforward and earned him the contumely of many of his fellow scientists. 'Those who assume', he wrote, 'that we are now acquainted with all, or nearly all, or even with any assignable proportion, of the forces at work in the universe, show a limitation of conception which ought to be impossible in an age when the widening of the circle of our definite knowledge does but reveal the proportionately widening circle of our blank, absolute, indubitable ignorance.'[27]

Home himself had expressed similar sentiments about seven years earlier.

Of those [phenomena] which are of a physical kind, such as the moving of furniture, the raps, the raising into the air, or levitation, and similar classes of phenomena, they are to be investigated and their uses ascertained by the man of science and the philosopher. At present such persons have fixed a priori that such things have never occurred, and are impossible and absurd; and for this reason, if for no other, it will be admitted that they are of the highest use in order to correct such notions of the relations between spiritual forces and natural things. There is no study which could be of such value to philosophers as that of facts now known to thousands, but which their present philosophy deems impossible. For their philosophy must be radically defective when that which they say is impossible is nevertheless of daily occurrence. The physical side, therefore, of these phenomena is to be studied by students of experimental science, in order to enlarge their views of material forces, and if this can be effected, as it has been in so many instances, by the movement of tables, and by the rapping sounds, and by the raising of bodies into the air without touch or contact, they will no longer complain of the triviality of such phenomena. Indeed, already so little are they trivial or unimportant that the noted men of science, such as the Faradays and Brewsters, have gone out of their way to inveigh against their possibility, and to bestow the name of credulous dupes upon those who have publicly stated what they have seen and heard. The very denial of these things by these men, and by the mass of the public, shows that they are not trivial to them, but that they are really of the utmost importance. For why are they denied by the men of science, but that they contradict all their previous knowledge of the laws of Nature, upsetting 'the philosophy of a lifetime', and are therefore impossible to them until they enlarge the present boundaries of their knowledge, and find out those higher laws under which these become not only facts, but possible facts.

But Home's abilities extended far beyond those displayed in Crookes's laboratory and included holding red-hot coals in his hands without injury, and levitating four or five feet from the ground, moving over the heads of his onlookers as he did so. When he was young, he had been subject to something resembling a poltergeist – loud raps coming from the head of his bed or the table at which he was sitting. These raps were investigated by three local church ministers, one of whom was convinced that they called for prayer to make them cease, while the second refused to discuss the phenomena any further and the third attributed the noises to the Devil. He was not alone. Home's aunt, too, considered them works of the Evil One, and when furniture began to move of its own accord, she put the family Bible on top of a moving table, saying, 'There! That will soon drive the devils away.' But it did not, and when the woman angrily climbed on top of the table to keep it still with her weight, both she and the table were lifted from the floor.[28]

These references to devils and the need for prayer to exorcise them reflect popular sentiment, not just in rural America where Home passed his childhood and youth, but in Europe and further afield as well where exorcism, for example, might still be considered an appropriate response to poltergeist phenomena. Ballechin House in Perthshire suffered from what sounded like musket explosions, banging, rapping, and shrieking, all of which were experienced by a Jesuit visiting in 1892. He tried sprinkling the rooms with holy water and praying for divine protection, but to no avail, and even exorcism by the Catholic Archbishop did not succeed in driving away what was generally taken to be a ghost rather than a poltergeist. Then in February 1897, a group of psychical researchers stayed in the house and employed a ouija board which produced a message telling them to go to a certain place at dusk. This they did and saw nothing; that is to say, none of them except a Miss Freer, who said she could see a female figure dressed as a nun. The same year, the *Madras Times* reported that in a house at Ootacamund, a hill station in the Nilgiri Hills, an exorciser had to be called in because the inhabitants were suffering from lithobolia and the breaking of glass articles. A young woman there exhibited some of the symptoms of being possessed, and it is clear from the reports that she was the focus of the poltergeistery which was not in the least affected by the exorciser's efforts, for it continued even as she and her father were packing up and preparing to move out. As in Scotland, one of the party – in this case, the affected young woman – claimed to see ghostly figures which were not visible to anyone else. Were they real, that is to say, were they genuine sightings of something external to both women, but perceptible only to them? Were they real but internal, that is, hallucinations or subjective projections? Or were they simply imaginings, in the sense of having no reality at all? The available evidence does not allow us to come to any definite conclusion, a timely lesson in the difficulty of pronouncing sensibly on any of these (or later) poltergeist episodes, when one is in the hands of witnesses whose testimony cannot be reliably tested.

What we can and should note, however, is that while confidence in orthodox religion, especially Christianity, declined in western Europe, technology dazzled and the fruits of imperial trade gave economics an allure which, during the twentieth century, would quickly turn buying and selling, particularly buying, into a kind of raison d'être for everyday existence. Yet poltergeists still managed to flourish and to do so via manifestations – visions, voices, and non-vocal forms of communication – which they had been employing for centuries. It was almost as though they were looking Science in the face and saying, 'Disbelieve as much as you like, but what do you make of *this*?'

This might be lithobolia, the appearance of a white hand thrust through a cut pane of glass, a hollow-sounding voice, practical jokery, and interference with people's victuals, such as happened in 1885 in a house in Dublin; or the misplacing of money and faeces, a deep gruff voice like that of an old man, written communication of obscenities, spontaneous fires, lithobolia, the throwing of various household articles, and a variety of appearances ranging from 'a tall, thin man with a crow's head, horns, tail, and a cloven foot' to a black dog and a handsome man dressed in white, all of which manifested in 1889 in Clarendon in Quebec; or moving planks, broken windows, a broken mirror, and a loud gruff voice uttering coarse abuse, which disturbed a house in Valence-en-Brie (Île de France). Gérard Encausse, a physician and occultist, remarked:

> Artless people who profess to explain everything have not failed to say, 'There was a ventriloquist hidden somewhere.' Now, one only needs to have studied ventriloquism to eliminate this idea. It is impossible to produce effects of this kind from the bottom of the cellar to the first floor, and if anyone in the house was master of this art, the phenomena would have ceased with the departure of this person, and such was not the case. In short, the householder made considerable

borings and excavations in his cellar to make sure that there were no electric wires, or acoustic apparatus of any kind connecting the cellar with the house. All those whom one interrogates in the near neighbourhood, whether they are credulous or not, affirm the reality of the voices heard: persons, the most respectable, the least capable of trickery, the most exempt by their age or temperament from any hallucination or influence of any kind, have distinctly heard the voice – Monsieur Hainot, Mayor of Valence, the teacher, and the priest who, by the way, does not see any diabolic activity in these strange phenomena.[30]

The priest may not have credited demons with this behaviour, but others most certainly did and continued to do so as the twentieth century teetered along its destructive path. It had been the hope of many nineteenth-century scientists to put to rest all notions of life-forms other than those which existed within the physical universe which they were becoming more and more adept at scrutinising. They did not succeed. Likewise, it had been the aspiration of the Society for Psychical Research to join hands with all sorts and conditions of men and women who wanted to believe and did believe in the spirit, angelic, and demonic worlds, and prove by the methods of science to such as jeered and denied, that those other worlds did indeed exist and not only existed, but communicated with human beings.[30] They too did not succeed, or at least did not succeed on the terms they would have wished, although the work of the Society still goes on. The twentieth century, therefore, inherited a sharply divided legacy and one might have expected that, with its attention diverted into other, mainly hostile channels, and with its inclinations firmly planted in the Victorian scientists' camp, the close of the second millennium would have the greatest of difficulty in taking the poltergeist seriously. One's expectations, however, appear to have been misplaced, although the seriousness of the seriousness can certainly be called into question.

10

Demons, Ghosts, and Something Else Unknown, 1901–Present

So far, the only consistent note in the poltergeist's history is the poltergeist's behaviour, and even that has been subject to quite a large range of variation. In essence, however, we can say that in spite of that variation, what distinguishes the poltergeist is its proclivity to make loud noises, cause objects to move through the air, and do damage to articles small and big. Its 'mood', if one can attribute such a thing to an unknown force or entity, is more violent than mischievous and more hostile than indifferent. As to whether the poltergeist is actually an entity rather than a force of some kind, available evidence is inconclusive, although the way in which it takes on characteristics sometimes of a ghost, sometimes of an evil spirit, and its apparent ability to communicate with humans via rapping, intelligible speech, and occasional writing, suggests an entity rather than merely a 'force'. On the other hand, if it sometimes appears to be a ghost or a demon, or if it seems to interact with its human subjects in ways they can understand, there is no guarantee that those same humans, or the human observers of the phenomena, are not interpreting what they observe and hear in ways which will impose sense on things which may not, in reality, possess the attributes given to them. The Middle Ages tended to treat poltergeists as a form of malevolent ghost; the early modern period, as a kind of demon; the nineteenth and twentieth centuries, either as ill-understood natural phenomena or as energy generated by emotionally disturbed and sexually awakening adolescents. Spirits of the dead, agents of Satan, electromagnetic interference and subconscious telekinesis: these, broadly speaking, represent at least one or two of the fundamental preoccupations of the respective centuries, and so interpreting poltergeist-like phenomena in accordance with them is only to be expected. It also means, of course, that in spite of the nineteenth and twentieth centuries' self-assurance that they had solved, or at least had the capacity to solve, questions of non-material origin or manifestation which had puzzled and intrigued previous ages, and to solve them in ways which brooked no contradiction, modern 'solutions' to the poltergeist enigma are no more finally authoritative than those of the Middle Ages or late Renaissance. The pretensions are there, but not a great deal else.

The last century, indeed, began with poltergeistery which would have been entirely familiar to the earlier centuries. In Monneville, a village in the north of France, for example, an old woman and her grandson were troubled by knocks, taps, rattling, and spontaneous movements of their beds at night. All this started to attract onlookers – nearly forty at one point, both within and outwith the house – and resulted in an attempt to communicate with the entity via rapping.

'Are you God?'
'No.'
'Are you the Devil?'
Hesitant no.
'Do you belong to his family?'
'Yes.'
'Was it a man who sent you?'
'No'.
'A woman?'
'Yes.'
'How old is she?'
'Thirty-four.'
'How many children has she?'
'Five.'

All this identified the source of the trouble as a witch (something everyone present accepted), and the excitement went on for at least a fortnight. So the old argument that a poltergeist was a demon-servant was still prevalent in the early 1900s, as was its assimilation to a ghost. Between 1905 and 1907, in Tackley, Oxfordshire, a Miss Sharpe's house (known as 'Beth-oni') was troubled by footsteps, raps, the sound of furniture's being dragged and of ripping wallpaper, and figures were to be seen in the various bedrooms. Since a farmer had died in the house thirty years or so previously, and Miss Sharpe herself took in dying villagers and nursed them to the end, it is perhaps not surprising that ghosts should have been associated with the place. Likewise, 1913–14 saw a lawyer in Transylvania harassed by stones and all kinds of small objects, including cigarettes and cigars, which fell from the air, and by rapid drumming upon a table and raps all round the walls. Communication was established via a ouija board and purported to reveal that the entity had once been a German baron, although further information about some buried treasure turned out to be futile.[1]

True to nineteenth-century occultist thinking, the notion that the dead were able to affect the living, perhaps not so much through their own manifestation in human form as through emotional energy they left behind after their death, could still form the basis of an attempted explanation of certain disconcerting experiences. 'Could we not', wrote Camille Flammarion in 1924, 'without undue audacity, suppose that the living leave behind them a certain residuum of force, of vital fluid impregnating the building, which, on effective contact with a sensitive, can undergo a revitalisation capable of producing these strange phenomena?' To this, by way of illustration, he attached an anecdote from a friend of his.

I remember having myself experienced, seventeen or eighteen years ago, a similar sensation in my room at my father's house when I was a young man, a year or two after my mother's death. A terrible noise in a large mirrored wardrobe kept me awake for several nights. It was certainly not the noise of wood warping, but loud detonations of great violence, like firearms. Although I was at the time naively atheistic, yet I received a great shock. I naturally refrained from talking to my father about these noises, as he would only have chaffed me. The phenomenon never repeated itself, but I have since then always had an insurmountable objection to sleeping in that room. My mother was very austere, rather prudish, and very pious. In her eyes I had the faults of a libertine, which, indeed, she did not forgive me even on her deathbed. I have often since then wondered whether these manifestations were not, according to your hypothesis, the revival of her displeasure which in her lifetime impregnated that room where I suffered in her presence, both physically and morally, for a long time. Here we are in the midst of unknown and mysterious things. There is nothing very daring in supposing that indefinite effluvia subsist after us. Everybody has observed that for many years perfumes remain attached to cut hair, to withered flowers, to articles of clothing. Let us also note that apparently slight causes can produce great effect. A cartridge can fire a formidable discharge of artillery, and the rubbing of a match can ignite an immense fire.[2]

But, regardless of what the poltergeist was thought to be, both exorcism and magic continued to be employed as counter-offensives, according to the cultural and religious ambience of the incident. On 1 May 1914, the *Gazette de Lausanne* reported that on 18 April an eleven-year-old boy had suffered a fit accompanied by stone-throwing and article-displacement. When the boy was taken to bed, he was violently pulled about and hit in the face with stones. A holy water stoup broke, and a blessed medal freed itself from the boy's neck and was thrown in the air. A Capuchin was called in to exorcise the house, but did not succeed in doing so, and in consequence the inhabitants called in a local magician, who 'read from a grimoire the prayers and invocations suitable to the occasion'. But he was no more successful than the friar, as stones continued to fall on his head and his book. On the other hand, the following day all the phenomena ceased, and so either the exorcism or the magic or both may have had an effect. Two years later, a member of the Royal Irish Constabulary met a farmer who told him that his house had been disturbed for the past week by some unseen spirit who was breaking things and even flung a bottle of ink over his youngest child, who lay dying in bed. The constable went and saw the damage for himself, and noted that the 'spook' (as he called it) was concentrating its hostility upon the farmer's wife and daughter.

> The woman and children said they would not remain when I left, so they started for the back door – the servant first, followed by the two children, then the farmer's wife, next the farmer, and I bringing up the rear. I had got across the kitchen near the end of the obstructing wall and was turning into the passage, but still in full view of the kitchen, when suddenly one of the horse-collars was flung from its position, high up on the wall, the whole length of the room, landing on the floor with a smack. The farmer turned, and after we had both examined the collar, he said, 'You must now believe', to which I assented. We passed into the yard, going towards the road, when a graip [dung-fork] was thrown across the yard by unseen hands.

A few days later Mass was said in the house, but even then the disturbance continued and in the end the farmer was obliged to build a new house and move his family out of the old one which, according to local belief, was being haunted by the angry ghost of someone the farmer had wronged in the past.[3]

The lack of fear or respect for sacred objects or rituals shown by these two poltergeists is paralleled elsewhere. We have come across this before in Reginald of Durham's biography of St Godric for example, and in Gerald of Wales's account of a disturbance in Pembrokeshire. But there is also a remarkable example of it from a Catholic community in southern India. The troubles lasted for just over a fortnight in March 1920, and consisted of outbreaks of fire in various places and objects' being thrown; but this poltergeist seemed to have a particular animus against religious symbols, for pictures of the Sacred Heart, the Blessed Virgin, and other saints were burned, chalk crosses were rubbed out with dung, one crucifix was thrown on a fire and a second disappeared, to be found later on the roof. Even when those afflicted moved to another house, the fires and the sacrilege followed. Various remedies were tried. Fermented palm juice was left as an offering to the spirit, but was rejected; a Brahmin was called in and wrote a small chit which was to be left for the 'devil' to find and answer. The chit disappeared, but next day symbols and three messages in Tamil were found on a lavatory wall: 'My name is Chief Mischief Maker. I shall not leave you'; 'If you don't run away from this house, I shall recommend you to my goddess for punishment'; 'Don't you know I am the King? I shall not leave this house, whatever the inmates do.' This last was preceded by what sounds like a threat against the clerk who translated the writings into English for the benefit of the house owner. The possibility that these were fraudulent is, of course, great, but for our purposes we should note that the poltergeist became particularly violent if anyone began to recite prayers.

> I recited the Apostles' Creed. After finishing it, I went to the middle hall and went towards the eastern room about ten feet off the hearth, with my boy aged two in one of my hands. He was also walking with me. The devil suddenly took another big piece of burning fire and threw it with great force between my legs. I at once turned back and saw the whole hall filled with fire.

Exorcism was tried and did not work; magic did not work, either, although a small packet wrapped in silk, which a magician sent to the homeowner, was left untouched while crucifixes and holy pictures were damaged or destroyed. Finally, Mass was said in the house and that had the desired effect, although not without one or two parting shots from the infesting spirit.[4]

Now, these examples show that the behaviour exhibited by poltergeists during the twentieth century differs not at all from that of previous centuries. Interfering with electrical equipment is, of course, a recent nuisance,[5] but essentially nothing has changed except people's attempts to explain what causes the phenomena. If we list a number of these attempts in the form of questions, we shall be able to see how they have been framed by the intellectual preoccupations of their various periods. (i) Are poltergeists a form of ghost in the sense of being the spirit of a dead person? (ii) Are they familiars, that is, spirits evoked by someone to carry out his or her wishes – in this case, do damage to another individual's property and person, and cause fright and distress? Connected with this is the direct question, are they manifestations of Satan himself? These are the options of 'ghost' and 'witchcraft' and have a continuous if intermittent history right up to the early years of the twentieth century. (iii) Are poltergeists non-existent, their phenomena explicable by reference to trickery of some kind? Fraud there undoubtedly has been in some cases, and fraud can be suspected in others. Indeed, a common first reaction from some of the earliest years of the poltergeist's recorded appearance has been suspicion that some mischievous or ill-natured person is playing a trick. Very frequently, however, further experience of the phenomena, coupled with careful investigation and the presence of several, sometimes a large number, of witnesses, had rendered the suspicion untenable.[6]

It is, however, characteristic of the twentieth century that, having discovered or uncovered fraud or the possibility of fraud, the psychology behind the fraud should be investigated. Hereward Carrington and Nandor Fodor provide a good example of this in a case from 1938, that of Mr and Mrs Forbes from Thornton Heath in South London. The principal phenomena consisted of apported objects – anything from cups and saucers, glasses, electric bulbs, vases, and egg cups – which would fly through the air, apparently unsupported. On close psychological examination of Mrs Forbes, Fodor discovered she was a highly disturbed individual with a history of repressed aggression directed against her husband. She agreed to come to the Institute for Psychical Research, where the showers of flying objects continued. She was then completely undressed in the presence of a committee of women, searched, and given a new set of undergarments, being watched carefully all the time, after which it became evident (says Fodor) that fraud was indeed being committed and that some of the objects were being concealed inside her body. 'The evidence', he adds, 'by the standards of psychical research, was damning and it invalidated all previous observations that were in her favour. Scientifically, the case was dead. Psychologically, it was beginning.' Mrs Forbes now underwent further psychological examination in sessions which purported to reveal that she had been violated as a child and that the discomfort of carrying apportable objects in her private parts was re-enacting the pain of the original rape.[7]

Perhaps it is not surprising that the committee of the Institute decided enough was enough and brought these sessions to a close, but Fodor himself was convinced that psychoanalysis could provide a key to better understanding of not just poltergeistery, but occultism involving mediumship in general.

Psychologists cannot be compromised by mediums because they are just as much interested in the mental processes which are active behind fraudulent phenomena as in those behind the genuine ones. Studying the whole of the medium's personality, they are not bound to partial commitment on some of the phenomena as, for instance, a physicist would be who might observe primarily the phenomena of energy discharge and the like. Psychologists will no more reject a medium for conscious or unconscious imposture than they would reject an analytic patient for lying. A medium may cheat for similar reasons that drive a kleptomaniac to stealing. He may produce valuable psychological phenomena as a neurotic produces his symptoms. Viewed as a conversion neurosis, mediumship may offer a novel and attractive field of inquiry. One can even venture to say that the mediumistic activity may represent a form of self-therapy, that it permits the affected persons an adjustment to life by sublimating individual traumata along channels of social usefulness, and by strengthening the importance of their ego.[8]

This concentration on the internal, psychic, or imaginative life of the individual in relation to poltergeists and other such phenomena is peculiar but not unique to the nineteenth and twentieth centuries. But it raises another question: (iv) are poltergeists spirits who possess the body of a disturbed human being and use his or her energies to give outward expression of that disturbance, or are they the effects of self-delusion? 'Self-delusion' may include conditions such as depression, hysteria, schizophrenia, multiple personality disorder, repressed sexual energies (as Fodor suggested in the case of Mrs Forbes), stress, and trauma, any of which, or any combination of which, may be thought to trigger the physical responses called 'poltergeistery'. Some of this, of course, may lead to a valid understanding of certain outbreaks, but they do not provide a catch-all explanation and should be treated with discretion. Hans Eysenck and Carl Sargent, for example, have called for caution in the case of a popular explanation, adolescent sexual tension, pointing out that 'in Europe and America the average age of focus people has gone up, while the average age at which puberty occurs has gone down'. Moreover, since poltergeist activity often falls away or ceases after intervention by a priest or doctor or psychic investigator, are we to think that these visits resolve that sexual tension? If so, why? Eysenck and Sargent also question the reliability of a psychiatrist's or psychoanalyst's attributing poltergeist activity to a young patient's psychological problems. 'Even if that person doesn't know the reason for the referral (most unlikely) and diagnoses the child as neurotic, the child may have become neurotic precisely because she is being persecuted by a poltergeist!'[9] Alan Owen, too, comes to the conclusion that 'connections with adolescence, sexual development, and menstruation may be psychological rather than physiological', and of course we have to bear in mind that poltergeist cases do not invariably involve the presence of children or young people.[10] Similarly, while schizophrenia, hysteria, and the rest may be considered to produce unusual energies capable of affecting the physical world round the source, it would be facile to try to explain every poltergeist case which is not, or may not be, a fraud by reference to such personal origins. Gauld and Cornell, for example, point to an English case from 1967–68 in which the phenomena consisted largely of thudding and rapping apparently focused on a twelve-year-old boy, Brian Connolly, and they come to the conclusion that Brian himself could not have produced all the reported phenomena, and neither could anyone else in the house or near neighbourhood. Moreover, 'once the phenomena had been triggered off in that place [Brian's bedroom] by Brian's presence, they might continue there even when Brian himself was under observation elsewhere'.[11]

John and Anne Spencer have suggested that frustration is an important consideration in evaluating poltergeist activity, frustration arising from a particularly strong degree of stress. Now, this may be centred upon or arise from an individual, but the manifestations of that stress may shift from the original focus to another – or to others, for the Spencers point out that 'just because it is clear that one individual is the focus of the poltergeist, it does not necessarily mean that only one individual is responsible … Perhaps the reason is that it takes a group dynamic to create a poltergeist.'[12] Here it is clearly implied that a poltergeist may be the sum of specific degrees of stress or frustration arising from one or more humans, and it may be implied further that the energies produced therefrom are capable of manifesting themselves in those phenomena typical of the majority of poltergeists – lithobolia, apportation, and breakage. Hence a fifth question: are poltergeists natural or anomalous forms of energy with no relation to or connection with spirits of any kind? Speculation about what these energies might be resulted in various theories, one of which posits the existence, under conditions ranging from 'poltergeistic' stress to inborn personal ability, of psychokinesis or telekinesis, a term coined at the end of the nineteenth century by Alexander Aksakov. Psychokinesis is, in fact, a broad term covering various types of ability, including those of moving physical objects by the mind alone and self-levitation, both of which appear in a number of poltergeist incidents. Since psychokinesis violates some laws of physics, modern scientists have been reluctant to admit its reality, although they have gone as far as to conduct experiments in an effort to prove its existence or non-existence, and substantial money prizes have been offered to anyone who can satisfactorily demonstrate the ability at work under specific, controlled conditions. ('Satisfactorily', of course, represents a potential stumbling block. Satisfactory to whom? The phrase *quis custodiet ipsos custodes* comes to mind.) A further term, PSI, was coined in 1942 to refer to what Daryl Bem and Charles Honorton describe as 'anomalous processes of information or energy transfer, processes such as telepathy or other forms of extraordinary perception that are currently unexplained in terms of known physical or biological mechanisms';[13] but again, many scientists are suspicious of the concept since it ventures well beyond the boundaries of what are generally conceived to be the fully established fields of valid scientific inquiry. Is this reasonable caution, or evidence of closed minds?[14]

But one also has to take into account the possibility that poltergeists may be spirits who possess the body of a disturbed human being and use his or her energies to give outward expression of their own malignity – and this, of course, suggests something identical with, or at least closely akin to, demonic possession. Scott Rogo reviews the Amherst case of 1878 and concludes that, as it was unlikely that the principal target of the attacks, Esther Cox, would have ruined her own life by deliberate or unwilling use of any psychokinetic ability she may have had – 'Did she destroy her own life in order to vent pent-up hostilities on others?' We should at least consider the possibility that she had been the subject of a psychic invasion. He also cites a case which was investigated during the late 1960s and notes that 'people who have an association with a poltergeist [that is, people other than the focus] often find that it will follow them back to their own homes. I doubt whether the simple "victim-projects-PK [psychokinesis]" explanations of the poltergeist can account for this phenomenon.' In cases of what appear to be poltergeist possession, then, Rogo proposes that 'we are dealing with some entity which produces the poltergeist phenomena, but which is both dependent and independent of the agent's mind'.[15]

In connection with this, Colin Wilson draws attention to elementals, which are spirits attached to, dwelling in, or having the nature of one of the four basic elements: earth, air, fire, water.[16] They are described by Paracelsus in his *Liber de nymphis, sylphis, pigmaeis, et salamandris* (although his view of them as half-human and half-spirit is peculiar to himself) and, more in accordance with Neoplatonic thought, by Cornelius Agrippa in *De Occulta Philosophia*, Book 3, chapter 19. But while Wilson connects the elementals with thought-forms produced by an individual in harmony with the cultural norms he or she has absorbed from traditions and the immediate social environment, if someone wishes to remove him or herself from the post-industrial world's growing obsession with relating everything to self, or maintaining that the self is the *fons et origo* of every non-physical phenomenon, he or she may find the notion of elemental-as-thought-form unsatisfactory as an explanation of the poltergeist, because it deliberately turns its back on the possibility that the entity is external to the human and not an internal construct. Nor is the malevolence of the poltergeist adequately explained by reference to elementals, whether these be taken as having a separate reality from human imagination or not.

More satisfying, if we wish to preserve the idea of a separate reality, are the *qlippoth* ('shells').[17] According to later Kabbalistic philosophy, the manifested primeval thoughts or forces (*sephiroth*) which represent the mediation between God and creation are mirrored by material elements and apparitions called 'the shells', and thus embody evil, destructive, impure impulses. Obviously akin to the concept of 'demons', these entities too may be conjured and deliberately evoked. We are therefore led to a sixth question pertinent to poltergeists: are they spirits of some kind who have entered the physical world by mistake, like a fish out of water or a non-swimmer fallen into the sea, and thrash about in growing terror until they find their way out again? 'By mistake' is the important modification. If they were summoned by an act of will, there is little reason to suppose they would be frightened by their new environment. Accidental entry, on the other hand, would create conditions necessary to blind panic with its uncomfortable or dire consequences for the human inhabitants of the sphere into which the spirit had stumbled, and growing fear might explain the increasing violence of poltergeist activity as the infestation continued. That said, however, this theory does not account for those examples of poltergeistery which show the entity as playful, nor those which tell of the poltergeist's entering into intelligible and intelligent discourse with human beings. If, therefore, we are to accept the notion of the poltergeist's being an entity separate and distinct from any human source, the variety of poltergeist behaviour suggests that perhaps more than one type of entity could be involved and that the term 'poltergeist' covers a numbers of different species of non-human beings. Of course, if we regard the poltergeist as the product or summation of forces released from a human source, or a particular form of hallucination, or an amalgamation of natural phenomena and mistaken reportage, some of these problems do not present themselves, although others – such as conversation and verbal or written threat and banter – are raised at once.

From the historian's point of view, however, these are all explanations and difficulties to be noted rather than solved, if indeed it is sensible to talk of 'solutions' in such a context. Rather, we may ask why reports of ghosts and poltergeists have burgeoned so considerably during these latter centuries when decline in both magical and religious beliefs in Western Europe, and the turning of night from a time of fearfulness and mystery into a busy, glittering imitation of day itself, should have banished awareness of and concern for such things from human consciousness. Perhaps, like children, we enjoy being frightened, provided what we regard as safety and normality are not far away; or perhaps the intrusion, or the possibility of intrusion, from other modes of existence is both exhilarating and intriguing, and a relief, however temporary, from the oppressive burden of a mechanistic material universe we have created for ourselves, or have had created for us. Which, indeed, is more appealing to the fundamental instincts of human nature: reassurance that we are 'seeing things' or 'hearing things' or that we are caught in an interplay of physical forces and our own misunderstandings, or the impulse which created that comforting plea addressed to the Ancient of Days, 'From ghoulies and ghosties and long-legged beasties and things that go bump in the night, good Lord, deliver us'?

Notes

Chapter 1

1. *Letter* 22.6 – *Corpus Christianorum, Series Latina*, Vol. 31, Turnhout: Brepols 2004, 55.

2. Constance de Lyon, *Vita Sancti Germani*, ed. R. Borius, Paris: Les Éditions du Cerf 1965, section 10.

3. The ancient world was well acquainted with puppets worked by strings. Herodotus, for example, describes their use during a religious festival in Egypt, *Historiae* 2.48. Cf. Lucian, *De Dea Syria* 1 and Xenophon, *Symposium* 4.55.

4. *Vita Sancti Germani* 7 & 8.

5. Gauld & Cornell, *Poltergeists*, 4.

6. When Mme du Deffand was told that Gautama, the Buddha, had taken three steps immediately after he was born, she observed drily, 'It's only the first one which is important.'

7. 22.1.9, my italics. Cf. 21.62.5–6; 22.36.7; 26.23.4–5; 28.27.16; 30.38.8–9; 34.45.6–8; 35.9.3–4; 36.37.1–4. Even when the stones appear by themselves, they are simply warning portents: 1.31.2; 7.28.7; 25.7.7; 38.36.4.

8. *Vita Caesarii Episcopi Arelatensis* 1.41 = *Monumenta Germaniae Historica Scriptorum Rerum Merovingicarum*, Vol. 3, Hannover: Hahn 1896, 473.

9. *Acta Sanctorum*, 22 April, p.58 = http://acta.chadwyck.co.uk/ 'Galatia' is now part of central Anatolia. St Theodoros died in 613.

10. This seems to have been an earlier form of the name 'Satan', as is clearly stated in Slavonic versions of the *Book of Enoch*, which are based on a lost Greek manuscript. See H.E. Gaylord, 'How Satanaël lost his "-el"', *Journal of Jewish Studies* 33 (1982), 303–4, 308.

11. *Tōn kellan eisduntos*. 'Kella' is borrowed from Latin *cella* which means 'a room in a temple, garret, larder, cubicle'. We are told that the house in question

had been built to house Basil, so as he was a monk, it included the equivalent of a monastic cell.

12. *Exōrkhēsato*. The verb means 'dance away, hop off', but was also used metaphorically (and in burlesque fashion) to suggest that someone had betrayed a secret. I have used the English phrase to give a sense of the informality of the Greek.

13. A.R.G. Owen follows both published English and French translations of this passage in suggesting that the earthquake came after the shower of stones, *Can We Explain the Poltergeist?* 403. But the Greek quite clearly says the phenomena happened together – *sunepelambane*, 'took part with, assisted'. Similar compound verbs indicate simultaneity: for example, *sunepideiknumi*, 'display at the same time'; *sunepiblepō*, 'regard at the same time'; *sunepibainō*, 'mount together'.

14. *Alexiad* 15.8.6–7. This may be dated to *c.*1100.

15. *Vita Sancti Willibrordi Traiectensis Episcopi* = Alcuin, *Opera Omnia*, ed. J-P. Migne, Paris 1863, Vol. 2, cols 705–706.

16. Nicolas Remy, *Demonolatry*, 82.

17. A Merovingian or Carolingian prayer composed for use on such an occasion describes what was involved. 'O God, the just judge, who are the author of peace and give fair judgement, we humbly pray you to deign to bless and sanctify this fiery iron which is used in the just examination of doubtful issues. If this man is innocent of the charge from which he seeks to clear himself, he will take this fiery iron in his hand and appear unharmed; if he is guilty, let your most just power declare the truth in him so that wickedness may not conquer justice, but falsehood always be overcome by the truth.' Quoted in R. Bartlett, *Trial by Fire and Water*, Oxford: Clarendon Press 1986, 1. The man had to pick up the iron, walk three paces, and then put it down. His hand was bandaged and sealed and then inspected after three days. If it had begun to heal cleanly, the man was innocent. If there was suppuration or other discolouration, he was guilty.

18. *Matthew* 10.26: 'So don't be afraid of them. For there is nothing hidden which will not be revealed, and [nothing] secret which will not be known.'

19. *Annales Fuldenses*, ed. G. Pertz, Hannover: Hahn 1891, 51–53.

20. Reading *singillatim* for *sigillatim*.

21. Reginald of Durham, *Libellus de vita et miraculis Sancti Godrici, heremitas de Finchale*, chap. 38 = Surtees Society 20 (1845), 93–95. St Godric died in 1170 and Reginald wrote his *Vita* not long after this.

22. This refers to Hugues de Saint-Calais who was Bishop of Le Mans from 1135 until 1142.

23. Calmet, *Traité sur les apparitions des esprits* 1.317–318. Cf. the English household spirits known as 'follets', described by Gervase of Tilbury, which threw kitchen utensils and other missiles at people. These, however, were not deterred by holy water. C.S. Watkins, *History and the Supernatural in Mediaeval England*, Cambridge: Cambridge University Press 2007, 61.

24. Giraldus Cambrensis, *Itinerarium Kambriae* Book 1, chap. 12 in *Opera*, ed. J.F. Dimock, Vol. 6 London: Longmans, Green Reader & Dyer 1868, 93–94.

25. Robert Kirk, *The Secret Commonwealth*, ed. S. Sanderson, Cambridge: D.S. Brewer Lyd. 1976, 85.

26. Quoted in D. Purkiss, *Troublesome Things: A History of Fairies and Fairy Stories*, London: Allen Lane, Penguin Press 2000, 154.

27. *Demoniality*, section 27.

28. 'Malkin' is a diminutive of 'Matilda', and among its other usages designated a female ghost or demon.

29. *Chronicon Anglicanum*, ed. J. Stevenson, London: Longman 1875, 120–121.

30. Other meanings are 'discussion' and 'interview'.

31. *Secret Commonwealth*, 55.

32. L. Henderson & E.J. Cowan, *Scottish Fairy Belief*, East Linton: Tuckwell Press 2001, 86, 128.

33. Purkiss, *Troublesome Things*, 118, 147. Henderson & Cowan, *Scottish Fairy Belief*, 171.

Chapter 2

1. C.W. Barlow (ed.), *Martini Episcopi Bracarensis Opera Omnia*, New Haven: Yale University Press 1950, 197–199.

2. The list is known as the *Indiculus superstitionum et paganiarum*. See further J.T. McNeill, *Mediaeval Handbooks of Penance*, New York: Columbia University Press 1938/1990, 419–420. Y. Hen, *Culture and Religion in Merovingian Gaul. AD 481–751*, Leiden: Brill 1995, 178–180, quotation, p.180.

3. *Anecdotes historiques*, ed. A. Lecoy de la Marche, Paris 1877, nos 370–371.

4. L. Châtellier, *The Religion of the Poor*, English trans. Cambridge: Cambridge University Press 1997, 94–95. J. Delumeau, *Catholicism between Luther and Voltaire*, English trans. Burns & Oates 1977, 161–162. See also C. Saunders, *Magic and the Supernatural in Mediaeval English Romance*, Cambridge: D.S. Brewer 2010, 87–99. T.B. de Mayo, *The Demonology of William of Auvergne*, Lampeter: The Edwin Mellen Press Ltd 2007, 55–89. Some practices have lasted from Classical times more or less to the present, even if meanwhile they

acquired a Christian coating. The sacred spring of Aphrodite at Kaisariani not far from Athens, for example, was believed to cure infertility, and at the beginning of the twentieth century sick people were still being brought there for remedy and women would drink from one of its streams and pray to bear children. See M. Hamilton, *Greek Saints and their Festivals*, London 1910, 151 sq.

5. Ovid, *Metamorphoses* 10.155–161. Vergil, too, refers to Ganymede's being 'snatched away', *Aeneid* 1.28. Dante, *La Divina Commedia: Purgatorio* Canto 9, vv.40–42, 73–94. In his *Hous of Fame*, Chaucer refers to Enoch, Elijah, and Ganymede in the same breath and in the same respect, 2.588–593.

6. *Ghosts in the Middle Ages*, 183. See also T.A. Dubois, *Nordic Religions in the Viking Age*, Philadelphia: University of Pennsylvania Press 1999, 75.

7. K. Briggs, *The Fairies in Tradition and Literature*, London & New York: Routledge 2002, 15–16.

8. T.S. Holmes (ed.), *The Register of John Stafford, Bishop of Bath and Wells, 1425–1443*, London 1915, 226.

9. See further S.A. Mitchell, *Witchcraft and Magic in the Nordic Middle Ages*, Philadelphia & Oxford: University of Pennsylvania Press 2011, 16–23. Many of Mitchell's observations made here are applicable to the wider field of Europe in general.

10. G. Henningsen, 'The Ladies from Outside: an archaic pattern of the witches' Sabbath' in B. Ankarloo & G. Henningsen (eds), *Early Modern European Witchcraft: Centres and Peripheries*, Oxford: Clarendon Press 1993, 195–203. Guillaume d'Auvergne, *De universo in Guillelmi Alverni Opera Omnia*, Paris 1674, 1.1066. See also Etienne de Bourbon, *Anecdotes historiques*, Paris 1877, 319–325.

11. *Descriptio Graecae* 6.6.11. Cf. the ghost of Caligula which terrified people at night in the house where he had been assassinated, Suetonius, *Vitae Caesarum: Gaius* 59.

12. *De anima* 57. Tertullian, however, is arguing that these may well be demons working through the dead for their own purposes.

13. *Philopseudes* 30–31. For examples from a different culture, see C. Blacker, 'The angry ghost in Japan' in H.R. Ellis Davidson & W.M.S. Russell (eds), *The Folklore of Ghosts*, Cambridge: D.S. Brewer 1981, 95–97.

14. Henderson & Cowan, *Scottish Fairy Belief*, 19–20, 46–47, 60–61, 137.

15. *Vitae Caesarum: Augustus* 6.

16. *Wizards: A History*, Stroud: Tempus Publishing 2004, 121–124.

17. D.J. Solla Price, 'Automata and the origins of mechanism and mechanistic philosophy', *Technology and Culture* 5 (1964), 18.

18. Nor was Boxley unique. Not far from the shrine of St Alban was a hollow statue whose eyes and head were made to move by means of wires. Robert Shrimpton, born in *c.*1505, remembered that when he was young he crawled into the statue many times and thus knew perfectly well how it worked. Groeneveld, 'A theatrical miracle', 39–40. Was the mechanism a closely guarded secret? Did Robert tell no one what he had seen and found? It seems, to say the least, most unlikely.

19. Maxwell-Stuart, *op. cit.* supra, 124.

20. Groeneveld, *op. cit.* supra, 39–44.

21. Quoted in D.D. Hall, *Witch-Hunting in Seventeenth-Century New England*, Boston: Northeastern University Press 1991, 208. An exception to the spirit's use of the human voice-box was recorded by Jean Boulaese in 1578. Referring to the possession of sixteen-year-old Nicole Obry in 1565 by the spirit of her dead grandfather, he noted, 'Speaking in Nicole, with her mouth open wide enough to allow the passage of a walnut, and with a swelling beneath the throat; or, to be more exact, in the throat beneath the chin; but in any case without either making use of or moving the lips, the grandfather replied loudly in a cracked voice, "I am from God, who endured death and suffering for us all, from the Virgin Mary, and from all the saints of Paradise. I am the soul of Joachim Willot".' Quoted in S. Connor, *Dumbstruck: A Cultural History of Ventriloquism*, Oxford: Oxford University Press 2000, 125.

22. *The Discoverie of Witchcraft* Book 7, chap. 13 = New York: Dover Publications 1972, 85.

23. Johannes Nider, *Formicarius*, Duaci 1602, 181–182.

24. Notice the contras with the Dagworth spirit seemingly allied to the concept of 'fairy' or 'human living temporarily with the fairies'. The spirit is a child and can be seen (if with reluctance on her part), as well as heard. Her audience is terrified before calming down and entering into amicable converse with her; and this child is perfectly willing to discuss Scripture with the clergy. If there was ventriloquism in use here, it would have had to come from someone who had a good reason to be present at each of the family conversations and those with Lord Osborne's chaplain, and someone who was sufficiently fluent in Latin to be able to talk theology with him. This is asking an extraordinary amount of an individual whose identity is never given or, it appears, suspected.

25. Part 2, question 1, chapter 7. Cf. the ninth-century canon *Episcopi* which refers to certain wicked women '[who] have been seduced by the illusions and phantasms of demons', and Bartolomeo della Spina who notes that the Devil can use air to construct a body which looks like a cat and so, 'by interposing an obstacle between the [observer's] eyes and the real bodies of humans, he

allows only the illusory [*phantasticum*] body to be seen'; or since 'the faculty of recognising images [*phantasia*] is a particular power of the soul connected to those organs of the body which receive illusory images [*phantasmata*] ... the Devil can move the faculty of recognising images whenever he wants to do so, just as he can move other physical things from one place to another. This is particularly true of the body's humours and the spirits [*spiritus*] which serve them, in which illusory images [*phantasmata*] are directly resident', *Quaestio de strigibus*, Rome 1576, 25–26.

26. 'The magical world view', *Journal for the Scientific Study of Religion* 1 (Spring 1962), 183–184.

Chapter 3

1. *A Monk's Confession*, 40–41.
2. D.J. Hufford, *The Terror that Comes in the Night*, Philadelphia: University of Pennsylvania 1982, 163. Reginald Scot, in common with some other people of his time, saw the Old Hag as physical in origin. A 'trouble of the mind', he called it, 'which of some is called The Mare, oppressing many in their sleep so sore, as they are not able to call for help, or stir themselves under the burthen of that heavy humour, which is engendered of a thick vapour proceeding from the crudity and rawness in the stomach: which ascending up into the head oppresseth the brain, in so much as many are much enfeebled thereby, as being nightly haunted therewith', *The Discoverie of Witchcraft*, London 1584, 86.
3. Dégh, *Legend and Belief*, 331.
4. Guibert, *op. cit.* supra, 54, 56, 64–69, 110.
5. The following account is based on Thurston, *Surprising Mystics*, 1–26.
6. Thurston, *op. cit.*, 105.
7. Thurston, 19.
8. Thurston, 18, 19.
9. Thurston, 7. The house shaking is not an impossibility if we accept that a wooden building, for example, is likely to reverberate and even move slightly more easily than one constructed from stone or brick.
10. Thurston, 13 and note 3.
11. Ian Wilson lists 91 stigmatic individuals between the thirteenth and twentieth centuries, *The Bleeding Mind*, 131–148.
12. Wilson, *op. cit.* supra, 92–95.
13. Third week, first day: Point 4, 'To consider what Christ our Lord suffers in His human nature, or is willing to suffer ... Here I should start to draw upon all my powers to grieve, to feel sorrow, and to weep'.
14. Thurston, *Ghosts and Poltergeists*, 15.

15. Both observations quoted in N. Fodor, *Encyclopaedia of Psychic Science*, London: Arthurs Press Limited 1933, sub 'Zügun, Eleonore'.
16. Gauld & Cornell, *Poltergeists*, 140.
17. 1 (1927), 148. The journal was discontinued in 1929.
18. *Surprising Mystics*, 21–22.
19. *Poltergeist*, 281. For an assessment of Eleonore in other terms, see P. Mulacz, 'Eleonore Zugun: the re-evaluation of an historic RSPK case', *Journal of Parapsychology* 63 (March 1999), 15–45. Rogo takes the line that poltergeist phenomena tend to spring either from the immediate sufferer or from someone closely associated with her or him. Anent Eleonore's case he observes that Romanian folk tradition associated the *dracu* with biting and scratching, and so 'unconsciously [Eleonore] was torturing herself with the fantasies that had been instilled in her as a very young child', *The Poltergeist Experience*, 79. He does not explain how the weals and scratches were produced on her body other than by referring to the experiences of volunteer subjects under hypnosis and this, of course, is not really applicable to Eleonore.
20. As Colin Wilson points out in *The Occult*, London: Watkins Publishing 2003, 580. The subconscious mind has become quite a favourite among people seeking a modern explanation of poltergeistery. The remark about Eleonore's not being 'consciously responsible' for producing marks on herself, made in the report from the National Laboratory of Psychic Research, is an early example of the genre. Even Herbert Thurston could not resist remarking that 'her subliminal consciousness was continually obsessed by the fear of some fiendish antagonist', *Surprising Mystics*, 26. It should be noted, in connection with Eleonore, that her brief association with Harry Price – not her own doing, since he came of his own accord to see her, largely, since he was a diligent self-publicist, to connect his name to her notoriety in occultist circles – should not be allowed to taint her reputation. It was not her fault that Price was a fraud or that he milked his acquaintance with her for his own ends. See further Morris, *Harry Price*, 96–98.
21. Thurston, 144. Clearly an adverse view might suggest that several of these manifestations could have been self-inflicted, but this depends on one's regarding Eustochium as a liar and a self-publicist, and the evidence for this is by no means either plentiful or conclusive.
22. Thurston, 158, 180–182; quotation, 182.

Chapter 4
1. Reference to an incident in Lagny in 1330, recorded by Calmet, *Traité sur les apparitions* 1.315–316, for example, contains nothing more than the

appearance of a dead woman who asks her relatives and friends to have certain Masses said for her soul, and assures them of her good faith by saying that a good angel is telling her what to say. One is puzzled to find any poltergeist-like behaviour in this.

2. The episode is recorded in Thurston, *Ghosts and Poltergeists*, 54–60. This quotation comes from p.59. See also Schmitt, *Ghosts in the Middle Ages*, 149–152.

3. Johannes Nider, *Formicarius* Book 1, chap. 2.

4. Spencer, *The Poltergeist Phenomenon*, 47–8.

5. Nider, *loc. cit.* supra. The date is *c.*1425.

6. Ross, 'A Mediaeval poltergeist that paid rent', 327–328. A poltergeist was said to have made coins – 'sometimes as many as five a day' – appear in a house in Cardiff during the late 1980s, as well as notes and coins to the value of £70, some of the notes being pinned to the ceiling by carburettor floats', Spencer, *The Poltergeist Phenomenon*, 64.

7. *De rerum varietate* (Basel 1557), Book 10, chap. 93. I have used the translation of Andrew Lang, *The Book of Dreams and Ghosts*, 288–291. The date of the incident may belong to the 1480s.

8. Spencer, *op. cit.* supra, 67–69.

9. The literature on this subject is potentially vast, but useful guides to the love of *mira* as a whole can be found in R. Bartlett, *The Natural and the Supernatural in the Middle Ages*, Cambridge: Cambridge University Press 2008, 71–110; C. Saunders, *Magic and the Supernatural in Mediaeval English Romance*, Cambridge: D.S. Brewer 2010; B. Bildhauer & R. Mills (eds), *The Monstrous Middle Ages*, Cardiff: University of Wales Press 2003; and A.L. Wilson, *Plots and Powers: Magical Structures in Mediaeval Narrative*, Gainesville, Florida: University Press of Florida 2001.

Chapter 5

1. *Dies Geniales* ('Happy Days'), Frankfurt 1594, 775.

2. Taillepied, *A Treatise of Ghosts*, 32. See also Maxwell-Stuart, *Ghosts*, 89. Schmitt, *Ghosts in the Middle Ages*, 146 and 258, note 66.

3. Wilson, *Poltergeist*, 103–107.

4. We may also care to ask why Alessandro's 'ghost' threw things around the room when it first appeared. Was this to keep people at a distance, or was it meant to suggest to them that the spectre was a kind of poltergeist?

5. Johann Weyer, *De praestigiis daemonum* (Basel 1583), Book 5, chap. 26. I have adapted the translation in H.C. Lea, *Materials towards a History of Witchcraft*, 3 vols. New York 1957, 2.519–520.

6. Gauld & Cornell, *Poltergeist*, 32–35.

7. Owen, *Can We Explain the Poltergeist?* 241. Roll, *The Poltergeist*, 30. Spence, *The Poltergeist Phenomenon*, 62.

8. *The Christian in Society IV* = *Luther's Works* Vol. 47, ed. F. Sherman, Philadelphia: Fortress Press 1971, 44; *Sermons on the Gospel of St John, Chapters 14–16* = *Luther's Works* Vol. 24, ed. J. Pelikan, Philadelphia: Fortress Press 1961, 76; *Lectures on Isaiah, Chapters 1–39* = Luther's Works Vol. 16, ed. J. Pelikan, Philadelphia: Fortress Press 1969, 205.

9. *Liber consolatorius de spectris, hoc est, apparitionibus et illusionibus daemonum* ('A reassuring book about ghosts, that is, about apparitions and the illusions of demons'), Wittenburg 1621, B3r–B4r.

10. *Table Talk*, 5 April 1538 = *Luther's Works* Vol. 54, ed. T.G. Tappert, Phildelphia: Fortress Press 1967, 279–280. See also C.M.N. Eire, 'Bite this, Satan! The Devil in Luther's Table Talk' in M.R. Forster & B.J. Kaplan (eds), *Piety and Family in Early Modern Europe*, Aldershot: Ashgate 2005, 70–93.

11. *Of Ghosts and Spirits Walking by Night*, 160. See also P. Marshall, *Beliefs and the Dead in Reformation England*, Oxford: Oxford University Press 2002, 188–220. B. Lewis, 'Protestantism, pragmatism, and popular religion: a case study of early modern ghosts' in J. Newton & J. Bath (eds), *Early Modern Ghosts*, Durham: Centre for Seventeenth-Century Studies 2002, 79–91.

12. Spencer, *The Poltergeist Phenomenon*, 94–95.

13. *Opus Epistolarum Desiderii Erasmi Roterodami*, ed. H.M. Allen & H.W. Harrod, Oxford: Clarendon Press 1941, 275. A female servant confessed to arson and to being a witch and was executed. This was not the only incident, apparently, as Erasmus adds, 'There is also talk of other things of this kind'.

14. Bayless, *The Enigma of the Poltergeist*, 113, 109. See also Rogo, *The Poltergeist Experience*, 164–176.

15. Gauld & Cornell, *Poltergeist*, 23–26. The case is also discussed by Timothy Chesters, *Ghost Stories in Late Renaissance France*, 35–40, where he points out that the whole story made a pointed contribution to the growing contemporary controversy over Purgatory and therefore over the reality or unreality of ghostly apparitions.

16. *Jardin de flores curiosas*, Salamanca 1570, quoted in Rémy, *Demonolatry*, Book 1, chap. 28.

17. Occasionally phenomena associated with poltergeistery, such as bed-shifting and levitation of a person, may appear in a witchcraft case, as in that which took place in Køge, a town in Zealand, south of Copenhagen, between 1608 and 1615. The twelve-year-old son of a wealthy merchant was attacked by an unseen spirit levitated and held so strongly in the air that four men

could not pull him down, and his bed was removed from his room and put in various unusual places. These events, however, took place amid a welter of other incidents clearly connected with *maleficium*, meetings with Satan, and sacrilege, and were prosecuted as 'standard' witchcraft, not as demonic possession or poltergeistery. The latter, in any case, was not an indictable offence. A clergyman, Johan Brunsmand, left a full account in 1674 in his *Energumeni Coagienses: sive, Admirabilis Historia de horrenda cacodaemonis tentatione quacum in Selendia Daniae, eiusque urbe* ('The Compulsions of Someone Possessed: or, An astonishing story about the dreadful attack of a wicked demon, which took place in Zealand in Denmark, and its city').

18. *Demonolatry*, Book 1, chap. 28. Cf. another instance recorded in the same place by Rémy. It relates to *c.*1575. In the village of Colmar, a 'demon' kept on throwing stones day and night at some servants who began to treat it as a joke and started to be rude and abusive. 'Therefore at the dead of night he set fire to the whole house in a moment, so that no amount of water was enough to prevent its being burned to the ground at once.' The similarity of the two stories is striking.

19. *The Travels of Pedro de Cieza de Leon*, ed. C.R. Markham, London: The Hakluyt Society 1864, 415–418. In 1557 in Toulouse, 'an evil spirit fell with thunder inside the house of Poudot, a shoemaker'. It also threw so many stones that they filled a large box. The doors and windows were closed, but the stones continued to fall, although they did not hurt anyone, Bodin, *De la demonomanie des sorciers*, Book 3, chap. 6.

20. Guazzo, *Compendium Maleficarum*, Book 1, chap. 17.

21. H.J. Schroeder (ed.), *Canons and Decrees of the Council of Trent*, English text, Rockford, Illinois: Tan Books 1978, 91. Jesuits were strong advocates of frequent confession and communion.

22. Guazzo, *op. cit.* supra, Book 3, chap. 4. The text mentions that the huge pitch-covered stones were handled by a Jesuit Father, as he himself reported.

23. Version given in C. MacKay, *Memoirs of Extraordinary Popular Delusions and the Madness of Crowds* (originally published in 1841), Ware: Wordsworth Editions 1995, 597–598. My italics.

24. C. Flammarion, *Haunted Houses*, 277–278.

25. Bueno, *Poltergeist: Una Incómoda Realidad*, 271–272. There is a misprint in the initial date given for this episode. It is later corrected to 1588.

26. Gauld & Cornell, *Poltergeist*, 27–31.

27. Price, *Poltergeist*, 31. These examples alone contradict Colin Wilson's assertion that there are no instances on record of a poltergeist's hurting anyone, *Poltergeist*, 148.

28. Quotations from Thurston, *Ghosts and Poltergeists*, 20–21.

29. Roll, *The Poltergeist*, 33. Hallowell & Ritson, *The South Shields Poltergeist*, 192.

30. See further B. Nischan, *Lutherans and Calvinists in the Age of Confessionalism*, Aldershot: Ashgate Variorum 1999, Essay VII, pp.1–20; quotation, p.11. H.C.E. Midelfort, 'The Devil and the German people: reflections on the popularity of demon possession in sixteenth-century Germany' in S. Ozment (ed.), *Religion and Culture in the Renaissance and the Reformation = Sixteenth Century Essays and Studies*, Kirksville, MO: SCJ Publications, Vol. 11 (1989), 113–133.

31. The rituals in Menghi's *Flagellum Daemonum* ('Scourge of Demons') are directed towards possessed individuals, but the format is easily adapted to other circumstances and gives a notion of the kind of exorcism probably used in this poltergeist incident.

32. Guazzo, *Compendium Maleficarum*, Book 3, chap. 4. Guazzo also includes another poltergeist episode in this Book and chapter, with a very similar message. A house in Trapani in Sicily was troubled by a stone- and household utensil-throwing poltergeist in 1585, and the local priest advised the householder to go to confession, receive the Eucharist, and to wear an *Agnus Dei*, an image of Christ as the Lamb of God stamped on blessed wax. These remedies proved effective and the poltergeist then left the family alone.

33. See further H.C.E. Midelfort, *Mad Princes of Renaissance Germany*, Charlottesville & London: University Press of Virginia 1994, 118–121. This suspicion had grown since the 1590s, although the Duke himself on occasion rebelled against the constant exorcisms inflicted on him, especially during 1604 and 1605. Notice, too, the full title of Guazzo's work: *Compendium Maleficarum: from which attention is drawn to the most abominable works of poisonous magic against the human race and the means whereby one may escape from them.* This suggests that the poltergeist incidents were seen in the light of witchcraft as well as demonic interference.

34. Pierre de Lancre, *L'incredulité et mescreance du sortilege plainement convaincue*, Paris 1622, 817–818.

35. *Disquisitionum magicarum libri sex*, Louvain 1599–1600, Book 2, question 27, section 2.

36. On this subject, see further T.J. Wengaert & P.D.W. Krey, 'A June 1546 exorcism in Wittenberg as a pastoral act', *Archiv für Reformationsgeschichte* 98 (2007), 71–83.

Chapter 6

1. These 'stages' refer to the sequence of Perreaud's narrative and not necessarily to that of the episode itself.

2. *L'antidemon de Mascon*, 4–6; quotation, 6.

3. *Op. cit.*, 7–9; quotation, 9.

4. *Op. cit.*, 9–12; quotations, 10 & 11.

5. *Poltergeist*, 241–242; quotation, 104. Cf. *Ibid.*, 110–111.

6. G. Modestin, 'Pays de Vaud' in R.M. Golden (ed.), *Encyclopaedia of Witchcraft: The Western Tradition*, Vol. 4, Santa Barbara: ABC-CLIO, 2006.

7. Labrousse, 'Le demon de Mascon', 17.

8. *L'antidemon de Mascon*, 13–19.

9. Quotations, *op. cit.*, 20, 21. Bresse is in the modern département of Ain and Bourg-en-Bresse is no more than ten miles away to the south-east of Mâcon.

10. *Op. cit.*, quotations, 21–23.

11. Once again the poltergeist could not resist giving the company private details, this time about the Tornus family. Perreaud tells us that François Tornus verified them in the memoirs he wrote of this whole poltergeist incident. Those memoirs do not seem to have survived.

12. *Op. cit.*, 25–26. Imprisoning demons in such things as rings and mirrors was a well-known theme in both religious and historical literature, from the pseudepigraphical *Testament of Solomon* to Jacopo da Voragine's *Legenda Aurea*, and the allegation that Pope Boniface VIII (reigned 1294–1303) made use of demons he had imprisoned in a ring, to Jean-Baptiste's *Traité des superstitions* in the seventeenth century.

13. Text given in P.C. Almond, *Demonic Possession and Exorcism in Early Modern England*, Cambridge: Cambridge University Press 2004, 281. Whether Somers was faking his behaviour or not is irrelevant to the question of the effect it had upon onlookers and those who later read the relevant pamphlet.

14. Hallowell & Ritson, *The South Shields Poltergeist*, 212–216. Wilson, *Poltergeist*, 146.

15. *L'antidemon de Mascon*, 28–29.

16. *Op. cit.*, 31–32.

17. At this point in his narrative, Perreaud tells us that the entity had said a great deal more – about religion, the state, the honour of several respectable individuals and families – as well as a number of foul and disgraceful things such as one expects from an evil spirit, and so he (Perreaud) has decided to leave them out, having said quite enough to illustrate his strange and extraordinary experience.

18. Poltergeists may well imitate unexpected but common sounds belonging to

the period in which they are active. Cf. an example from the twentieth century in which a haunted house provided evidence of the sound of a motorbike revving up in an upstairs room, Rae-Ellis, *True Ghost Stories*, 244.

19. Quoted in Fodor, *Encyclopaedia of Psychic Science*, 12. See also Roll, *The Poltergeist*, 33, 40–41, 97. Rogo, *The Poltergeist Experience*, 141.

20. Quoted in Owen, *Can We Explain the Poltergeist?* 280.

21. Lullier had a further experience which Perreaud includes in his narrative, although he does not connect it directly with the poltergeist. Lullier and Claude Rapai were making their way home from Perreaud's house at about midnight when they saw a woman, all by herself, outwith a tavern called The Black Head and near a street corner known as 'the money-earner'. (One presumes, therefore, that the woman either was or looked like a prostitute.) She was dressed like a village woman, but in rather a novel way, and was twisting thread from her distaff by the light of the moon. The moment and Lullier and Rapai approached, however, she vanished. This sounds very much like a ghost-sighting and has nothing to do with the poltergeistery Perreaud was suffering.

22. Burr, *Narratives of the Witchcraft Cases*, 34–37, 58–77. Rogo, *The Poltergeist Experience*, 143. Quotation anent Canvey Island in Gauld & Cornell, *Poltergeists*, 215. Cf. Sciacca in Sicily in 1890. '[My grandmother] saw a priest come in to exorcise the house ... Black smoky stones were hurled at him. Grandmother watched the stones materialise in midair; they positively did not come through windows, walls, or ceiling. She picked some, they were not and sooty', Roll, *The Poltergeist*, 41–42. Cf. also Spencer, *The Poltergeist Phenomena*, 97.

23. Roll, *op. cit.* supra, 42.

24. *L'antidemon de Mascon*, 46–47.

25. Perreaud also mentions two episodes, one in Lyon, the other in Mâcon, in which a demon in the form of a young girl had seduced men. Both episodes, it seems, had been published, almost certainly in the form of pamphlets.

26. See further A. Soman, *Sorcellerie et Justice Criminelle* (16–18e siècles), Hampshire: Ashgate Variorum 1992, Essays I and III.

27. *L'antidemon de Mascon*, 50–58. The various quotations come from within these pages.

28. This would have been to hold a sample of urine, since medicine at the time placed great store in the appearance, smell, and taste of a patient's urine as a guide to diagnosis.

29. 'In the Divell's likenesse', 73. See also Chesters, *Ghost Stories in Late Renaissance France*, 29–35.

30. *Malleus Maleficarum*, Part 2, question 2, introduction. R. Merrifield, *The*

Archaeology of Ritual and Magic, London: B.T. Batsford Ltd 1987, 120, 173. Cf. S. Hukantaival, 'Hare's feet under a hearth: discussing ritual deposits in buildings' in V. Immonen, M. Lempiaiïen & U. Rosendahl (eds), *Hortus Novus: Fresh Approaches to Mediaeval Archaeology in Finland* 14 (2007), 66–75.

31. E.W. Monter, *Witchcraft in France and Switzerland*, Ithaca & London: Cornell University Press 1976, 217–218, 223–224, 212–213.

32. Quoted in Thurston, *Ghosts and Poltergeists*, 40. It is, of course, true to observe that Boyle and Perreaud were of similar mind in the confession of their religion, but that does not necessarily invalidate Boyle's assessment of Perreaud's character.

33. This is attached to *L'antidemon de Mascon*, 76–77.

34. Ludwig Lavater, *Of Ghosts and Spirits Walking by Night*, 191–192.

35. *Ghosts and Poltergeists*, 46. It may be worth noting that Father Thurston was a Jesuit and therefore not inclined by religious confession to be partial in his assessment.

36. Thurston, *op. cit.* supra, 40. Labrousse, *Conscience et Conviction*, 23–25; quotation, 25, note 32.

37. *L'antidemon de Mascon*, 75.

38. *The Certainty of the World of Spirits Fully Evinced*, London: Joseph Smith 1834, 16–17.

39. Quoted by Labrousse, *Conscience et Conviction*, 41.

Chapter 7

1. Cf. the title of George Sinclair's book, published in 1685, *Satan's Invisible World Discovered: or, a choice collection of modern relations providing evidently, against the atheists of this present age, that there are devils, spirits, witches, and apparitions.*

2. The account is taken from Chambers, *Domestic Annals of Scotland*, Vol. 2, chap. 3c; Ashton, *The Devil in Britain and America*, 72–76; Seth, *In the Name of the Devil*, London: Jarrolds 1969, 75–89.

3. George and Thomas Hutcheson had founded a grammar school there in 1641. This may have been the school Thomas Campbell was attending.

4. I.e. 'Never mind what other people say about an individual.'

5. *The Encyclopaedia of Witchcraft and Demonology*, London: Spring Books 1959, 224–226.

6. Owen is inclined to accept these memoirs as genuine, *Can We Explain the Poltergeist?* 43. My account has been based on his discussion of the episode, *Ibid.* 33–45.

7. Owen points out that even after 1660, any joker might feel obliged to keep his

identity secret, since 'Presbyterians, Independents, and other Parliamentarians were still entrenched in all parts of the country, enjoyed property acquired during the rebellion, and occupied valuable posts and positions of patronage.'

8. A. Rowlands, *Witchcraft Narratives in Germany: Rothenburg, 1561–1652*, Manchester & New York: Manchester University Press 2003, 162–164.

9. Gauld & Cornell, *Poltergeists*, 147–148.

10. *Extracts from the Presbytery Book of Strathbogie*, Aberdeen 1843, 50–51.

11. Glanvill, *Saducismus Triumphatus*, 255–257. These poltergeist phenomena attracted onlookers, of course. One of them gave Fox some money which he put into a handkerchief. But it did not remain there long and flew out into the middle of the room.

12. Price, *The Poltergeist*, 65–66.

13. St John D. Seymour, *Irish Witchcraft and Demonology*, New York: Dorset Press 1992, 105–131; quotation, 112–113. Nicholas may have been in Florence's cell during the evening because he was keeping watch on her. This was sometimes done in witchcraft cases to make sure the accused witch did not escape by turning herself into a creature small enough to fly or crawl away, or summon up her familiar who would assist her to escape in some fashion.

14. *Essais*, ed. P. Villey, Pris: Presses Universitaires de France 1965, 1029–1030.

15. This is often dated to 1661, largely because of a mistake by Joseph Glanvill, but see Price, *Poltergeist*, 388–399. My account here is based on Glanvill, *Saducismus Triumphatus*, Part 2, 49–62.

16. Glanvill, *Saducismus Triumphatus*, 55. It is a measure of Glanvill's honesty that he tells the reader he had not included this part of his narrative in earlier editions of his book because some people might say that he and the friends who were with him were in a state of fright and therefore liable to fancy they heard noises rather than actually doing so. But he protests he was not nervous at all and so stands by his assessment of this episode.

17. See further Hunter, 'New light on the Drummer of Tedworth', 11.

18. Glanvill, *op. cit.* supra, 59. Rollins, *The Pack of Autolycus*, 121.

19. *A Philosophical Endeavour in the Defence of the Being of Witches and Apparitions*, London 1668, 4–5.

20. Whether Hartlieb was influenced by the notion of a Rosicrucian Society which had excited much of intellectual Europe during the late 1610s and 1620s is open to discussion. See further T. Churton, *The Invisible History of the Rosicrucians*, Rochester, Vermont: Inner Traditions 2009, 286–295. C. McIntosh, 'The Rosicrucian legacy' in R. White (ed.), *The Rosicrucian Enlightenment Revisited*, Hudson, New York: Lindisfarne Books 1999, 249–264.

21. *Thinking With Demons*, Oxford: Oxford University Press 1997, 296. It is worth reading Clark's whole chapter on this subject, 294–311. See also R. Porter, 'Witchcraft and magic in enlightenment, romantic, and liberal thought' in B. Ankarloo & S. Clark (eds), *The Athlone History of Witchcraft and Magic in Europe*: Vol. 5, *The Eighteenth and Nineteenth Centuries*, London: Athlone Press 1999, 197–199. I. Bostridge, *Witchcraft, its Transformations, c.1650–c.1750*, Oxford: Clarendon Press 1997, 73–78.

22. Hunter, 'New light on the Drummer of Tedworth', 6. The letter to Mompesson's cousin, *Ibid.*, 24. A Cambridge case in April 1694 saw five Fellows of St John's College, who had come along to a house plagued by lithobolia, loud noises, and the hurling of money into one of the rooms, decided to warn off what they took to be a prankster by discharging their pistols in the direction of any noise they happened to hear. Sir Isaac Newton tetchily observed to some scholars he saw outwith the house, 'Oh ye fools, will you never have any wit? Know ye not that all such things are mere cheats and impostures? Fie, fie! Go home for shame', Abraham de la Pryme, *Diary*, 19 May, 1694.

23. *Op. cit.* supra, 27.

24. *Saducismus Triumphatus*, Part 2, 61.

25. Pointed out by Chambers, *The Cock Lane Ghost*, 65–66.

26. Mather in Burr, *Narratives of Witchcraft Cases*, 32–33. Beaumont, *An Historical, Physiological and Theological Treatise*, 306–311; quotation, 309. An apologetic account, ('apologetic' in its modern sense) of Glavill's investigations into occult phenomena is given by Greenslet, *Joseph Glanvill*, 144–176, although Greenslet would have done well to heed his own questions (p.176), 'How far are all our opinions only the products of the convention and fashion of our age?'

27. Ashton, *The Devil in Britain and America*, 60–64.

28. Sinclair, *Satan's Invisible World Discovered*, 21–25.

29. Crowe, *The Night Side of Nature* 2.269–270; Baxter, *The Certainty of the World of Spirits*, 58–59; *News from Puddle-Docke in London*, 1674; Ashton, *The Devil in Britain and America*, 64–68.

30. Valletta, *Witchcraft, Magic, and Superstition*, 63–93. Burns, *An Age of Wonders*, 1–9.

31. Burr, *Narratives of the Witchcraft Cases*, 25. The whole episode is described on pp.23–32. See further D.D. Hall, *Witch-Hunting in Seventeenth-Century New England*, Boston: Northeastern University Press 1991, 230–259.

32. Burr, *op. cit.* supra, 27.

33. Burr, *op. cit.* supra, 96–97. See also A. Walsham, *Providence in Early*

Modern England, Oxford: Oxford University Press 1999, 176–203.

34. Burr, *op. cit.* supra, 35–37. Many more details are given *Ibid.*, 58–77.

35. See J. Demos, *The Enemy Within: A Short History of Witch-Hunting*, New York: Penguin Books 2008, 81–86; E. Reis, *Damned Women: Sinners and Witches in Puritan New England*, Ithaca & London: Cornell University Press 1997, 4, 58; R. Godbeer, *The Devil's Dominion: Magic and Religion in Early New England*, Cambridge: Cambridge University Press 1992, 91–97.

36. Burr, *op. cit.* supra, 131–134; quotations, 131, 133.

37. Burr, *op. cit.* 99–131. This took place in Boston, Massachusetts in 1688–89 and is also taken from Cotton Mather's *Memorable Providences*.

38. Burr, *op. cit.*, 37–38. This comes from Increase Mather's *Remarkable Providences*.

39. Burr, *op. cit.*, 305–306. Cotton Mather was incensed and confided his ire to his diary. 10 June 1698: 'Moreover, the Lord is furnishing of me with one special opportunity for the exercise of His graces under a trial of a very particular importance. There is a sort of Sadducee in this town, a man who makes little conscience of lying, and one whom no reason will divert from his malicious purposes. This man, out of enmity to me, for my public asserting of such truths as the Scripture has taught us about the existence and influence of the invisible world, hath often abused me with venomous reproaches and most palpable injuries. I have hitherto taken little notice of his libels and slanders, but this contempt enrages him. I understand that he apprehends the shortest way to deliver people from the belief of the doctrines which not I only, but all the ministers of Christ in the world have hitherto maintained, will be to show the world what an ill man I am. To this end, I understand, he hath written a volume of invented and notorious lies, and also searched a large part of the books which I have published, and with false quotations of little scraps here and there from them endeavoured for to cavil at them. This volume he is, as I understand, sending to England that it may be printed there.' 4 December 1700: 'My pious neighbours are so provoked at the diabolical wickedness of the man who has published a volume of libels against my father and myself that they set apart whole days of prayer to complain unto God against him, and this day particularly.' 28 December 1700: 'The Lord has permitted Satan to raise an extraordinary storm upon my father and myself ... First Calef's book and then Coleman's do set the people in a mighty ferment.'

40. Burr, *op. cit.*, 310–311, 314, 337–338.

41. Gauld & Cornell, *Poltergeists*, 161–167.

42. C. L'Estrange Ewen, *Witchcraft and Demonism*, London: Heath Cranton

Ltd 1933, 459.
43. *The Book of Dreams and Ghosts*, 118.

Chapter 8
1. *Confessions*, Paris: Garnier-Flammarion 1968, Vol. 1, p.196.
2. Many people did not cope, in fact, and sought relief in suicide. See further Knights, *The Devil in Disguise*, 197–205.
3. *The Phantom World* 2.288–293, 296, 251–263.
4. *Réflexions sur le Traité des Apparitions de dom Calmet*, ed. G. Banderier, Grenoble: Éditions Jérôme Millon 2008, 56.
5. *The Phantom World* 1.xxiii–xxiv. *Traité* 1.iii–iv.
6. The thought that he was the Devil may have crossed her mind. Satan was commonly represented as having red hair and grotesquely deformed feet.
7. R. Wodrow, *Analecta*, Edinburgh: Maitland Club 1842, Vol. 1, pp.95–97; quotations, 96.
8. Gauld & Cornell, *Poltergeist*, 118. Thurston, *Ghosts and Poltergeists*, 17. Owen, *Can We Explain the Poltergeist?* 98. Thurston, *op. cit.*, 193–194. Owen, *op. cit.*, 97–98. Gauld & Cornell, *op. cit.*, 40–41.
9. Quoted in Price, *Poltergeist*, 85. The letters are dated 12, 19, and 25/27 January 1717.
10. Quotations, *op. cit.* supra, 87, 89.
11. *Op. cit.*, supra, 95, 97.
12. *Op. cit.*, supra, 102–103, 107. John Wesley's summary of events also notes that Samuel had once called the entity a 'deaf and dumb devil' and bade it cease to disturb the children, *Ibid.*, 97. On 'conjuring' as exorcism, note that the Bishop of Winchester recommended it in *c.*1770 to get rid of a supposed ghost in Hinton Hampner. Sitwell, *Poltergeists*, 253.
13. Introduction to Dudley Wright, *The Epworth Phenomena*, ix. Frank Podmore absolves her (just) from the charge of trickery, but clearly maintains that the explanation for everything would turn out to be natural, *Mediums of the Nineteenth Century*, 39. Hetty was nineteen at the time of the disturbances and not in the least neurotic or troubled. Indeed, so attractive and pleasant was her disposition, and so striking her intelligence, that by her mid-twenties she had received several offers of marriage.
14. *Poltergeists*, 82–83, 84. See also *Ibid.*, 55, 84–86, 94, 109.
15. Cowper quoted in Knights, *The Devil in Disguise*, 162. Sacheverell, woodcut 1709, reproduced in Knights, *op. cit.*, 174. The taste for 'Gothic' or supernatural fiction which dominated the second half of the century in England especially – one thinks of Horace Walpole's *Castle of Otranto* (1765) and

Anne Radcliffe's *Castles of Athlin and Dunbayne* (1789), *A Sicilian Romance* (1790), and *The Mysteries of Udolpho* (1794) – responded to this peculiar psychology, as did the theatre which, both in its repertoire and its acting style, catered to the popular taste for the paranormal. See further E.J. Clery, *The Rise of Supernatural Fiction, 1762–1800*, Cambridge: Cambridge University Press 1995, 37–49.

16. C.K. Sharpe, *A Historical Account of the Belief in Witchcraft in Scotland*, London & Glasgow 1884, 177–180; quotation, 179. Heinisch's choice of Kobold to designate his troublesome entity may be compared with Calmet's *folet* in a chapter devoted to examples of their mischievous behaviour. In 1740, for example, the curé of an Alsatian parish found that pots were being moved, stones thrown, glass broken, plants uprooted and scattered, and kitchenware displaced: in a way, typical poltergeist disturbances. Agents of the local landowner attributed all this to hostile magic, as did the curé himself, although Calmet dismisses the idea, *The Phantom World* 1.200–203; *Traité* 1.225–228. Nevertheless, he wonders whether magic of some kind may not lie behind some of the *folets*' similar nuisance-making, *Ibid.*, 208. These thoughts, however, do not appear in the revised French edition of 1737.

17. R.H. Robbins, *The Encyclopaedia of Witchcraft and Demonology*, London: Spring Books 1959, 362–363. Gauld & Cornell, *Poltergeists*, 181.

18. M. Summers, *The Geography of Witchcraft*, London 1927, 506–516. Details also come from a sermon preached after her execution by the Jesuit Georg Gaar: *Christliche Anred nächst dem Scheiter-Hauffen worauf der Leichnam Mariae Renatae einer durchs Schwerdt hingerichteten Zauberin, den 21 junii anno 1749*, Würzburg 1749.

19. The following account is based on Paul Chambers's detailed investigation of the affair, *The Cock Lane Ghost*.

20. *Journal*, 25 May 1768. Jonathan Barry observes that 'Wesley could be pragmatic about whether the "discourse of spirits" would or would not forward his evangelistic mission in particular cases and with particular audiences', 'Public infidelity and private belief?' 138. See also Davies, 'Methodism, the clergy, and popular belief in witchcraft and magic', 252–258. Chambers, *The Cock Lane Ghost*, 47–54.

21. Addison, *The Spectator*, 14 July 1711. Blackstone, *Commentaries on the Laws of England*, 4 vols. Oxford 1769, 4.60.

22. *Curieuse und wahrhaffte Nachricht oder Diarium*, 15, 42. Interestingly enough, Hänell's account speaks of more than one entity and calls them 'ghosts' (*Spuken*): hence the reference to a ghost and a poltergeist in his title.

23. Durbin, *Witchcraft at the Lamb Inn*, 14–15.

24. See also Barry, 'Public infidelity and private belief?' 118–131. Gauld & Cornell, *Poltergeists*, 118–124. Spencer, *The Poltergeist Phenomenon*, 17–19. Thurston, *Ghosts and Poltergeists*, 17–26.

25. See further J. Black, *The English Press in the Eighteenth Century*, 104–108, 245. H. Barker, 'Catering for provincial tastes: newspapers, readership, and print in late eighteenth-century England', *History* 69 (1999), 42–61. On the pretensions of the would-be educated and socially elevated, see further R.A. Houston, *Madness and Society in Eighteenth-Century Scotland*, Oxford: Clarendon Press 2000, 296–300.

26. *An Authentic, Candid, and Circumstantial Narrative*, 5. My italics. Further quotations, *Ibid.*, 17, 18, 20–21.

27. Alan Gauld records a story dating to 1826 that someone claimed to have known Ann Robinson some years after 1772, and that she had told him she had been responsible for the phenomena, using wires, horsehairs, and so forth. Gauld dismisses this as nonsense, agreeing with Price that the sheer practicalities of distributing wires etc. round the house, unseen, and then manipulating them undetected militate against any belief either in the story or the explanation it offers, *Poltergeists*, 87–88. Price, *Poltergeist*, 153.

28. The following account is based on those letters and narratives recorded in Sitwell, *Poltergeists*, 230–267. See also Price, *Poltergeist*, 129–144.

29. Sitwell, *op. cit. supra*, 256.

30. Poltergeists also made their way into autobiography. We have already seen examples of the kind in works by Alessandro Alessandri and François Perreaud. Another can be found in the fascinating, but perhaps not altogether reliable *Vida, ascendencia, nacimiento, crianza y aventuras del doctor don Diego de Torres y Villarroel*, published in separate parts between 1743 and 1758. In this he writes that in 1723 he was once staying with the condesa de los Arcos, and for eleven continuous days listened, with the rest of the household, to thunderous poundings throughout the mansion. Pictures fell from the wall and lamps were extinguished suddenly. No cause was ever found, nor did Don Diego succeed in getting rid of the mischievous nuisance, although in fairness it should be added that neither did the Condesa's chaplain who had invited Don Diego to stay with her in the first place. See Bueno, *Poltergeist*, 272–274.

31. *An Historical, Physiological, and Theological Treatise*, 306.

32. *Poltergeists*, 216–217.

33. St John Seymour, *Irish Witchcraft and Demonology*, 200–221.

34. Price, *Poltergeist*, 113–120; quotation, 117. It is perhaps indicative of Ockley's religious adherence that he designated his experience a test laid upon him by divine Providence.

234

35. Wilson, *Poltergeist*, 220, quoting Allan Kardec.
36. *The Female Thermometer*, 159.
37. *Letters on Demonology and Witchcraft*, Ware: Wordsworth Editions 2001, 221.
38. See further Leigh Schmidt's illuminating essay on the history of ventriloquism in relation to changing historical attitudes towards religion, 'From demon possession to magic show', 274–277, 281–292.

Chapter 9

1. *Fallacy of Ghosts, Dreams, and Omens, with Stories of Witchcraft, Life-in-Death, and Monomania*, London 1848, 10, 13, 7. Cf. Frank Podmore's attempts to suggest that lithobolia was done by 'naughty little girls surreptitiously [throwing] stones, crockery, and other articles', and that the reason witnesses often describe the stones as moving slowly through the air is that the excitement of the moment produces in them 'a slight dissociation of consciousness, dreaminess'. 'We judge', he goes on, 'of course of the speed of external movement mainly by the sensation of movement in our own eye muscles in following the object from point to point. A man in the early stages of chloroform or haschisch intoxication would see a stone or a saucer moving slowly through the air', *The New Spiritualism*, London: T. Fisher Unwin 1910, 84, 85.
2. Crowe, *The Night Side of Nature* 2.274–292; quotations, 281, 289. This is reproduced in Sitwell, *Poltergeists*, 307–317. Gauld & Cornell, *Poltergeists*, 247. Brad Steiger's popular re-telling of the story offers the pubertal son of the castle's caretaker and Kern's putative post-traumatic shock from his experiences at the battle of Jena as possible sources of the psychic energy needed to create these events, *Strange Guests*, San Antonio, Texas: Anomalist Books 2006, 122.
3. Iceland: Lang, *The Book of Dreams and Ghosts*, 249–253. England: Ingram, *Haunted Homes and Family Traditions*, 548–555; quotations, 550, 551, 554–555.
4. Wilson, *Poltergeist*, 108–116. Rogo, *The Poltergeist Experience*, 50–54.
5. His doctor, who knew him for seventeen years, testified that neither hallucination nor exhaustion nor dementia were in the least applicable to this case because Monsieur Vianney possessed 'perfect regularity of all the functions of the organism, a serenity of ideas, a delicacy of perception, a sureness of view and judgement, a mastery of all his powers, and the maintenance of that miraculous health which hardly ever failed him, notwithstanding the incessant labour that absorbed his life', Trochu, *The Curé d'Ars*, 252, note 5.
6. *Op. cit.* supra, 250–264; quotations, 253, 259.

7. See further H. Evans, *Seeing Ghosts: Experiences of the Paranormal*, London: John Murray 2002, 77–80. C. Green & C. McCreery, *Apparitions*, London: Hamish Hamilton 1975, 152–155.

8. Sitwell, *Poltergeists*, 189–213; quotations, 195, 207, 211, 212–213. The case is also discussed briefly in Gauld & Cornell, *Poltergeists*, 195–199.

9. *Op. cit.*, 615–618; quotations, 615, 617, 618. He would have agreed with the later view of Charles Ollier who, as we have seen, believed that superstition began in a child's earliest years. 'Mothers and grandmothers, aunts and nurses, begin the cheat; and, from little horrors and hideous stories of bugbears, mormoes, and fairies, raw-head-and-bloody-bones, walking lights, will-o'-the'wisps, and hobgoblins, they train us up by degrees to the belief of a more terrible ghost and apparition. Thus instructed, *or thus imposed upon*, we begin to listen to the old legendary and traditional accounts of lcoal ghosts, which, like the genii of the ancients, have been reported, time immemorial, to haunt certain particular family seats and cities, famous for their antiquity and decay', *Fallacy of Ghosts, Dreams, and Omens*, 9. His italics.

10. See further Leonard, *People from the Other Side*, 17–29, 32–54. Pearsall, *The Table-Rappers*, 29–41. Gauld, *The Founders of Psychical Research*, 3–18.

11. Carrington & Fodor, *Haunted People*, 85–91. Spencer, *The Poltergeist Phenomenon*, 141. Carrington and Fodor, quoting Frank Podmore, say that the message to Eliakim was in 'strange writing', but do not say what the message was.

12. *Poltergeist*, 136.

13. Hallowell & Ritson, *The South Shields Poltergeist*, 107–108. Wilson, *op. cit.* supra, 53. Writing also appeared in Borley Rectory in the early years of the twentieth century, but considerable doubt attends the phenomena reported from there. See Morris, *Harry Price*, 124–130.

14. Flammarion, *Haunted Houses*, 84–86; quotation, 85–86.

15. Thurston, *Ghosts and Poltergeists*, 28–32, 87–90. Flammarion, *op. cit.* supra, 149–153. Thurston, *op. cit.*, 177–181. Cf. poltergeistery in a house in Corrèze (Limousin) in 1895. Among the apported objects were a statue of the Virgin and a crucifix, Flammarion, *Haunted Houses*, 119.

16. *Report on Spiritualism*, 260–263; quotation, 261–262.

17. W.B. Carpenter, for example, a Fellow of the Royal Society, wrote of the astronomer William Huggins, later President of the Royal Society, that he was a scientific amateur who suffered from a 'want of that broad basis of general scientific culture'. See Lamont, 'Spiritualism and a mid-Victorian crisis of evidence', 912.

18. Quoted in Lamont, *op. cit.* supra, 920.

19. Quoted in J. Oppenheim, *The Other World: Spiritualism and Psychical Research in England, 1850–1914*, Cambridge: Cambridge University Press 1985, 84.

20. Gauld, *The Founders of Psychical Research*, 146–147. Salter, *The Society for Psychical Research*, 5–12.

21. Quoted in Gauld, *op. cit.* supra, 47. Cf. Francis Galton, *English Men of Science: Their Nature and Nurture*, London 1872, 24: 'The pursuit of science is uncongenial to the priestly character'.

22. Quoted in Flammarion, *Haunted Houses*, 326.

23. See further J. Warne Monroe, *Laboratories of Faith: Mesmerism, Spiritism, and Occultism in Modern France*, Ithaca & London: Cornell University Press 2008, 206–211. Richet himself summarised his experiences and mature thought in his *Traité de Métaphysique* (Paris 1922), translated into English under the title *Thirty Years of Psychical Research*, New York: Macmillan 1923.

24. *Demon Possession and Allied Themes*, 401–406; quotations, 9, 242.

25. Thurston, *Ghosts and Poltergeists*, 90–94. A case from 1885 in Finland, however, which involved objects' being thrown and broken, planks' and breadsticks' dancing, and a candle-holder's whirling in circles, also came to trial, but this was on a charge of employing demonic powers to cause the phenomena, with a view to increasing the accused's sales of brandy to the inquisitive crowds who came to see them. Gauld & Cornell, *Poltergeists*, 71–76.

26. Gauld & Cornell, *Poltergeists*, 68–71.

27. Roy, *The Eager Dead*, Sussex: Book Guild Publishing 2008, 70. See also P. Lamont, *The First Psychic*, London: Little & Brown 2005, 203–206. D.D. Home, *Incidents in My Life*, New York: A.J. Davis & Co. Ltd 1864, 308.

28. Home, *op. cit.* supra, 23–25.

29. St John D. Seymour & H. Neligan, *True Irish Ghost Stories*, Dublin: Hodges, Figgis & Co. Ltd 1914, 21–27. Thurston, *Ghosts and Poltergeists*, 162–171. Flammarion, *Haunted Houses*, 229–231; quotation, 230.

30. See further O. Davies, *Witchcraft, Magic, and Culture, 1736–1951*, Manchester: Manchester University Press 1999, 35–39.

Chapter 10

1. Thurston, *Ghosts and Poltergeists*, 175–177. Gauld & Cornell, *Poltergeists*, 183–186. See also Price, *Poltergeist*, 327–328. Carrington & Fodor, *Haunted People*, 92–96.

2. *Haunted Houses*, 174–175.

3. Flammarion, *op. cit.* supra, 301–303. Thurston, *op. cit.* supra, 172–175; quotation, 174.

4. Thurston, 61–79; quotations, 68, 70–71. Exorcism was also used during incidents in Tanzania in 1923 and Vietnam in 1924–25. Gauld & Cornell, *Poltergeists*, 31–32; Bayless, *The Enigma of the Poltergeist*, 184. Bayless discusses exorcism and the poltergeist *Ibid.*, 187–197.

5. Wilson, *Poltergeist*, 159–160. Roll, *The Poltergeist*, 100–103. Hallowell & Ritson, *The South Shields Poltergeist*, 212–216.

6. Cf. Gauld & Cornell, Poltergeists, 312–318 on a case from 1957 in England. They consider opportunities for fraud, including the possibility that one or the other of the investigators might have produced the phenomena fraudulently, or that they conspired to do so. 'To this we must confess that we cannot find a ready answer. No sceptic worth his salt wuld accept our avowals of honesty, even if supported by evidence as to our moral characters, as refuting the hypothesis of fraud, for he could always conceive of overriding motives which might have impelled us to throw our habitual scruples to the winds – the desire for publicity, for instance, or the sheer joy of deceiving other people. To such dedicated disbelief there is in the last resort no answer', (318).

7. *Haunted People*, 117–134; quotation, 123. Fodor discusses this case in detail in his book, *On the Trail of the Poltergeist*.

8. *On the Trail of the Poltergeist*, 221.

9. *Explaining the Unexplained*, 101.

10. *Can We Explain the Poltergeist?* 361–363; quotation, 365. Cf. Roll, *The Poltergeist*, 169–178.

11. *Poltergeists*, 275, 277.

12. *The Poltergeist Phenomenon*, 266–270; quotation, 270–271.

13. 'Does psi exist? Replicable evidence for the anomalous process of information transfer', *Psychological Bulletin* 115 (1994), 4.

14. William Roll, however, describes his testing these various possibilities in a number of cases from the 1950s and 60s and comes to the conclusion that recurrent spontaneous psychokinesis (RSPK) may explain at least some poltergeist effects, *The Poltergeist*, 158–168. See also Eysenck and Sargent, *Explaining the Unexplained*, 109–112. Roll & Persinger, 'Investigations of poltergeists and haunts', 126–153.

15. *The Poltergeist Experience*, 196–202, 215–224; quotations, 202, 208, 224. John and Anne Spencer reject the notion of a poltergeist separate from the individual and, after very briefly wondering whether the human mind can actually construct a thought-form which becomes independent of its creator, prefer to suggest that psychokinesis of some kind or another is enough to satisfy questions about the origin of a poltergeist, *The Poltergeist Phenomenon*, 181–186. Whether Rogo's entity should be called a 'demon' depends on one's

theological persuasion, since that particular nomenclature is reserved to religion, whether Christian or not.

16. *Poltergeist*, 332–351.

17. So called because in Kabbalistic philosophy, seven of the first set of ten sephiroth proved too weak to hold the divine emanating creative force and broke, and their 'shells', retaining a residue of that creative force, remained in existence, but in conflict with the divinity which had created them in the first place. See further the mid-thirteenth-century *Treatise on the Left Emanation* by Isaac ha-Cohen in R.C. Kier, *The Early Kabbalah*, New York: Paulist Press 1986, 172–182. Cf. the magical text *Sepher Rezial Hemelach*, ed. & trans. S. Savedow, San Francisco: Weiser Books 2000, 82–83.

Illustrations

1. A fourteen-year-old domestic servant, Thérèse Selles, experiences a poltergeist. The cover of the French magazine, *La Vie Mystérieuse*, 1911.
2. A poltergeist frightens a priest. Nineteenth-century engraving.
3. Poltergeists in the nursery. Nineteenth-century painting.
4. Velitrae, modern Velletri. The Emperor Augustus's nursery in the villa here was reputed to be infested by a poltergeist. From Georg Braun & Franz Hogenburg, *Civitates Orbis Terrarum*, 6 vols, 1572–1617. Vol. 3 (1582).
5. Poland, Slawiecice, Slawentzitz, Ehrenforst. Castle entrance. This castle was the scene of a major poltergeist outbreak in the nineteenth century.
6. Outbreak of lithobolia in a Paris street during the building of a road between the Sorbonne and the Pantheon in 1846. Contemporary engraving.

Select Bibliography

Alderson, J., *An Essay on Apparitions in which their appearance is accounted for by causes wholly independent of preternatural agency*, London 1823.

Anon., *An Authentic, Candid, and Circumstantial Narrative of the Astonishing Transactions at Stockwell in the County of Surrey*, London 1772.

Ashton, J., *The Devil in Britain and America*, London: Ward & Downey 1896.

Baker, D.C., 'Witchcraft, Addison, and the Drummer', *Studia Neophilologica* 31 (1959), 174–181.

Barry, J., 'Public infidelity and private belief? The discourse of spirits in enlightenment Bristol' in O. Davies & W. de Blécourt (eds), *Beyond the Witchcraft Trials: Witchcraft and Magic in Enlightenment Europe*, Manchester & New York: Manchester University Press 2004, 117–143.

Bath, J., 'In the Divells's likenesse: interpretation and confusion in popular ghost belief' in J. Newton (ed.), *Early Modern Ghosts*, Durham: Centre for Seventeenth-Century Studies 2002, 70–78.

Baxter, R., *The Certainty of the World of Spirits Fully Evinced*, London 1691.

Bayless, R., *The Enigma of the Poltergeist*, New York: Ace Books Inc. 1967.

Beaumont, J., *An Historical, Physiological, and Theological Treatise of Spirits, Apparitions, Witchcrafts, and Other Magical Practices*, London 1705.

Black, J., *The English Press in the Eighteenth Century*, Beckenham: Croom Helm 1987.

Bovet, R., *Pandaemonium: or, the Devil's cloister being a further blow to modern Sadduceeism, proving the existence of witches and spirits, in a discourse deduced from the fall of the angels, the propagation of Satan's kingdom before the Flood*, London 1684.

Bueno, L.F., *Poltergeist: Una Incómoda Realidad*, Madrid: Ediciones Nowtilus 2002.

Burns, W.E., *An Age of Wonders: Prodigies, Politics, and Providence in England, 1657–1727*, Manchester & New York: Manchester University Press 2002.

Burr, G.L., *Narratives of the Witchcraft Cases 1648 to 1706*, Cornell University 1914.

Calmet, A., *The Phantom World: or, The Philosophy of Spirits, Apparitions, etc.*, English trans. 2 vols. London: Richard Bentley 1850.

Carrington, H. & Fodor, N., *Haunted People: The Story of the Poltergeist down the Centuries*, New York: E.P. Dutton & Co. Inc. 1951.

Chambersm P., *The Cock Lane Ghost: Murder, Sex, and Haunting in Dr Johnson's London*, Stroud: Sutton Publishing 2006.

Chambers, R., *Domestic Annals of Scotland*, 3rd ed. 3 vols. Edinburgh & London 1874.

Chesters, T., *Ghost Stories in Late Renaissance France*, Oxford: Oxford University Press 2011.

Crowe, C., *The Night Side of Nature: or, Ghosts and Ghost Seers*, London: T.S. Newby 1848.

Davies, O., 'Methodism, the clergy and popular belief in witchcraft and magic', *History* 82 (1997), 252–265.

Dégh, L., *Legend and Belief: Dialectics of a Folklore Genre*, Bloomington & Indianapolis: Indiana University Press 2001.

Dingwall, E.J., Goldney, K.M. & Hall, T.H., *The Haunting of Borley Rectory: A Critical Survey of the Evidence*, Proceedings of the Society for Psychical Research 51 (1956).

Dodds, E.R., 'Supernormal phenomena in Classical antiquity', *Proceedings of the Society for Psychical Research* 55 (March 1971), 189–237.

Durbin, H., *Witchcraft at the Lamb Inn, Bristol*, Leicester: Vance Harvey Publishing 1971.

Eysenck, H.J. & Sargent, C., *Explaining the Unexplained: Mysteries of the Paranormal*, London: Prion 1993.

Finucane, R.C., *Appearances of the Dead: A Cultural History of Ghosts*, London: Junction Books 1982.

Flammarion, C., *Haunted Houses*, London: T. Fisher Unwin Ltd 1924.

Fodor, N., *On the Trail of the Poltergeist*, New York: The Citadel Press 1958.

Gauld, A., *The Founders of Psychical Research*, London: Routledge & Kegan Paul 1968.

Gauld, A. & Cornell, A.D., *Poltergeists*, London: Routledge & Kegan Paul 1979.

Green, C. & McCreery, C., *Apparitions*, London: Hamish Hamilton 1975.

Glanvill, J., *Saducismus Triumphatus: or, A Full and Plain Evidence concerning*

Witches and Apparitions, 3rd ed. London 1700.

Greenslet, F., *Joseph Glanvill: A Study in English Thought and Letters of the Seventeenth Century*, New York: Columbia University Press 1900.

Groeneveld, L., 'A theatrical miracle: the Boxley Rood of Grace as a puppet', *Early Theatre* 10 (2007), 11–50.

Guazzo, F.M., *Compendium Maleficarum*, English trans., New York: Dover Publications 1988.

Guibert de Nogent, *A Monk's Confession: The Memoirs of Guibert of Nogent*, English trans. Pennsylvania: Pennsylvania State University Press 1996.

Hänell, H.G., *Curieuse und Wahrhaffte Nachricht oder Diarium von einem Gespenst und Poltergeist*, Hamburg: Thomas Wiering 1722.

Hastings, R.J., 'An examination of the Borley Report', *Proceedings of the Society for Psychical Research* (March 1969), 65–175.

Hallowell M.J. & Ritson, D.W., *The South Shields Poltergeist*, Stroud: The History Press 2009.

Henderson, J-A., *The Ghost that Haunted Itself: The Story of the MacKenzie Poltergeist*, Edinburgh & London: Mainstream Publishing 2001.

Houran, J. & Lange, R. (eds), *Hauntings and Poltergeists: Multidisciplinary Perspectives*, Jefferson & London: McFarland & Co. 2001.

Hunter, M., 'New light on the Drummer of Tedworth: conflicting narratives of witchcraft in Restoration England', London: Birkbeck ePrints. http://eprints.bbk.ac.uk/archive/00000250

Ingram, J.H., *The Haunted Homes and Family Traditions of Great Britain*, London: Reeves & Turner n.d.

Jennings, P., *Haunted Ipswich*, Stroud: The History Press 2010.

Knights, M., *The Devil in Disguise: Deception, Delusion, and Fanaticism in the Early English Enlightenment*, Oxford: Oxford University Press 2011.

Lamont, P., 'Spiritualism and a mid-Victorian crisis of evidence', *The Historical Journal* 47 (2004), 897–920.

Lang, A., *Cock Lane and Common-Sense*, London: Longmans, Green, & Co. 1894.

———, *The Book of Dreams and Ghosts*, London: Longman, Green, & Co. 1897.

Leonard, M., *People from the Other Side: The Enigmatic Fox Sisters and the History of Victorian Spiritualism*, Stroud: The History Press Ltd 2008.

McCorristine, S., *Spectres of the Self: Thinking about Ghosts and Ghost-Seeing in England, 1750–1920*, Cambridge: Cambridge University Press 2010.

Morris, R., *Harry Price: The Psychic Detective*, Stroud: Sutton Publishing 2006.

Neuber, W., 'Poltergeist the prequel: aspects of otherworldly disturbances in early modern times' in C. Göttler & W. Neuber (eds), *Spirits Unseen: The Representation of Subtle Bodies in Early Modern European Culture*, Leiden & Boston: Brill 2008, 1–17.

Nickell, J., 'Phantoms, frauds, or fantasies?' in J. Houran & R. Lange (eds), *Hauntings and Poltergeists*, q.v. 214–223.

Owen, A.R.G., *Can We Explain the Poltergeist?* New York: Garrett Publications 1964.

Pearsall, R., *The Table-Rappers*, London: Michael Joseph 1972.

Perreaud, F., *L'antidemon de Mascon*, Geneva 1653.

Podmore, F., *Mediums of the Nineteenth Century Part 1*, Hyde Park, New York: University Books 1963, first published 1902.

Rae-Ellis, V., *True Ghost Stories of Our Own Time*, London: Faber & Faber 1990.

Rogo, D.S., *The Poltergeist Experience*, London: Penguin Books 1979.

Roll, W.G., *The Poltergeist*, New York: Paraview 2004, originally published 1972.

Roll, W.G. & Persinger, M.A., 'Investigations of poltergeists and haunts: a review and interpretation' in J. Houran & R. Lange (eds), *Hauntings and Poltergeists* q.v. 123–163.

Rollins, H.E. (ed.), *The Pack of Autolycus*, Cambridge, Mass: Harvard University Press 1927.

Ross, D.J.A., 'A Mediaeval poltergeist that paid rent', *Modern Language Review* 48 (1953), 327–328.

Salter, W.H., *The Society for Psychical Research: An Outline of its History*, London 1948.

Schmidt, L.E., 'From demon possession to magic show: ventriloquism, religion, and the enlightenment', *Church History* 67 (1998), 274–304.

Schmitt, J-C., *Ghosts in the Middle Ages: The Living and the Dead in Mediaeval Society*, English trans. Chicago & London: University of Chicago Press 1998.

Sinclair, G., *Satan's Invisible World Discovered: or, a choice collection of modern relations, proving evidently, against the atheists of this present age, that there are devils, spirits, witches: that marvellous story of Major Weir*, Edinburgh 1789.

Sinistrari, L.M., *Demoniality: or, Incubi and Succubi*, Latin text & English trans, Paris 1879.

Sitwell, S., *Poltergeists: An Introduction and Examination followed by Chosen Instances*, New York: University Books 1959.

Spencer, J. & A., *The Poltergeist Phenomenon: An Investigation into Psychic*

Disturbance, London: Headline Book Publishing 1996.

Taillepied, N., *A Treatise of Ghosts*, English trans. London: The Fortune Press n.d.

Tarlow, S., *Ritual, Belief and the Dead in Early Modern Britain and Ireland*, Cambridge: Cambridge University Press 2011.

Thurston, H., *Ghosts and Poltergeists*, Chicago: Henry Regnery Co. 1954.

———, *Surprising Mystics*, London: Burns & Oates 1955.

Trochu, F., *The Curé d'Ars: St Jean-Marie-Baptiste Vianney*, Charlotte, North Carolina: TAN Books 1977, originally published 1927.

Turner, F.M., 'The Victorian conflict between science and religion', *Isis* 69 (1978), 356–376.

Valletta, F., *Witchcraft, Magic, and Superstition in England, 1640–70*, Aldershot: Ashgate 2000.

Willin, M., *The Paranormal Caught on Film*, Cincinatti, Ohio: David & Charles 2008.

Wilson, C., *Poltergeist: A Study in Destructive Haunting*, London: Caxton Editions 2000.

Wilson, I., *The Bleeding Mind*, London: Weidenfeld & Nicolson 1988.

Wright, D., *The Epworth Phenomena*, London: William Rider & Son 1917.

Also available from Amberley Publishing

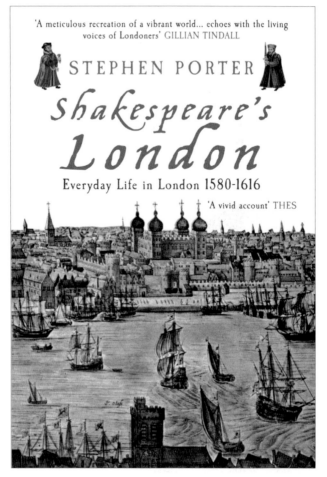

'A meticulous recreation of a vibrant world... echoes with the living voices of Londoners' GILLIAN TINDALL

STEPHEN PORTER

Shakespeare's London

Everyday Life in London 1580-1616

'A vivid account' THES

Everyday life in the teeming metropolis during William Shakespeare's time in the city (c.1580-1616), the height of Queen Elizabeth I's reign

'A vivid account' THES

'A lucid and cogent narrative of everyday life' SHAKESPEARE BIRTHPLACE TRUST

Shakespeare's London was a bustling, teeming metropolis that was growing so rapidly that the government took repeated, and ineffectual, steps to curb its expansion. From contemporary letters, journals and diaries, a vivid picture emerges of this fascinating city, with its many opportunities and also its persistent problems.

£9.99 Paperback
127 illustrations (45 colour)
304 pages
978-1-84868-200-9

Available from all good bookshops or to order direct
Please call **01453-847-800**
www.amberleybooks.com

Also available from Amberley Publishing

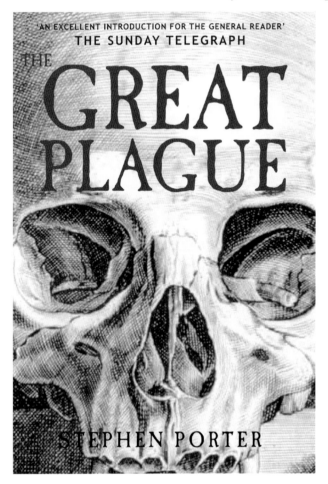

'An excellent introduction for the general reader'
THE SUNDAY TELEGRAPH

The bubonic plague epidemic which struck England in 1665-6 was responsible for the deaths of almost a third of London's population. Its sheer scale was overwhelming and it was well-recorded, featuring in the works of Pepys and Defoe and described in terrible detail in the contemporary Bills of Mortality. Stephen Porter describes the disease and how people at the time thought it was caused. He gives details of the treatments available (such as they were) and evokes its impact on the country. We will probably never know the reasons for the disappearance of the bubonic plague from England after 1665. What is clear is the fascination the subject still holds.

£12.99 Paperback
61 illustrations
192 pages
978-1-84868-087-6

Available from all good bookshops or to order direct
Please call **01453-847-800**
www.amberleybooks.com

Also available from Amberley Publishing

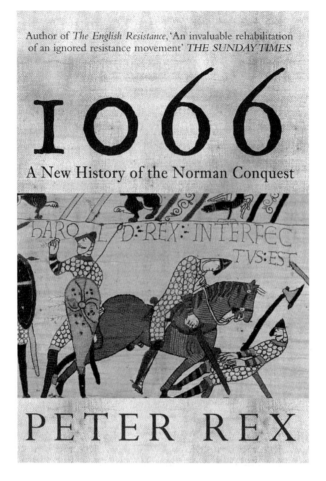

Author of *The English Resistance*, 'An invaluable rehabilitation of an ignored resistance movement' *THE SUNDAY TIMES*

1066
A New History of the Norman Conquest

PETER REX

A radical retelling of one of the most important events in Englsh history

'A gripping re-evaluation of those turbulent times… Rex vividly conjures up the ebb and flow of the battle' THE MAIL ON SUNDAY

Peter Rex tells the whole story of the Conquest of England by the Normans from its genesis in the deathbed decision of King Edward the Confessor in January 1066 to recommend Harold Godwinson as his successor, to the crushing of the last flickers of English resistance in June 1076.

£20 Hardback
40 colour illustrations
336 pages
978-1-84868-106-4

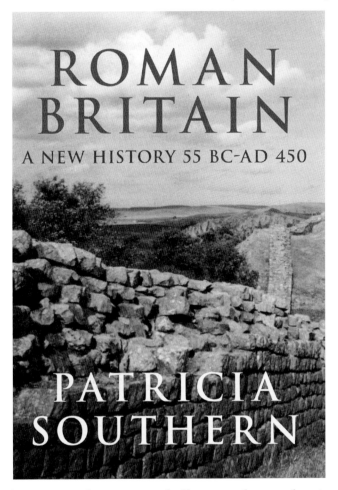

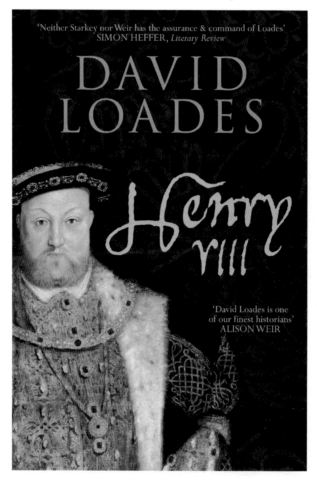

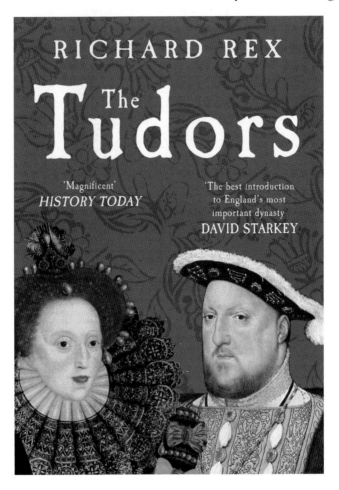

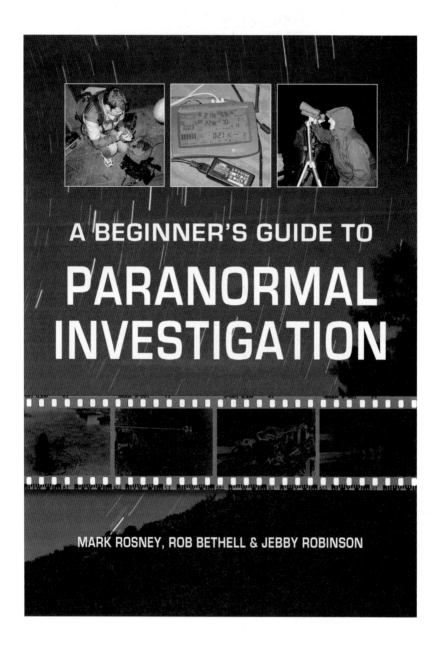

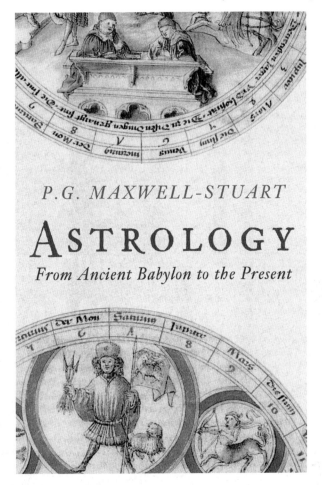

Available December 2011 from Amberley Publishing

'Devilish' *TLS*

Satan
A Biography

P.G. MAXWELL-STUART

The story of Devil from antiquity to the present

'A learned and fascinating book… devilish' *PROFESSOR JAMES SHARPE, TLS*

The Devil, like the poor, is always with us. Evil has been personified in every religion and culture, and Christianity in particular developed a highly graphic view of him from its earliest period.

This book follows the Devil through his various, sometimes surprising incarnations from the ancient world to the present, and shows that his reign is by no means over, even in the West.

£12.99 Paperback
36 illustrations
240 pages
978-1-4456-0575-3

Available December 2011 from all good bookshops or to order direct
Please call **01453-847-800**
www.amberleybooks.com

Index